TRANSACTIONS OF THE

AMERICAN PHILOSOPHICAL SOCIETY

HELD AT PHILADELPHIA

FOR PROMOTING USEFUL KNOWLEDGE

VOLUME 68, PART 2 · 1978

Power, Authority, and the Origins of American Denominational Order

The English Churches in the Delaware Valley 1680–1730

JON BUTLER

ASSISTANT PROFESSOR OF HISTORY, UNIVERSITY OF ILLINOIS AT CHICAGO CIRCLE

THE AMERICAN PHILOSOPHICAL SOCIETY

INDEPENDENCE SQUARE: PHILADELPHIA

February, 1978

Copyright © 1978 by The American Philosophical Society

Library of Congress Catalog
Card Number 77–91661
International Standard Book Number 0–87169–682–7
US ISSN 0065–9746

ACKNOWLEDGMENTS

Many people helped me complete this study. Among them were Frederick B. Tolles, John M. Moore, J. William Frost, and Jane Rittenhouse, Friends Historical Library, Swarthmore College; Elizabeth Trittle, Quaker Collection, Haverford College; Edward C. Starr, American Baptist Historical Society; Lillian Tonkin, Library Company of Philadelphia; Reba McMahon, Historical Commission, Southern Baptist Convention; Nathaniel N. Shipton, Rhode Island Historical Society; Ellis E. O'Neal, Jr., Andover Newton Theological School; Rev. T. S. H. Elwyn, Baptist Historical Society, England; John D. Cushing, Massachusetts Historical Society; James Mooney, American Antiquarian Society and Historical Society of Pennsylvania; Norman H. Maring, Eastern Baptist Theological Seminary; Alice P. Allen and Laura L. Reid, Department of Records, Philadelphia Yearly Meeting; Robin Burt, Library, California State College, Bakersfield; and many anonymous people at the Historical Society of Pennsylvania, the Presbyterian Historical Society, the Minnesota Historical Society, Wilson Library at the University of Minnesota, the Library at the University of Illinois at Chicago Circle, and the Newberry Library, Chicago.

At the University of Illinois at Chicago Circle, Lillie Brewton arranged for secretarial help and Susan Robinson and Florence Henry patiently typed my manuscript. Earlier, at California State College, Bakersfield, Vincent Ponko, Jr., Dean of the School of Humanities, and Homer Chaney, Jr., Chairman of the Department of History, always helped facilitate my research and the California State College, Bakersfield, Foundation offered important financial help. Two fellow graduate students, Robert Scholz and Paul Lucas, helped me early in my study and I learned much from their work.

Professors J. William Frost, William McLoughlin, Eric Monkkonen, John Howe, Timothy L. Smith, and Darrett B. Rutman read part or all of this study and clarified many points. However, I alone am responsible for all errors and omissions.

Two people deserve special mention. One of them is my former graduate adviser, Darrett B. Rutman, whom I first met as a student at the University of Minnesota and who now teaches at the University of New Hampshire. Over several years he maintained great faith that this project was worthy of continued labor and constantly offered me encouragement and criticism. In all ways he has been a model adviser and friend whose goodness and skill should be acknowledged publicly.

The other person who deserves special mention is my wife, Roxanne. She helped with research, worked while I studied, and encouraged me to finish. She could not have done more.

J. B.

Portions of Chapters II and III first appeared as an article in the *William and Mary Quarterly,* 3d ser., **31** (1974): pp. 431–452, and are here reprinted through the courtesy of the editors.

Dates have been modernized by naming rather than numbering the months and by beginning the new year in January rather than March.

ABBREVIATIONS

ABHS	American Baptist Historical Society, Rochester, N.Y.
CPEHS	*Collections of the Protestant Episcopal Historical Society for the Year 1851* (New York, 1851).
FHL	Friends Historical Library, Swarthmore College, Swarthmore, Pa.
HSP	Historical Society of Pennsylvania, Philadelphia, Pa.
MPBA	*Minutes of the Philadelphia Baptist Association from A. D. 1707 to A. D. 1807,* A. D. Gillette, ed. (Philadelphia, 1851).
RPC	*Records of the Presbyterian Church in the United States of America Embracing the Minutes of the General Presbytery and General Synod 1706–1788* (Philadelphia, 1904).
SPG MSS.	Manuscripts of the Society for the Propagation of the Gospel in Foreign Parts, London. Microfilm edition by Micromethods, Ltd., Wakefield, England.

POWER, AUTHORITY, AND THE ORIGINS OF AMERICAN DENOMINATIONAL ORDER

The English Churches in the Delaware Valley, 1680–1730

Jon Butler

> I remember I was once talking to a shee quaker who was for taking away all the externall references and circumstances of Religion, and was only for the spirit and substance and I told her she was like one that would lay the skin and haire from off a living creature, that nothing but the mere substantiall and vitall parts of the animal might remaine, and asked her how well she thought the animal could live, upon which she [was wrapt?] and smiled, but said nothing.

Henry More to Lady Jane Conway
September 15, 1670

CONTENTS

I. INTRODUCTION: THE DELAWARE VALLEY AND AMERICAN DENOMINATIONAL ORDER

One of the major problems of colonial American history concerns the fate of traditional English values and institutions in the New World, and hence, the origins and character of early American culture. Eighty years ago Frederick Jackson Turner suggested that the frontier transformed hierarchical patterns in European government, economics, and social interrelationships into open, dynamic, democratic American ones. Other historians, although a minority, have rejected this formulation. They have argued that the colonists' cultural baggage proved more important to making New World society than did any transforming effects of the frontier, and that while American society changed and emerged as distinct from European society, democracy still was not its hallmark. Rather, hierarchic and aristocratic models, although differing from their European counterparts, still best described American society throughout the colonial period.[1]

This study measures the fate of English values and institutions in America by describing how settlers in the Delaware valley organized religious affairs there between the settlement of Pennsylvania in 1681 and the coming of the Great Awakening in the 1730's. In doing so, it proposes to fill a major gap in early American denominational and regional history. Of the four religious groups described here, historians have given sustained attention only to Quakers. Scholarly work on Delaware valley Baptists is limited to one modern book on New Jersey. The studies published in the 1930's and 1940's by Guy S. Klett and Leonard J. Trinterud remain the only substantial works on early Delaware valley Presbyterianism. The only books on Delaware valley Anglicanism treat New Jersey and Delaware but not Pennsylvania. Finally, no broad cross-denominational study of the region's religious culture before the Great Awakening exists at all, although several essays by the Quaker historian, Frederick Tolles, make some headway in this direction.[2]

---

[1] Turner's essay was read at the 1893 meetings of the American Historical Association and is reprinted in his collection of essays, *The Frontier in American History* (New York, 1920), pp. 1–38. One of the most powerful modern explications of Turner's emphasis on democracy still remains Robert E. Brown, *Middle-Class Democracy and the Revolution in Massachusetts, 1691–1780* (Ithaca, N.Y., 1955). Two of the more forceful dissents include James A. Henretta, *The Evolution of American Society, 1700–1815: An Interdisciplinary Analysis* (Lexington, Mass., 1973) and John M. Murrin and Rowland Berthoff, "Feudalism, Communalism, and the Yeoman Freeholder: The American Revolution Considered as a Social Accident," *Essays on the American Revolution*, Stephen G. Kurtz and James H. Hutson, eds. (Chapel Hill, N.C. and New York, 1973), pp. 256–288.

[2] Frederick B. Tolles, *Quakers and the Atlantic Culture* (New York, 1964); Leonard J. Trinterud, *The Forming of an American Tradition: A Re-Examination of Colonial Presbyterianism* (Philadelphia, 1949); Guy S. Klett, *Presbyterians*

The lack of denominational and regional histories is surprising because the Delaware valley was so crucial to the shaping of American denominational life. Between 1685 and 1707 three of the four English denominations prominent in the colonies organized their most important disciplinary meetings in Philadelphia. The Philadelphia Yearly Meeting originated there in 1685 and quickly became the most powerful Quaker gathering in the colonies. The Presbytery of Philadelphia met there in 1706 as the first, and for twenty years the only, presbytery in the colonies. A year later in 1707 the Philadelphia Baptist Association met for the first time and thus became the first continuing Baptist association in the colonies. These meetings usually limited their formal jurisdiction to the Delaware valley—Philadelphia and the surrounding Pennsylvania counties, nearly all of West Jersey, much of East Jersey, and Delaware, or the so-called "three lower counties" of Pennsylvania. Little wonder then that in his recent *Religious History of the American People,* Sydney E. Ahlstrom writes that in Pennsylvania alone many of the religious groups important to American denominational development first "experienced the difficulties and discovered the possibilities for fruitful coexistence that American democracy was to offer. Within the borders of no other state was so much American church history anticipated or enacted." [3] Thus, while we look to New England to view the rise and decline of American Puritanism, we ought to look toward the Delaware valley to understand the rise of English denominational order in the colonies.

Ahlstrom's linking of American democracy with Pennsylvania's religious pluralism and its denominational development suggests another point as well. Historians generally fit American religious history into Frederick Jackson Turner's democratic interpretation of American political and cultural development. This is an old habit. A host of writers on American religion from Robert Baird in the 1840's to Sydney Ahlstrom, Sidney Mead, and Timothy Smith in the 1960's have argued that the colonial denominations very early manifested the democratic culture that would set America apart from Europe by the time of the American Revolution. [4] Thus, in *The Lively Experiment,* Sidney Mead argued that the "voluntaryism" of the colonies—meaning the absence of state coercion in religion that was especially prominent in Pennsylvania —stimulated startling growth in the denominations, led

to dynamic competition among them, promoted popular and democratic revivalism, and so thoroughly undermined European theological stuffiness that the denominations' "common thrust . . . was toward '*no creed but the Bible*' and the right of 'private judgment' in its interpretation," tendencies that produced a new religious culture in America different from that of Europe and which became a vital part of the new American society. [5]

Mead never explicitly used the term "democracy" to describe the denominations and the denominationalism he wrote about, although, like Turner, he emphasized the transforming effects of the wilderness in making a new American religious order. [6] Timothy L. Smith did, however. In a seminal 1968 essay in the *William and Mary Quarterly,* the leading journal of early American history, Smith described the origins of that democracy in a way that corrected Mead on some points while extending his general interpretation. [7] Smith argued that the colonial denominations, including those organized in the Delaware valley, were democratic because they were "created at the prompting of the congregations themselves." Their organizational thrust came from the bottom up, not from the top down. They were created "without regard to the doctrines of church government they had espoused before," meaning that members of the congregations changed their European notions about the exercise of power. This transformation occurred because in America the congregations continually met the needs of new settlers as they helped maintain public order, family stability and spiritual vitality on the frontier. As a result, democracy emerged in the congregations. In turn, congregations created democratic denominations. According to Smith, "denominational structures eventually arose in response to the demands of such congregations" and these structures strengthened the "democratic tendency in all communions."

This study tests the democratic interpretation of the colonial denominational order by examining English religious groups in the Delaware valley. No area is better suited to the task. No state-supported churches existed there, state coercion in religion was minimal, the number of competing religious groups multiplied rapidly, and the area assumed the kind of heterogeneity in religion and ethnic identity that typified much of American society later. In addition, the

---

in Colonial Pennsylvania (Philadelphia, 1937). See the brief discussions at the beginning of each chapter for more information on this point.

[3] Sydney E. Ahlstrom, *A Religious History of the American People* (New Haven and London, 1972), p. 213.

[4] For a superb discussion of the manner in which belief in a rising religious freedom in America has dominated American religious history see Jerald C. Brauer, "Changing Perspectives on Religion in America," in: *Reinterpretation in American Church History,* Jerald C. Brauer, ed. (Chicago, 1968), pp. 1–28.

[5] Sidney E. Mead, *The Lively Experiment: The Shaping of Religion in America* (New York, 1963), p. 109.

[6] Mead's views on the importance of the frontier in shaping American religious life are found in *ibid.,* pp. 107–108.

[7] Timothy L. Smith, "Congregation, State and Denomination: The Forming of the American Religious Structure," *William and Mary Quart.,* 3d ser., 21 (1968): pp. 155–176. Smith corrected Mead in suggesting that "voluntaryism" emerged only after colonial governments stopped using congregations to uphold the social order in the earliest years of settlement, at which point the congregations created their particular denominational institutions.

groups we want to study competed actively for support there and did so in two ways. They competed individually—Quakers against Baptists, Baptists against Presbyterians, Presbyterians against Anglicans—and they competed in a collective fashion, namely as Dissenters against Anglicans.

The denominational competition of the Delaware valley has come to be important in the mythology of American history because Dissenters won the clash, a fact historians frequently use to wax eloquently on what they take to be its moral: that the hierarchical polity practiced by the Church of England failed while the more democratic polity of the Quakers, Baptists, and Presbyterians succeeded. Since much Quaker, Baptist, and Presbyterian activity in the colonies stemmed from decisions taken in Philadelphia, and since the Church of England through the Society for the Propagation of the Gospel in Foreign Parts worked to counter that activity, this study should be able to assess their confrontation and the traditional explanations of it in ways that noncomparative studies cannot.

Testing the degree to which American colonists freed themselves of European ideas and formed democratic denominations in an increasingly democratic culture necessarily requires an excursion into English history. Thus the second chapter here examines the ways the denominations first exercised power and ordered their affairs in England. The result reminds us how fluid the English past was. American historians write too freely about the breakdown of European ideas in the New World and emphasize a nonexistent uniformity in European and English behavior and practices. After all, ideas "broke down" there too, just as they would in America, in part because they never were as well "fixed" as we might like to imagine.

Still, within this flux I have tried to locate the broad themes that characterized English denominational order. Here, and to my surprise, I discovered that a cohesive pattern of ministerial authority characterized the polity of all these groups, including even Quakers and Baptists. Within it each group worked out particular institutional expressions best suited to their theological inclinations and organizational desires. Again, this general commitment to a pattern of ministerial dominance never created order everywhere and its institutional expressions changed over time. But the general pattern provides a standard against which the histories of the denominations in the Delaware valley can be measured.

The ministerial command of English denominational order naturally focuses primary attention on the role ministers played in America. Did congregations —meaning laymen—create the New World denominations? If so the change from the English pattern was fundamental. Did the denominations become increasingly democratic and help create a popular democratic culture in America? Would such tendencies among Dissenters help explain the failure of Anglicanism?

Of course the fact that colonial denominations might have given much authority to ministers, as was the case in England, does not necessarily mean they were not democratic. Smith, Mead, and Ahlstrom always have acknowledged the importance of ministers in the making of denominational order. But they have never specified exactly how the ministers fitted the denominations' democratic thrust. What rightly determines denominational democracy in both England and America is not whether a clerical leadership existed in them, but whether laymen ultimately selected, shaped, and controlled that leadership. Did laymen determine who would and who would not enter the ministry? Did laymen determine which ministers would lead? Did laymen determine where ministerial authority stopped and lay authority began? And if laymen exercised power in the denominations, which laymen did and which laymen did not? A mob need not have ruled to make the denominations democratic. But since by all reasonable measures democracy involves the ability of those who are ruled to approve and disapprove the actions of those who govern—even to remove governors from office—democracy in all groups, including denominations, is measured best by determining whether such action was possible and whether it ever occurred.[8]

In this study the character of denominational order is measured by polity rather than by prayer or doctrine. I have done this because this is the way seventeenth- and eighteenth-century Quakers, Baptists, Presbyterians, and Anglicans viewed the problem.[9] Polity, and the institutional gatherings that implemented it, never expressed the whole of denominational life. But together they became the cutting edge of denominational definition. English men and women of the seventeenth century seldom used the term "denomina-

---

[8] The concept of democracy used here to measure the behavior of the English religious groups is an extremely modest, even conservative one, that should allow for considerable flexibility of discussion and judgment. It by no means approaches even the requirements set out in Robert A. Dahl, *A Preface to Democratic Theory* (Chicago, 1956), a work that itself takes a middle of the road position on the problem and is generally regarded as a conservative and certainly nonradical point of departure.

It should also be said here that the "needs" test used by Smith to measure democracy in the congregations is unsatisfactory because, lacking regular or institutionalized mechanisms through which laymen could judge ministers, it is impossible to determine whether the ministers' good works really satisfied them.

[9] Mead does the same thing himself by using a conceptualization of the denomination that emphasizes organization rather than theory. In fact, it makes no reference to religion at all. Thus he describes the denomination as "a voluntary association of like-hearted and like-minded individuals, who are united on the basis of common beliefs for the purpose of accomplishing tangible and defined objectives," a view that describes businesses as well as it describes churches. See Sidney E. Mead, *The Lively Experiment: The Shaping of Religion in America* (New York, 1963), p. 104.

tion" to mean anything much more than "label." This was true in America too, as when dissident Quakers admitted during the so-called Keithian schism that although they had come to Pennsylvania "under the denomanation [*sic*] of Quakers," they now rejected that label.[10] It was the acceptance of a disciplinary structure and the authority of meetings that most often determined whether one could take the label Quaker, Baptist, Presbyterian, or Anglican upon himself or have it applied by others. Meetings determined what stances of polity *and* doctrine would guide group behavior. And polity explained the authority of the meetings. Thus English Protestant groups always tolerated considerable doctrinal heterodoxy within their ranks, as recent studies by Christopher Hill, Keith Thomas, and Geoffrey Nuttall have shown.[11] But few people called themselves Quakers, Baptists, Presbyterians, or Anglicans who refused to accept the authority of Quaker meetings, Baptist associations, Presbyterian presbyteries, or Anglican bishops.

Doubt about the importance of polity in shaping denominational attachment is best dispelled by examining the behavior of dissidents. Typically, dissidents become schismatics when they refuse to accept decisions made in traditionally important denominational meetings. This usually happens long after they have adopted "unorthodox" ideas. And typically also, these same dissidents become a separate denomination or sect when they have created a new disciplinary structure, that is, if they do not in the meantime join some other existing denomination or sect. Thus in the early 1690's the Quaker dissident George Keith became a schismatic when he refused to accept the authority of the Philadelphia Meeting of Ministers and the Philadelphia Yearly Meeting. He then turned his followers, called "Christian Quakers," into a new denomination by creating new disciplinary meetings. Later, he returned to England where he adopted Anglican theological views. But by the standards of the day he did not "become" an Anglican until he accepted the authority of a bishop.[12]

As with the chapter on England, I have tried to analyze denominational order in the Delaware valley by looking at the actual exercise of authority in denominational meetings. I have tried not to rest the

analysis on abstract statements of polity handed down in only the most prestigious meetings, however, although this has not been possible everywhere. The major documentary materials on Delaware valley Presbyterianism seldom extend beyond proceedings of the Synod of Philadelphia and its constituent presbyteries, since only two congregations own even a fragmentary set of their records covering affairs before 1740. Elsewhere most sources used here were consulted in manuscript depositories. The minutes of the Pennepek Baptist Church, for example, constitute one of the most remarkable sets of congregational records surviving from any of the American colonies, including New England, and are here used systematically for the first time since they appeared in Morgan Edwards' *Materials Towards a History of the American Baptists* (Philadelphia, 1770). It is hoped that these materials will give breadth to the study and demonstrate how much still can be done by way of analyzing organized religion outside colonial New England.

Ultimately, the study extends a point made about the meaning of the frontier long ago by Clifford K. Shipton. Shipton argued that what was most remarkable about early America was the way colonists reproduced rather than rejected their English past in the colonies.[13] Similarly, this study argues that those who successfully maintained denominations did so by manipulating a tradition of ministerial dominance that already had stimulated denominational growth in England. Of course, this interpretation conflicts with the more democratic ones advanced by Mead, Ahlstrom, and Smith. I do not mean to pummel those views. But readers should know that their authors probably would explain the events described here quite differently than I have.

Of course, I hope the study will fulfill several useful ends. The first is to reveal similarities in the behavior of religious groups in an area where collectively, and sometimes individually, they have won relatively little attention. Because the meaning and significance of things often emerge out of complex processes of comparison, I also hope the initial emphasis on similarity will in the end better pinpoint differences that still made Quakers, Baptists, Presbyterians, and Anglicans distinctive, and that the entire examination will remind us how, in the English case at least, a vital, pluralistic denominational life nonetheless emerged from common channels of tradition and experience.

II. MINISTRY, AUTHORITY AND DENOMINATIONAL ORDER: THE EVOLUTION OF ENGLISH MODELS IN REFORM AND CHURCH GOVERNMENT, 1580–1720

In November, 1682, Philadelphia's newly arrived Friends moved to establish denominational order in

---

[10] Things transacted by a Congregation usually met at Powels house, in Minutes, Brandywine Baptist Church, Chadds Ford, Pa. (microfilm copy from Southern Baptist Historical Society, Nashville, Tenn.)

[11] Christopher Hill, *The World Turned Upside Down: Radical Ideas During the English Revolution* (New York, 1972); Keith Thomas, *Religion and the Decline of Magic* (New York, 1971); and Geoffrey T. Nuttall, *Richard Baxter* (London, 1965). Nuttall's work is especially important in illustrating how Baxter purposefully ignored doctrinal divisions to organize ministerial associations on a professional ministerial basis in the 1650's.

[12] See below, chapters 3 and 6, as well as an article, Jon Butler, "Into Pennsylvania's Spiritual Abyss: The Rise and Fall of the Later Keithians, 1693–1703," *Pennsa. Mag. History and Biography,* 101 (1977): pp. 151–170.

[13] Clifford K. Shipton, "The Frontier in New England," *New England Quarterly,* 10 (1937): pp. 25–36.

Pennsylvania by laying out a number of disciplinary meetings to handle Quaker affairs in the infant colony. The meetings were, by 1682, an identifying mark of English Quakerism and leaders of this American enterprise hoped that meetings there could duplicate "that godly and Comely Practice and Example which they had receiv'd and Enjoyed with True Satisfaction amongst their Friends and Brethren in the Land of their Nativity." When Pennsylvania Friends increased the number of meetings in the colony seven months later, they named a committee to report further on the English practice and "draw up a Brief (yet Full) Account [of] the good Order of Truth as it is Practis'd in the Men and Women['s] Meetings of Friends in England." Using it, they might better plant similar meetings in America.[1]

The process by which colonial American Protestants cast their eyes back toward England when facing New World problems was repeated many times in the Delaware valley. Baptists sought advice from London at all the crucial points in their history. Presbyterians hoped for money and good ministers from both England and Scotland. Anglicans pleaded for direction from the Bishop of London and from the Society for the Propagation of the Gospel in Foreign Parts. The frequency of these contacts reveals an important truth about colonists. They were Europeans before they were Americans and they drew upon their European past when preplexed because it was dynamic and malleable—a superb tool for sustaining denominational order in the difficult early years of settlement and an equally important one for propelling denominational activity into the American future.

But what kind of past? The principles that underwrote denominational order in the Delaware valley first were laid down in England, and to understand them we need to explore the formation and early history of Dissenters and of reforming groups among Anglicans at home. In the process, we will discover that all these groups shared surprisingly common notions about the exercise of power and authority in religion, despite the attention long given to their mutual hostility and opposition. Specifically, all of them rested the major burdens of denominational order squarely on the shoulders of persons in the ministry who had shaped the dynamics of religious reform in England since the Elizabethan period.

Unfortunately, two major difficulties stand in the way of appreciating the connection between the dynamics of English religious reform and denominational order in the Delaware valley. One concerns the English past itself. Nothing seems more chaotic than does the course of religion in sixteenth- and seventeenth-century England. From Elizabeth's refusal to broaden reform in the 1560's, to the angry Hampton Court

conference of 1603, when James I warned he would harry reformers "out of this land or else do worse," then through the Civil War and the Restoration, established authorities tried many ways to induce conformity in religion.[2] None succeeded, and when the Act of Toleration passed Parliament in 1689 it meant that toleration had not so much been achieved as the search for religious conformity had been abandoned.

In fact, heterogeneity infected English Christianity throughout the seventeenth century. Baptists split with Baptists, Presbyterians from Presbyterians, Independents from Independents, and Quakers from Quakers. Miscellaneous sects flowered and died with a frightening regularity. New solutions to the nation's spiritual crisis tumbled off the presses as though England were a giant cornucopia bursting with a multitude of visionary fruits. Even George Fox, later to be the leader of the Quakers, complained in the 1640's that reformers were as much responsible for religious chaos as were Anglicans because it was the reformers who "blowed the people about this way and the other way, from sect to sect."[3]

A second difficulty in connecting English patterns with the Delaware valley's denominational order stems from the way historians write history. Many divide Tudor-Stuart England into Puritan and non-Puritan camps and describe the wall separating them as high, strong, and unassailable. In a different vein, denominational historians usually slight the Puritan and non-Puritan division, but till a single denominational garden, seldom peering into the next plot to observe plants grown there. As a result, both English and American religious development remains mired in a minutiae of exaggerated differences—usually denominational ones—and similarities are difficult to appreciate.[4]

In matters of church government, however, a surprising number of English religious groups adhered to a common tradition in the exercise of authority that also underwrote the denominational institutions later established in the Delaware valley. This tradition rested on reformed English Protestant concepts of the ministry and of ministerial authority. In the late Tudor and early Stuart periods a broad agreement emerged among reformers about the relationship of the minister and ministerial labor to the making of Christian faith. The minister was no mere function-

---

[1] Minutes, Philadelphia Quarterly and Monthly Meeting, 9 January, 1683; 5 June, 1683, FHL microfilm copy.

[2] Quoted in David Harris Willson, *King James VI and I* (New York, 1967), p. 207.

[3] *The Journal of George Fox*, John L. Nickalls, ed. (Cambridge, Engl., 1952), p. 36; A. G. Dickens, *The English Reformation* (New York, 1964), pp. 325–340; Christopher Hill, *The World Turned Upside Down: Radical Ideas during the English Revolution* (New York, 1972), pp. 148–185, 223–230; W. K. Jordan, *The Development of Religious Toleration in England* (4 v., London, 1938) 3: pp. 119–131, 160–170, 253–266.

[4] As an example see John F. H. New, *Anglican and Puritan* (Palo Alto, Calif., 1964).

ary. Although he was often described as a "messenger," the very nature of his task made him the center of much reformed Protestant discussion for the next century. After all, he brought *God's* word to secular society. Thus the influential Puritan William Perkins called ministers not only messengers, but "Angels," "Ambassadours . . . of the high god," "God's Interpreter to the people, and the peoples to God." Richard Sibbes asserted that ministers were "Christ's Mouth" and that Christ was "either received or rejected in his Ministers."[5] The Elizabethan reformer Edward Dering put the matter even more directly. To Dering the minister was "the eye of the body, the workman of the harvest, the messenger that calleth unto the marriage, the prophet that telleth the will of the Lord, the wise man that teacheth to discern between good and evil, . . . the dispensers of the mysteries of God . . . the minister by whom the people do believe."[6]

These views illustrate a simple point. However bitter the attacks on priests, or however strong the Protestant appeal to the authority of laymen, the minister became the nexus of the English reformation. From him one heard doctrine. By him the scriptures were read and explicated. Through him men sinful since Adam were received into the church by baptism and the Lord's Supper. To him came individuals for advice, for counsel, for words of consolation, sometimes even for words that frightened. It is not surprising then that so many general arguments about religion centered on the roles clerics would play. What were the duties of a clergyman? What spiritual authority did he possess? What was his relationship to his parish? Did he merely preach the Word or did he effect God's work in the souls of men and women? Should he abandon the parish with its reprobate inhabitants and minister instead to a gathered congregation of saints? And what of discipline, or the politics of the church, of relations between clergymen and communicants or interrelationships between clerics themselves? What justified setting one minister over another, or a group of ministers over a single cleric? Worse, if every listener, though perhaps not a priest, was capable of understanding God's demands and promises, could ministers even be justified? And, should many persons minister—not merely a few?

Understandably, concern about the minister extended deep into the English population. Precisely because this was an age when most men and women were illiterate, the symbolism of clerical gowns and relics was not lost on Elizabethan parishioners. Thus Patrick Collinson argues that the "vestments" controversy, one of the major religious disputes of the Elizabethan period, broke out when laymen demanded that clerical dress be lean and plain, not elaborate and

full like the gowns that still hung from the shoulders of many Anglican clerics.[7] Yet lay influence rose and waned. Although lay men and women were important to the growth of religious reform in Tudor-Stuart England, especially by establishing lectureships for reforming ministers, they never institutionalized this influence in ways that would allow them to rule over the ministers to whom they faithfully listened. As a result leadership in Elizabethan reform commonly passed to the very ministers who were so much the center of religious debate. As we shall see, the organizational patterns they developed while pursuing this leadership laid down fundamental patterns of denominational order that later would characterize American development in the Delaware valley.

Of course, the best known example of ministerial reform comes not from England but Scotland. There the Reformation has always been associated with the growth of a Presbyterian ecclesiastical system dominated by clerics who ruled congregations sternly and sustained their power through regional and national church gatherings called presbyteries and synods. This system had limited influence in Elizabethan England, however. Even in Scotland, Gordon Donaldson has pointed out that the presbyteries gained power slowly, to emerge only in the 1580's and 1590's as clerical bodies that supervised ministerial labor, tried heretics and examined the financial and disciplinary affairs of local congregations.[8] Although two prominent English reformers, Thomas Cartwright and John Field, tried to extend this emerging Presbyterianism to England, their effort failed. Among the English clergy, Presbyterianism seemed too much concerned with polity, too little concerned with piety. And to Elizabeth, the system was politically dangerous. How would she control presbyteries and a national synod of ministers when her own bishops sometimes undermined ecclesiastical order?[9]

In fact, English reform was not dependent on Scottish Presbyterianism at all. Rather, it was rooted in local "prophesyings," reformed worship services that emphasized sermonizing and public discussion of doctrine and faith. Brilliantly uncovered and described by Patrick Collinson in his *Elizabethan Puritan Movement*, they furnish the first example of the form and

---

[5] Quoted in Charles H. George and Katherine George, *The Protestant Mind of the English Reformation, 1570–1640* (Princeton, N.J., 1961), p. 325.

[6] Quoted in Patrick Collinson, *The Elizabethan Puritan Movement* (Berkeley and Los Angeles, Calif., 1967), p. 106.

[7] *Ibid.*, pp. 93–94; H. C. Richardson, *Puritanism in North-West England: A Regional Study of the Diocese of Chester to 1642* (Manchester, Engl., and Totowa, N.J., 1972), pp. 74–114. Claire Cross, *Church and People, 1450–1660: The Triumph of the Laity in the English Church* (London, 1976) was published as this study was in press and reaches quite different conclusions about the power laymen exercised in Tudor-Stuart religious reform. However, she pays little attention to the actual exercise of power in the Dissenting denominations and instead concentrates on what she terms the laymens' "influence" in those bodies and in the Church of England.

[8] Gordon Donaldson, *The Scottish Reformation* (Cambridge, Engl., 1960), pp. 183–225.

[9] C. G. Bolam, *et al.*, *English Presbyterians from Elizabethan Puritanism to Modern Unitarianism* (London, 1968), pp. 29–33.

method that would characterize the emerging English tradition of ministerial authority in church reform and government.

The prophesyings began in the 1560's under the direction of reforming Anglican bishops seeking to extend Protestant worship to large numbers of laymen. Backed by town and county officials, Anglican ministers gave sermons in public squares and markets and often engaged their audiences in public discussions of issues raised by their sermons. Then the ministers commonly withdrew to private rooms to discuss the sermons among themselves. The public prophesyings drew enormous audiences and often produced intense debates in which a whole crowd, "all of them, men and women, boys and girls, labourers, workmen and simpletons," argued over the notions they had imbibed.[10] Although Elizabeth outlawed the prophesyings in 1577, saying they were seditious, one crucial part of them survived. The ministers who led the public gatherings used their private discussions of the sermons as models for organizing private, extra-legal ministerial conferences. These began meeting in the 1580's. Now the old public sermons were heard only by ministers, while the ministers' discussions were broadened. For example, the conference or "classis" that met at Dedham between 1582 and 1589 heard one sermon at each meeting, evaluated it in the absence of the speaker, then conversed about problems encountered in imposing reformed worship on their parishes. The procedure marked a considerable advance toward formal organization. Not only were the earlier gatherings after the public prophesyings more casual, but now the ministerial conferences kept minutes of their deliberations, a feature Patrick Collinson argues produced a "case law" of reformed practice for interested clerics.[11]

Two special features of organization and activity are of special interest to us here. On the one hand, the meetings stimulated and reinforced an intense personal fellowship among participating ministers. This stemmed from the conferences' immersion in worship itself. If, as William Haller argued long ago, Elizabethan reformers stressed the growth of a dynamic relationship between ministers and laymen, the clerical meetings extended this relationship to the ministers themselves. The reforming conference emerged as a "congregation" of ministers who, in pursuit of their parish duties and concern for lay religiosity, heard sermons, debated doctrine, agonized over theology and gave out with advice for the stimulation of reform that could be used by each minister individually and considered by all of them collectively. Thus, what

Haller called the "cure of souls," an intensely demanding worship affecting all the religious senses and practiced by reforming clerics in their parishes, was extended to the clergymen gathered in the conferences.[12]

On the other hand, the conferences did not yet act as formal agents of church government. They were composed of Anglicans, not Separatists, and they evinced strikingly little interest in national reform through parliamentary schemes. In fact the conferences thrived on English localism. They seemed content to push reform in their home parishes through the existing church structure. In 1587 the Dedham conference refused even to discuss a "Book of Discipline" proposed for national use by the ministerial conference in London. The Dedham conference also rejected interference in local affairs even from fellow reformers. When the London conference suggested that each conference limit its membership to ten ministers each, the Dedham ministers answered that those "best privy in our conference," meaning themselves, not London clerics, would determine the size of their meetings. Of course, such occurrences are difficult to explain if the conferences are viewed as quasi-Presbyterian. But if they are understood as modest vehicles for the solidification of local reform among Anglicans infected with some amount of simple provincialism, their behavior seems more comprehensible.[13]

Unfortunately, it is difficult to follow ministerial conferences into the seventeenth century. No one has done for these years what Patrick Collinson has accomplished for the Elizabethan period. But many signs, some discovered by Collinson himself, point to their continuing existence and to their importance for the rise of Stuart Puritanism. As before, they sustained local reform by promoting regular conversations among ministers. In the 1610's they again became associated with public preaching. Public sermonizing, with its accompanying ministerial conferences, was reported in the Diocese of Lincoln in 1614 and 1616; the mayor and leading citizens of Leicester defended the public preaching of reforming ministers on market and fast days in 1617; in East Anglia ministerial panels containing upwards of thirteen clerics maintained reformed worship into the 1620's; and Thomas Shepard reported in his *Autobiography* that a

---

[10] Quoted in *ibid.,* p. 175.

[11] *Ibid.,* pp. 208–239; H. C. Richardson, *Puritanism in North-West England: A Regional Study of the Diocese of Chester to 1642* (Manchester, Engl., and Totowa, N.J., 1972), pp. 18–19.

[12] William Haller, *The Rise of Puritanism, Or, The Way to the New Jerusalem as set forth in Pulpit and Press from Thomas Cartwright to John Lilburn and John Milton, 1570–1643* (New York, 1957), pp. 27–33, 54. Haller discounted the ministers' formal organization, a point revised by Collinson.

[13] Patrick Collinson, *The Elizabethan Puritan Movement* (Berkeley and Los Angeles, 1967), pp. 229, 319–329. The implications of this narrow habit of mind for New England history is discussed by Timothy H. Breen, "Persistent Localism: English Social Change and the Shaping of New England Institutions," *William and Mary Quart.* 3d ser., **32** (1975): pp. 3–28.

reformed ministerial conference operated in Essex through the 1630's.[14]

Here was the birthplace of Stuart Puritanism and a crucial source of ecclesiastical or "denominational" order in the later Separatist and Puritan movements. Since in the main Puritanism was reforming Anglicanism made illegal, it is understandable that in some respects it never escaped its origins. While many reformers received a common training at Cambridge, they worked out their Puritanism in their parishes and much of the credit for their success was due to the conferences to which many of them belonged. Thus when Archbishop Laud forced the most insistent reformers to leave England in the 1620's and 1630's, they easily turned to the conference tradition to support religious reform in their new surroundings. Policy for exile congregations in the Netherlands was made through a ministerial conference unwittingly chartered by James I in 1621, while in New England it often emerged from ministerial gatherings called "consociations." In both places the connection to the English conference was personal as well as intellectual. John Cotton, Richard Mather, Thomas Shepard, Thomas Hooker, and Ezekiel Rogers all had belonged to conferences in England before moving to America, while Hooker, Hugh Peter, and John Davenport had been members of the English classis in the Netherlands. Understandably then, New England ministers used a vocabulary familiar in old England to justify formation of their consociation. The 1636 "Model of Civil and Church Gov[ernment]" stoutly defended the ministerial meetings because of "needs of Each others helps, in regard of daily emergent troubles, doubts and controversies," but especially because of the "Love of each others Fellowship . . . [and the] great blessing and Special presence of God upon such Assemblies hitherto."[15]

Exile ministers found it difficult to add new responsibilities in church government to the old pleasures of conversation, however. In the Netherlands the English classis possessed coercive powers "to suppresse those who tooke upon them the function of preachers without lawfull vocation or Admission to the Ministry. And 21y. to examine, restraine, and punish the ill manners of such as give scandall by the vitious lives." Such purposes reflected the reformed ministers' long concern for clerical purity. But the exercise of government also drove them toward discord. Lack-

ing any real experience with governance in the English conferences, the opportunity to judge and condemn led the ministers toward internal argument and disputes with Dutch ministerial conferences. As a result, the classis meetings lapsed. Thus when James I happily revoked the classis charter in 1629 he was able to do so on the embarrassing ground that although it was given power to remove "all jealousies of innovation, separation, faction or schism," it had instead heightened them.[16]

In New England the consociations fared better, probably because they pretended to less. In an important study of the New England consociations, Robert Scholz counts some 160 ministerial conferences there between 1633 and 1672. They were most useful when they concentrated on the adjustment of relatively narrow issues. The ministers reconciled differences among and within congregations, censured laymen (usually non-church members), petitioned and advised the Massachusetts legislature, supervised public fasts, and recommended standards for clerical ordination, all while discussing doctrine and theology among themselves. Efforts to fashion a more rigid New England way proved less successful, however. Their products —the Cambridge Platform of 1648 and the Half-Way Covenant of 1662—spoke as much of the ministers' differences as of their agreements. Each document skirted important issues or was ignored by individual ministers and many congregations. Thus, New England Puritanism finally looked much like old English reformism. Even though the authority of the Anglican Church had effectively been evaded, New England ministers still gathered in consociations to promote reform and to discuss common problems. But local variation and an inability to create a common mind on religious questions frustrated those who hoped a New England way might guide Christian reformers elsewhere.[17]

This period of reform activity also saw the fixing of important ecclesiastical principles among English Separatists. B. R. White argues correctly that Separatists and Anglican reformers agreed on a surprising number of issues despite the apparent tension between them. But they clearly disagreed in their under-

---

[14] Patrick Collinson, *The Elizabethan Puritan Movement* (Berkeley and Los Angeles, 1967), pp. 209–210; *God's Plot: The Paradoxes of Puritan Piety, Being the Autobiography and Journal of Thomas Shepard,* Michael McGiffert, ed. (Amherst, Mass., 1972), p. 46.

[15] Quoted in Robert F. Scholz, "Clerical Consociation in Massachusetts Bay: Reassessing the New England Way and Its Origins," *William and Mary Quart.,* 3d ser., **29** (1972): pp. 391–414; Raymond P. Stearns, *Congregationalism in the Dutch Netherlands: The Rise and Fall of the English Congregational Classis, 1621–1635* (Chicago, 1942), pp. 9–17, 21–22.

[16] Raymond P. Stearns, *Congregationalism in the Dutch Netherlands: The Rise and Fall of the English Congregational Classis, 1621–1635* (Chicago, 1942), pp. 10, 71–76, 83–84; Keith L. Sprunger, *The Learned Doctor William Ames: Dutch Backgrounds of English and American Puritanism* (Urbana, Ill., 1972), p. 223.

[17] Robert F. Scholz, "Clerical Consociation in Massachusetts Bay: Reassessing the New England Way and Its Origins," *William and Mary Quart.,* 3d ser., **29** (1972): pp. 405–408. See also Robert F. Scholz, "The Reverend Elders: Faith, Fellowship and Politics in the Ministerial Community of Massachusetts Bay, 1630–1710" (unpublished Ph.D. dissertation, University of Minnesota, 1966), pp. 154–206, and Robert E. Wall, Jr., *Massachusetts Bay: The Crucial Decade, 1640–1650* (New Haven and London, 1972), pp. 32–34, 61–63, 84, 89–92.

standings of spiritual leadership. In theory Separatists tended to reduce the clerical authority stressed by reforming Anglicans by placing both ministry and authority at the disposal of congregations. Thus the Separatist John Smyth argued that the religious life of England had been so corrupted that no true ministers or churches then existed there. Therefore, in order to form a Christian church he had to baptize himself, then baptize others, then encourage the newly baptized persons to organize a congregation which would in turn select a minister from within its own ranks. But Smyth also believed that the last step was only a matter of convenience and that the entire congregation could exercise the ministerial office collectively. Its members could "preach, pray, sing psalms, . . . administer the seals of the covenant . . . admonish, convince, excommunicate, absolve, and [perform] all other actions either of the kingdom or priesthood." In Smyth's view then, every congregation was its own master. Not only could it choose the kind of minister it wished to utilize—and hence, what if any minister it wished to hire—but it also could reject the advice of any person or group outside its membership.[18]

Even among Separatists John Smyth's views were more often read than practiced. Between 1620 and 1640 most Separatist congregations rejected the collective exercise of the ministry and named ministers, elders, and deacons to preach and govern in the congregations. Yet their theoretical position on the ministry was well reflected in Smyth's thinking and established important, and to some people irritating, principles in seventeenth-century English religious life. Separatists tended to emphasize an egalitarianism in congregational organization that became especially important for their view of the ministry. It also pointed up the startling conservatism of their reforming Anglican and Puritan colleagues on the point. Separatists insisted that ministers were servants of the congregations that made them. Their office gave them no monopoly over the explication of the Word. Thus as a result, Separatists did not encourage the narrowly based clerical conferences that characterized reforming Anglicanism and Puritanism. Indeed, they compared the latter's emphasis on clerical authority to that of Catholicism, and among Baptists, later used their quasi-egalitarian tendency as the basis for even more radical provisions for ministry, authority, and denominational order after 1640.[19]

Between 1640 and 1660 the patterns for promoting reform developed in earlier decades became models for fashioning denominational order and institutions in a Commonwealth increasingly given to sectarian divisions. Reforming Anglicans and Puritans experienced both frustration and success in attempting to utilize the old models. On the one hand, despite their command of Parliament, they obviously failed to reform the Church while still preserving its place in society and government. Part of the failure surely stemmed from the fact that the reformers were not committed to identical notions of church government. Thus the Westminster Assembly of Divines divided bitterly over the question of importing Presbyterianism from Scotland.[20] But some reformers also seemed perplexed by the very terms of the debate on church polity. Richard Baxter, later to become a major Commonwealth cleric but then very young, wrote that until he attended the Westminster Assembly he "never thought what Presbytery or Independency was, nor spoke with a man who seemed to know about it." [21] His comment usually is adduced by historians to mean that the two positions were not as well defined then as they would be later. It also points up the localism that still characterized English religious reform in the 1640's. Whatever the pet theories of the most prestigious clerics, the experience of many reformers was little more than regional and the aims that tied them together—the practice of spiritual and liturgical reform in their parishes and among themselves—called up no necessary discussion of polity or national ecclesiastical policy.

Thus, whether from internal division or sheer unfamiliarity with what later were fundamental issues, the Westminster divines vacillated until 1645, when the desperate need to secure allies forced them to accept a Scottish Presbyterianism many did not want and some did not understand. The scheme established four bodies to govern church affairs. They were organized in hierarchical fashion—weekly assemblies in each parish, monthly "classical prebyteries" in the counties, provincial assemblies that would meet twice each year, and a national assembly or synod that would meet at the call of Parliament. Although each was to contain both ministers and laymen, John Milton correctly caught the tendency for ministerial dominance when he observed that in this scheme "New Presbyter is but old Priest writ large." [22]

If Milton had meant reforming priest, which he did not, his judgment would have been more accurate. As a national plan the scheme was a failure. In most parishes ministers refused to share power with laymen and laymen refused to submit to the rule of lay elders, who by law could act much like village constables.

---

[18] Quoted in B. R. White, *The English Separatist Tradition: From the Marian Exiles to the Pilgrim Fathers* (Oxford, 1971), p. 127.

[19] *Ibid.*, pp. 142–143, 155.

[20] C. G. Bolam *et al., English Presbyterians from Elizabethan Puritanism to Modern Unitarianism* (London, 1968), pp. 34–46; Patrick Collinson, *The Elizabethan Puritan Movement* (Berkeley and Los Angeles, 1967), pp. 296–302.

[21] Quoted in Robert F. Scholz, "Clerical Consociation in Massachusetts Bay: Reassessing the New England Way and Its Origins," *William and Mary Quart.,* 3d ser., **29** (1972) : p. 402.

[22] Quoted in C. G. Bolam *et al., English Presbyterians from Elizabethan Puritanism to Modern Unitarianism* (London, 1968), p. 43.

But in a few areas the scheme worked more effectively than many historians have admitted. This success occurred, however, at the expense of lay power because, where this new Presbyterian establishment operated, it worked on the old reforming Anglican model. The classis at Nottingham agreed that "nothing shall be determined concerning government but in the presence of four or three ministers at least." But it only required the presence of "as many ruling elders as can be" to validate decisions.[23] Similarly, in London the division between laymen and clerics was institutionalized. The city's Fourth Classis instituted one set of meetings for joint worship and discussion with laymen where ministers always served as moderators and gave the sermons (no layman prophesied here). At the same time the ministers met privately to handle such professional matters as ordinations, a rite the London ministers in no way shared with the lay elders.[24]

The only other successful attempt to sustain order in the Commonwealth church came from extra-legal ministerial associations organized in the 1650's in several counties—Westmoreland, Cumberland, Wiltshire, Dorsetshire, Somersetshire, Hampshire, and Essex. Their prototype was the association established by Richard Baxter in Worcestershire in 1653. Unwilling to join the Presbyterian system and perplexed by spiritual chaos in the Commonwealth, Baxter sought to reclaim old ground in the associations. He viewed reform itself as a ministerial problem. He told one audience in 1655 that "churches either rise or fall as the Ministry doth rise or fall" and argued that, if clerics would reform their own ranks and set ministers "on their Duties zealously and faithfully, the People would certainly be reformed."[25] But he never believed in an empty-minded clericalism. "The bare authority of the Clergy will not serve the turn," he wrote, "without overtopping ministerial abilities." Only when ordained ministers impressed the generality with their skill and knowledge as well as with their piety could the religious life of the parish be reformed. To sway his own listeners, Baxter himself "did usually put in something in My Sermon which was above their own discovery, and which they had not known

before . . . that they might be kept humble, and still perceive their ignorance, and be willing to keep in a learning state." In this way Baxter not only promoted local religious renewal but simultaneously inhibited any egalitarian tendencies that might be encouraged elsewhere. This was an important point because Baxter believed deeply that, if ministers failed to intimidate their listeners, "the People will be tempted to turn Preachers themselves, and think that they have learnt all that the ministers can teach them."[26]

In turn, the associations Baxter organized promoted clerical reform as the foundation of parish reform. They did so first as self-policing professional bodies. The ministers of the Cambridge association, for example, agreed to "yeeld our selves to brotherly exhortations, admonitions, and reproofes" in order to improve individual skills. The Worcestershire association announced that it would hear "any complaint that any people have against any member of our association, for scandal, false doctrine or Maladministration" as a way of gaining public confidence for their endeavors. But of course the ministers judged the complaints themselves. Indeed, the Cambridge association even warned laymen against consulting non-clerical competitors on spiritual matters—"wiches, wizard[s], and fortune tellers"—even while it rejected doctrinal tests for membership, believing that the minister's clerical status and his willingness to promote reform were sufficient tests of his orthodoxy.[27]

The associations also promoted much fraternal intercourse among the ministers. Geoffrey Nuttall quotes Baxter as distinctly remembering that "every first Thursday of the month was the Ministers meeting for Discipline and Disputation." "When we had dined together, we spent an Hour or two in Disputation on some Question which was Chosen the Week before."[28] These gatherings gave Baxter much satisfaction, because they created what he termed the "unanimous faithful ministers." Their meetings and activities between 1653 and 1660 comprised what he later remembered as "the confortablest time of all my life."[29]

The associations also promoted a reformed congregational life. For Baxter the involvement of the association in parish reform was real and personal. The same year he organized his Worcestershire association, he also imposed a new discipline on his Kidderminster parish, beginning what he called "the Work of Personal Conference with every Family" and tight-

---

[23] *Minutes of the Bury Presbyterian Classis, 1647–1657*, William A. Shaw, ed., *Remains Hist. and Lit. Chetham Soc.*, n.s., **36** (Manchester, Engl., 1896) : p. 154.

[24] *The Register-Booke of the Fourth Classis in the Province of London, 1646–59*, Charles E. Surman, ed., *Publications of the Harleian Society* 82 (London, 1952) : pp. xvi-xvii, 18.

[25] *Reliquiae Baxterianae: or Mr. Richard Baxter's Narrative of the Most Memorable Passages of his Life and Times*, Matthew Sylvester, ed. (London, 1696), p. 115. See also Geoffrey F. Nuttall, *Richard Baxter* (London, 1965), pp. 64–66; Geoffrey F. Nuttall, "The Worcestershire Association: Its Membership," *Jour. Ecclesiastical History* 1 (1950) : pp. 197–206; *The Life of Adam Martindale, Written by Himself,* . . . Richard Parkinson, ed., *Remains Hist. and Lit. Chetham Society* 4 (Manchester, 1845) : pp. 112–118.

[26] Quoted in Frederick J. Powicke, *A Life of the Reverend Richard Baxter, 1615–1691* (London, 1924), pp. 105–106.

[27] *Ibid.*, p. 166; "Minutes of the Cambridge Classis," in: *Minutes of the Bury Presbyterian Classis, 1647–1657*, William A. Shaw, ed., *Remains Hist. and Lit. Chetham Soc.*, n.s., **41** (Manchester, Engl., 1898) : p. 198.

[28] Geoffrey F. Nuttall, *Richard Baxter* (London, 1965), p. 69.

[29] *Reliquiae Baxterianae: or Mr. Richard Baxter's Narrative of the Most Memorable Passages of his Life and Times*, Matthew Sylvester, ed. (London, 1696), p. 150.

ening discipline by using lay elders to admonish erring communicants.[30] Both practices were directly connected with the organization of the association. Baxter saw the catechizing of families as an extension of the association's work with ministers and even used the association to bolster the disciplining of individual church members. Again, Geoffrey Nuttall, quoting Baxter, writes that "if offenders 'could not be prevailed with to repent' by Baxter and his assistant, 'we required them to meet all the ministers at [this] other monthly Meeting, which was always the next Day after [the] parochial Meeting.' "[31]

Associations elsewhere aimed for similar ends. The Cambridge association agreed that local reform was promoted best by "diligent and constant preaching" or "by frequent private conference to instruct persons of all sorts," and the association in Cornwall agreed to supply ministers bi-weekly during the summer of 1656 for the same ends, and to "consult about some present supply of vacant places, especially [those] most populous and next to us."[32]

A look in a different direction at Baptists and Quakers ought by most standards to take us far from the clerical domination in church government practiced by reforming Anglicans and Puritans. But in fact it will demonstrate how fluid, and hence useful, this English reforming tradition was. It will illustrate how ministerial labor could be conceptualized in other ways and yet remain within this tradition, and how two quite different groups joined ministry with authority in new ways to create new forms of denominational order in Commonwealth England.

The Baptists' long accepted radicalism during the Commonwealth period clearly stemmed from their concept of the ministry and its implications for authority, church government, and denominational institutions. One of the most popular anti-Baptist tracts of the 1650's—Daniel Featley's *The Dipper Dipt, or the Anabaptists Duckt and Plunged over Head and Ears*—lays down the elemental charge against the Baptists. Featley claimed that they denied all distinctions between laymen and ministers and that their preachers needed only an infusion of the Holy Spirit to validate their work. He observed that among Baptists "not the meanest citizen, not the illiterest day labourer but holds himself sufficient to be a master builder in

Christ's Church," thus making them anarchists and egalitarians whose suppression was necessary to the Puritan Commonwealth.[33] But in fact, Featley misunderstood the Baptist concept of the ministry and greatly underestimated the Baptist commitment to institutions promoting denominational order.

The foundation of denominational order among England's Particular Baptists—the major English Baptist group important to the religious development of the Delaware valley—was established in a *Confession of Faith* drawn up by representatives from seven Baptist congregations meeting in London in 1644.[34] Since the Particular Baptist movement emerged out of a dispute over the rite of baptism among Independents or Congregationalists, it is scarcely surprising that the *Confession* stressed the importance of individual congregations. These were deemed to be autonomous bodies, "every one a compact and knit Citie in it selfe," so that no single congregation was subject to the rule of another congregation or to the rule of a group of congregations. Yet the *Confession* also recognized the need for a broader discipline, for common rules among the congregations, and for "the counsell and help one of another in needful affairs of the church."[35]

The *Confession* solidified a decentralized view of the ministry far different from that espoused by reformers like Richard Baxter. As B. R. White notes, the *Confession* devalued the authority of any single minister in a congregation. But this was accomplished by discussing the ministry in terms of work and duties—preaching the Word, administering baptism and the

[30] Quoted in Frederick J. Powicke, *A Life of the Reverend Richard Baxter, 1615–1691* (London, 1924), p. 105.

[31] Geoffrey F. Nuttall, *Richard Baxter* (London, 1965), p. 63. Nuttall argues that the connection was direct, and that "catechizing and discipline together were, moreover, the basis for the Association of ministers which he formed in Worcestershire and which became a model for many other counties throughout the country." *Ibid.*, p. 57.

[32] "Minutes of the Cambridge Classis," in: *Minutes of the Bury Presbyterian Classis, 1647–1657*, William A. Shaw, ed., *Remains Hist. and Lit. Chetham Soc.*, n.s., 41 (Manchester, Engl., 1898): pp. 193–194; "Minutes of the Cornwall Classis," in *ibid.*, pp. 176, 183, 187.

[33] Quoted in Robert Barclay, *The Inner Life of the Religious Societies of the Commonwealth* (3d ed., London, 1879), p. 297. The radical character of the early Baptist movement was emphasized by nineteenth-century historians who connected it with Continental Anabaptism. Now, however, even recent historians who connect the Commonwealth Baptists with Commonwealth political radicals dismiss the Continental connection. See Donald F. Durnbaugh, "Baptists and Quakers—Left Wing Puritans," *Quaker History* 42 (1973): pp. 67–82; Jack Birdwhistell, "The Continental Anabaptists and the Early English Baptists: A Review and Analysis of Research," *Quart. Review: A Survey of Southern Baptist Progress* 34 (1974): pp. 47–58; Christopher Hill, *The World Turned Upside Down: Radical Ideas During the English Revolution* (New York, 1972), pp. 11–12, 302–305; B. S. Capp, *The Fifth Monarchy Men: A Study in Seventeenth-Century English Millennarianism* (Totowa, N.J., 1972), pp. 14–15, 79; B. R. White, *The English Separatist Tradition: From the Marian Exiles to the Pilgrim Fathers* (Oxford, 1971), pp. 161–164.

[34] See Alfred C. Underwood, *A History of the English Baptists* (London, 1947), p. 73.

[35] The document is printed in *Baptist Confessions of Faith*, W. L. Lumpkin, ed. (Valley Forge, Pa., 1969), pp. 153–171. The quotations are from article 47. B. R. White argues that the Baptist view on assemblies was very close to the consociation theory developed by John Cotton in his *Keyes of the Kingdom of Heaven* in 1644 and important to the development of New England. B. R. White, "The Doctrine of the Church in the Particular Baptist Confession of 1644," *Jour. Theological Studies*, n.s., 19 (1968): p. 587.

Lord's Supper, and disciplining the faithful—and by referring to the many people who would perform such duties in the congregations—"Pastors, Teachers, Elders, Deacons." The 1644 *Confession* then replaced the noun, "minister," with the verb, "to minister," and divided the work of the ministry among many members of the congregation. The administration of baptism, which aside from the Lord's Supper was the most important rite among Particular Baptists, was given over to someone called a "preaching Disciple," because as the *Confession* put it, the rite was "no where tyed to a particular Church, Officer, or person extraordinarily sent." Thus anyone who preached—a great many people indeed—might also baptize.[36]

The need for "counsell and help one of another" led to the creation of the first Particular Baptist "denominational" meetings in the late 1640's and early 1650's. Although these meetings were attended by a broad range of persons from the congregations, they remained ministerial in character because those who attended them were engaged in the multi-sided work of the ministry. Thus the meetings reveal that Baptists had not abolished the distinction between laymen and ministers, as Daniel Featley had charged, but had simply enlarged the ministerial ranks while still preserving the essential distinction.

At the same time, the meetings promoted a special kind of ministry—the work of those who preached to the general public and who usually, but not always, were called "pastors." This development reflected the emergence of a subtle ranking of ministerial activity among Commonwealth Baptists. In 1654 the Particular Baptist meeting in Wales wrote that among all church officers "the greatest charge lay on pastors." They were more fully involved in ministerial labor than others were, tended to assume a great responsibility for the health of their local congregations, and if they traveled were the ones who organized new congregations. Thus in both Wales and western England general meetings sought out pastors, raised money for their expenses, and promised help from others in the ministry. Indeed, in the Midlands Particular Baptists criticized congregations with an abundance of pastors. They "ought not to suffer other churches to wante," the Midlands Baptists wrote. Rather, all Baptists should be able "to partake of their giftes as they apeare to have need both in speritualles and temporalles." [37]

Unlike reforming Anglicans and Puritans, and in partial contrast to the Particular Baptist case itself in the 1690's, pastors in the 1650's never institutionalized a superior authority in their congregations or in the general meetings. Through a series of scholarly errors, one of the best known pastors, Thomas Collier, was long thought to have been "superintendent" of Particular Baptist congregations in western England and to have been one of many such officials among Commonwealth Baptists. This never happened. As B. R. White has now shown, Collier was only the foremost of several western pastors and was ordained in 1654 "for the performance of that worke that hee hath beene a long tyme exercised in, namely, in gathering and confirming the church," meaning the work of a pastor, not for any newly created office.[38]

This sharing of ministry, authority, and discipline combined to produce a vital cohesion among Particular Baptists. As Thomas Collier himself put it, Particular Baptists were "fellow members of one body though in distinct congregations." [39] There individuals heard the Word, received baptism, listened to the problems of their fellow members and were offered the Lord's Supper, thus making for the vibrant discipline so sensibly described by Michael Walzer's *Revolution of the Saints*.[40] And in the denominational meetings those who shared the work of the ministry sought to extend it by promoting the activity of pastors as well as by answering "queries" from individual congregations. Sometimes the questions were obscure, as when in 1656 a congregation asked "whether Astrology in matters of physick be lawfull" (Baptists were told to be "very cautious how they meddle with the practice of it"). More often they concerned the problems of ministry and authority that were central to the maintenance of Particular Baptist discipline.[41]

The relatively broad sharing of ministry and authority among Particular Baptists also promoted denominational cohesion in which all individual activity was legitimized by its connection with the discipline of the whole body. This produced a corporate impulse quite the opposite of the anarchy for which Daniel Featley had castigated the Baptists. In this context individualist tendencies brought quick censure. In 1654, for example, the western Particular Baptist meeting determined that baptism should be confirmed in congregational membership. It was not designed to allow individuals to go their own spiritual way.

[36] *Baptist Confessions of Faith*, W. L. Lumpkin, ed. (Valley Forge, Pa., 1969), pp. 166, 167. See also B. R. White, "The Organization of the Particular Baptists, 1644–1660," *Jour. Ecclesiastical History* 17 (1966) : pp. 208–225.

[37] *Association Records of the Particular Baptists of England, Wales and Ireland to 1660*, B. R. White, ed. (London, 1971–1973), pp. 3, 11, 25.

[38] *Ibid.*, pp. 103, 109.

[39] *Ibid.*, p. 77. The quotation is from Collier's epistle to the western Baptist congregations of 1656.

[40] Michael Walzer, *The Revolution of the Saints: A Study in the Origins of Radical Politics* (Cambridge, Mass., 1965), pp. 219–224. For an example see *Records of the Churches of Christ, Gathered at Fenstanton, Warboys, and Hexham, 1644–1720*, Edward B. Underhill, ed., *Publ. Hanserd Knollys Soc.* 9 (London, 1854), or *The Records of a Christ of Christ in Bristol, 1640 to 1687*, Roger Hayden, ed., *Publ. Bristol Record Soc.* 27 (Bristol, Engl., 1974).

[41] *Association Records of the Particular Baptists of England, Wales and Ireland to 1660*, B. R. White, ed. (London, 1971–1973), p. 65.

Preaching also was tied to the congregations. In 1657 Midlands Baptists were asked whether a gifted member could "go out to preach at [his] owne will at the time of the church meeting." The meeting rejected the suggestion. It was a "disorderly practice" and if the member persisted in it the church had an obligation to "deale with him as an offender." Thus, as Michael Walzer has argued, among these Baptists the congregation—not the individual—was the center for the achievement of Christian discipline and the touchstone of the Christian experience. It scarcely is surprising then that Midlands Baptists concluded their advice to the inquiring congregation by advising simply that "all those gifted are the church's"—a notion that in its emphasis on membership in a corporate structure sharply conflicts with the view of many historians that Commonwealth Baptists manifested modern individualist tendencies in the seventeenth century.[42]

The denominational order developed by Commonwealth and Restoration Quakers also thrived on a corporate emphasis. But it strayed far from the Baptist pattern by the enormous power Quakers gave to ministering Friends. Of course, this argument stands traditional Quaker historiography on its head, because the Quaker ridicule of the "hireling clergy," their repudiation of ordination, traditional ecclesiastical offices, and the sacraments, and their belief in an "Inward Light" that could be cultivated by all Friends, has led most historians to describe Quakerism as lacking ministers in any customary sense. Most historians also have thought of Quakerism as a democratic movement, with authority centered in local meetings, not in national ones or among ministers. If oligarchic tendencies set in, this happened after a formal meeting system was established in the late 1660's and after Friends stopped seeking converts in the 1680's and 1690's. As we shall see, however, Friends not only had a powerful clerical order—ministers called "Public Friends"—but its members dominated the movement until at least 1690 through their control of a hierarchical meeting system that first emerged in the Commonwealth period.[43]

To appreciate the magnitude of the Quaker achievement it is first important to understand how Friends retained ministers. They did so not in the usual Protestant sense—they always decried ordination and clerical ceremonies—but in a special Quaker way.[44] Friends believed that the Inward Light could be fully received and understood by everyone, a tenet that might even further relieve them of the need for a ministerial group. But as early as 1653 the great Quaker leader, George Fox, noted "diversities of gifts" within the Light, and this idea played an important role in the development of the Quaker denominational order.[45] There was a place for everyone in the church, "some threashing, some ploughing, and some to keep the sheep."[46] One such role was in the explication of the Inward Light. Here Quakers discovered and used a "gift" to speak about the Holy Spirit and bring others to Quakerism. This was the "talent" possessed by the earliest Public Friends, the First Publishers of Truth who brought the movement into being in the 1650's. To Fox they were preachers and "prophets of the Lord" whom God had "made to be his mouth," and in the forty years after 1650 they became better known for their labor, especially their arduous travels and stays in the English jails, than for the office they occupied, so that Quakers emphasized the verb "to minister" rather than the noun when discussing their service.[47]

Between 1651 and 1655 the First Publishers of Truth grew from a handful of followers surrounding Fox to a group of more than seventy persons. More important, by 1655 they had developed a corporate fellowship that fostered discipline among them and encouraged the coordination of their activities. Their earliest endeavors in northern England testified to a penchant for careful planning. In Yorkshire the village of Malton received two visits from pairs of Quaker ministers in 1652 in which the first cultivated a large audience for the second, and in 1654 John Audland and John Camm traveled to Bristol only after details of their mission had been worked out in a meeting of ministers then combing London for converts.[48] Indeed, Public Friends met so often at

---

[42] Ibid., p. 34.

[43] Thus both Ernest A. Taylor, The Valiant Sixty (London, 1947) and William C. Braithwaite, The Beginnings of Quakerism (2nd ed., Cambridge, Engl., 1961), treat early Quaker leaders as evangelists but not as ministers. For treatments that give at least some suggestion of the latter see Arnold Lloyd, Quaker Social History, 1669–1738 (London, 1950); Frederick B. Tolles, "The Transatlantic Quaker Community in the Seventeenth Century: Its Structure and Functioning," in: Tolles, Quakers and the Atlantic Culture (New York, 1960), pp. 21–35; Richard T. Vann, The Social Development of English Quakerism, 1655–1755 (Cambridge, Mass., 1969), pp. 96–101; Lucia K. Beamish, Quaker Ministry, 1691 to 1834 (Oxford, privately printed, 1967). Christopher Hill connects a growing conservatism in the Friends after 1660 with their interest in organization and institutional authority in The World Turned Upside Down: Radical Ideas During the English Revolution (New York, 1972), pp. 302–306.

[44] Fox to Friends in the Ministry, 1653, in: Selections from the Epistles of George Fox, Samuel Tuke, comp. (Cambridge, Mass., 1879), pp. 19, 34–35; The Memorable Works of a Son of Thunder and Consolation . . . Edward Burroughs [sic] (London, 1672), p. 441.

[45] Fox to Friends in Cumberland, Bishoprick and Northumberland, 1653, in: Selections from the Epistles of George Fox, Samuel Tuke, comp. (Cambridge, Mass., 1879), p. 29.

[46] Fox to [Friends], 1652, ibid., p. 13.

[47] Fox to Friends in the Ministry, 1653, ibid., p. 19; Fox to Friends in the Ministry, 1654, ibid., pp. 34–35.

[48] Hugh Barbour, The Quakers in Puritan England (New Haven, 1964), pp. 37–56; William C. Braithwaite, The Beginnings of Quakerism (2nd ed., Cambridge, Engl., 1961), pp. 28–77; Henry J. Cadbury, "First Publishers of Truth in London," Jour. Friends Hist. Soc. 36 (1936): pp. 52–58; Francis Howgill to Robert Widders, 23 September, 1654, in: "Letters,

Swarthmore, the Cumberland home of Fox's later wife, Margaret Fell, that one Friend represented his convincement as beginning with a visionary instruction to join them there. "Go thy ways to Swarthmore," the Lord told him, "where my Lambs and Babes and Children of Light will be gathered together to wait upon my Name." [49]

By the mid-1650's the ministers had developed an internal discipline to match their external organization. Stung by a falling out with James Nayler that dramatized unexpected flaws in ministerial discipline, George Fox probed additional sources for discipline. Although warnings against individual excesses had been expressed earlier, after Nayler "ran into imaginations," Fox began to speak systematically about the uses of silence for Friends. For every Quaker there was a "time of Waiting, . . . a time of Receiving, . . . a time of Speaking." Not until a Friend knew these times and was free from his own vanity and self-deception should he presume to exercise a public ministry. Until then, every Friend was encouraged to cultivate an inner faith and as Fox put it, to "mind where the watching is." [50]

The exhortations against an immature ministry were paralleled by the rise of a kind of ministerial apprenticeship in which those who wanted to work in the ministry were supervised by those already accepted as ministers. An example can be seen in the career of John Burnyeat. Convinced as a Friend in 1653, Burnyeat spent the next few years close to his local meeting. Then with great fear he challenged local Anglican and Puritan clergymen to debates and took a short trip to Ireland. He next journeyed to Scotland in the company of a more experienced minister, Robert Lange, and on this journey nurtured a desire to minister in America. Since such an undertaking would require much skill and preparation, he went to London in 1660 to consult about it with Fox and other important ministers. Unfortunately the discussion did not go well. The ministers did not approve the trip and Burnyeat resisted their verdict, experiencing "great travail in spirit and deep exercise in mind be-

fore I gave up," he later wrote. Still the desire remained and two years later he traveled to London again to seek the "counsel and countenance of my elder brethren." Although the ministers' verdict is not clear, Burnyeat still did not go to America until 1664, or until he had completed preaching tours of Yorkshire and Cumberland. But according to his *Journal* Burnyeat considered these last trips, especially the American one of 1664, to mark his full entrance into the Quaker ministry, a ministry he exercised until his death in 1690. [51]

Using their own discipline as their principal foundation, between 1655 and 1660 the Quaker ministers created a denominational order that turned a ragged collection of listeners into a cohesive and feared religious movement. They did so by exercising an authority in church government that paralleled their power in preaching. As they won converts across England the ministers began to advise the growing number of meetings for worship. At first this happened incidentally. But in 1656 and again in 1659 some of the Public Friends issued formal recommendations to strengthen discipline and order in local proceedings. Friends should adopt uniform practices for worship, business matters, marriages, recordkeeping, and the collection of funds. In 1656 the ministers denied that their advice was a demand or was laid down "as a rule or form to walk by." It was given "so in the light walking and abiding, these things may be fulfilled in the Spirit, not in the letter, for the letter killeth, but the spirit giveth life." In 1659, however, the ministers' advice carried no such apology, not even as a postscript. [52]

Between 1660 and about 1700 Quaker denominational order was increasingly sustained in a formidable array of meetings and committees, so much so that as we shall see, in the 1690's it became a model for reforming Anglicans. For Friends, however, the evolution meant that a relatively fluid movement first held together by the authority of the First Publishers of Truth quickly became a church distinguished for astonishing institutional complexity. This change had secular as well as religious implications. By the end of the seventeenth century Quakers were behaving in a distinctly ghetto-like fashion. In worldly matters they shielded themselves behind institutions and self-

&c., of Early Friends," A. R. Barclay, ed., *Friends Library* 11 (1847) : p. 330; Edward Burrough to Margaret Fell, September, 1655, in: *Early Quaker Writings, 1650–1700*, Hugh Barbour and Arthur O. Roberts, eds. (Grand Rapids, Mich., 1973), pp. 476–478.

[49] Quoted in Geoffrey F. Nuttall, *Studies in Christian Enthusiasm Illustrated from Early Quakerism* (Wallingford, Pa., 1948), p. 22.

[50] See "An Epistle to All the People in the Earth," in: *Gospel-Truth Demonstrated, in A Collection of Doctrinal Books, Given forth by that Faithful Minister of Jesus Christ, George Fox* (London, 1706), pp. 91–101; Geoffrey F. Nuttall, "James Nayler, A Fresh Approach," *Jour. Friends Hist. Soc.,* suppl. 26 (1954) ; *The Journal of George Fox,* John L. Nickalls, ed. (Cambridge, Engl., 1952), pp. 268–269; Fox to Friends in the Ministry, 31 March, 1657, in *Early Quaker Writings, 1650–1700,* Hugh Barbour and Arthur O. Roberts, eds. (Grand Rapids, Mich., 1973), pp. 489–491.

[51] "Journal of the Life and Gospel Labours of John Burnyeat," *Friends Library* 11 (1847) : pp. 121–134. See also *The History of the Life of Thomas Ellwood* (London, 1714), pp. 108–110.

[52] These epistles are printed in "Letters, &c., of Early Friends," A. R. Barclay, ed., *Friends Library* 11 (1847) : pp. 409–411, where the first is misdated 1657. Braithwaite summarized them in *The Beginnings of Quakerism* (2nd ed., Cambridge, Engl., 1961), pp. 311–316, but was not especially concerned about their authorship. A partial text also appears in *Early Quaker Writings, 1650–1700,* Hugh Barbour and Arthur O. Roberts, eds. (Grand Rapids, Mich., 1973), pp. 549–550.

imposed identifying customs long in the making. In church government it involved a decline in the power held by the Quaker ministers.

Quakers faced new difficulties after the Restoration of 1660. They experienced persecution by the state, internal dissension, and the loss of important ministers through death or imprisonment. To meet these challenges Friends reorganized existing meetings into the now famous system of monthly, quarterly, and yearly meetings.[53] What was important in this system was not so much the creation of new meetings but the successful integration of all Quaker meetings, new or old, into a smoothly working scheme that Friends could use easily to transact business under trying circumstances. In all the meetings a great emphasis was placed on selectivity of membership and the legitimacy of hierarchical authority. The London Yearly Meeting was established in 1661 as the most powerful of all the meetings and was attended only by Public Friends until 1678. Although monthly and quarterly meetings contained persons outside the ministry they were attended by only a small proportion of the Quakers who attended meetings for worship. The London Yearly Meeting justified the practice in 1673 simply by noting that among Friends "a general care be not laid upon every member touching the good order and government in the Church's affairs."[54]

Authority in the expanded Quaker meeting system flowed down from the top, not up from the bottom. Ministers in the London Yearly Meeting passed their directions on to quarterly meetings, which in turn sent them down to monthly meetings. The effect was dramatically evident in financial matters. Even in the early 1670's the Gainsborough Monthly Meeting in Lincoln, for example, passed half the funds it collected in meetings for worship on to the quarterly meeting above it. Although some of the money occasionally found its way back to Gainsborough, most of it was sent on to London, where it was redistributed.[55]

The authority of the Public Friends in the Quakers' hierarchical scheme of church government appeared even in the design of meetinghouses. In the country meetinghouses Friends built pulpits that were raised above the floor and faced by a panel that hid the lower portions of the minister's body as he spoke. In larger meetinghouses the ministers sat in galleries that contained several rows of seats, also raised above the floor and usually placed along the side of the room. In the largest meetinghouses the galleries were, in fact, balconies, from which the ministers could gaze down on their audience. They delivered their "openings" from them and waited there for what George Fox had once called the "gathering of the simple-hearted ones."[56]

After 1660 new meetings serving specialized tasks added to the complexity of the Quakers' institutional structure. In the early 1660's a new committee of London ministers assumed the management of a fund for ministerial expenses originally established by Margaret Fell in 1654. Then in 1679 this committee was in turn replaced by a committee of the London Yearly Meeting.[57] The London Second Day Morning Meeting, a wholly ministerial body, began its work in the 1670's. It controlled all ministerial activity in and around London but became especially powerful because it controlled the publication of all Quaker books and pamphlets in England through its use of broad censorship powers.[58] The Meeting for Sufferings organized in 1675 coordinated Quaker resistance to persecution. It divided itself into four groups, each of which met weekly for three months in the space of a year to consider reports received from correspondents stationed throughout the country. Formation of the Meeting for Sufferings encouraged the development of an even more efficient arrangement for carrying on Quaker church government. While the Yearly Meeting in London established general policy for English Quakerism, the Meeting for Sufferings became the Quaker executive body. It developed tactics to counter-

[53] For Fox's view of the change see *The Journal of George Fox*, John L. Nickalls, ed. (Cambridge, Engl., 1952), p. 511, and his long epistle in *Selections from the Epistles of George Fox*, Samuel Tuke, comp. (Cambridge, Mass., 1879), pp. 122–135. See also William C. Braithwaite, *The Second Period of Quakerism* (2nd ed., Cambridge, Engl., 1961), pp. 215–222.

[54] Quoted in William C. Braithwaite, *The Second Period of Quakerism* (2nd ed., Cambridge, Engl., 1961), p. 294. See also *ibid.*, pp. 276–277, and Arnold Lloyd, *Quaker Social History, 1669–1738* (London, 1950), p. 27. Vann argues that the monthly and quarterly meetings were not formally limited in membership but admits that only the more prestigious local Friends regularly attended them. Richard T. Vann, *The Social Development of English Quakerism, 1655–1755* (Cambridge, Mass., 1969), pp. 105–121. For a glimpse at the size of monthly meetings in Bristol, where Friends were numerous, see *Minute Book of the Society of Friends in Bristol, 1667–1686*, Russell Mortimer, ed., *Publ. Bristol Record Soc. 26* (Bristol, Engl., 1971): pp. 41–68, 162–174. In the 1670's the monthly meetings sometimes were attended by as many as twenty persons, but by the 1680's usually less than ten persons were present.

[55] *The First Minute Book of the Gainsborough Monthly Meeting of the Society of Friends, 1669–1719*, Harold W. Brace, ed., *Publ. Lincoln Record Soc. 38* (London, 1948): pp. 7, 58.

[56] Fox to Friends, 1651, in: *Selections from the Epistles of George Fox*, Samuel Tuke, comp. (Cambridge, Mass., 1879), p. 8; Richard T. Vann, *The Social Development of English Quakerism, 1655–1755* (Cambridge, Mass., 1969), p. 100; Hubert Lidbetter, *The Friends Meeting House* (York, Engl., 1961), pp. 26–28. Lidbetter dates the construction of the Quaker buildings but not their interiors.

[57] Isabel Ross, *Margaret Fell, Mother of Quakerism* (London, 1949), pp. 63–66; Arnold Lloyd, *Quaker Social History, 1669–1738* (London, 1950), p. 158; *Early Quaker Writings, 1650–1700*, Hugh Barbour and Arthur O. Roberts, eds. (Grand Rapids, Mich., 1973), pp. 475–476.

[58] Luella M. Wright, *The Literary Life of the Early Friends, 1650–1725* (New York, 1932), pp. 97–109.

act persecution, hired lawyers to defend imprisoned Quakers, and engaged lobbyists to press Court and Parliament for legislation to end the persecution.[59] As a result, institutions reinforced belief. The unity of the meeting structure paralleled the "unity in the Light" which the First Publishers of Truth proclaimed. Together they cleared away the confusing minutiae of life, straightened the spirit, and created order in denominational affairs.[60]

In all of this a simple theme persisted: Quaker ministerial authority and the denominational order that flowed from it was corporate in character. One hears little about individual ministers asserting "right" against other ministers or setting one meeting for worship against another, problems that often plagued other Protestant groups. Rather, a Quaker remained "in the ministry" only as long as he was associated with a ministerial meeting like London's Second Day Morning Meeting. The Public Friends returned ceaselessly to these meetings for directions and sustenance. There they consulted on all the matters that concerned them—tactics, discipline, effectiveness, financing—and this cooperation made theirs a peculiarly joint ministry.[61] Seldom did a Quaker minister act alone. Rather, he or she traveled and spoke in the company of other Public Friends. Moving across England in pairs and on itineraries approved by their ministerial meetings, they were living examples of the "unity of the Light." [62]

This ministerial cohesion was especially valuable in times of crisis. When John Perrot threatened to divide the Quakers in the 1660's he centered many of his attacks on the ministers. He called them self-serving and vain and suggested that they were more interested in increasing the number of their followers than in the work of the Holy Spirit. As an antidote to their pretensions he urged that Friends stop their proselytizing. One of his followers argued that Friends should observe a "time of keeping at home . . . every one to sit down under his own vine, and quietly to enjoy the fruit of his labour." [63] Not surprisingly, the ministers attacked Perrot. He was first con-

demned by eleven of them, meeting in London, in a verdict that contained a strong defense of their own ministerial prerogatives. Quakers were told that the ministers were persons "whom God hath called to labour and watch for the eternal good of your souls." Perrot's egalitarianism was rejected as an "abominable pride that goes before destruction." Authority and judgment were needed in a sinful world, and the ministers asserted their right to exercise both. "When we testify in the name of the Lord," they wrote, their opponents were to be "rejected, as having erred from the Truth." [64] However extreme this last claim, it reflected the widely held view that the Quaker ministers held the movement together with their prophecy, travel, and authority.

After about 1680, however, the ministers began to lose their sole command of Quakerism. The most obvious cause was the death of nearly all the remaining First Publishers of Truth, including George Fox, who died in 1691. While some impressive individuals replaced them, like the much neglected George Whitehead, the later leaders were less dynamic and certainly less colorful than their predecessors. Equally important was the fact that ministerial labor also changed. As the complexity of Quaker institutions increased, the work of committees and meetings in London became routinized. Account books needed auditing, funds had to be collected and distributed, decisions regarding policy toward the government and courts had to be made and implemented.[65] As a result, the stereotyped image of the "new" Quaker leader of the late seventeenth century in fact approached reality. Men like William Penn or Thomas Rudyard, the so-called "Quakers' lawyer," demonstrated a sophistication, urbanity, and success at lobbying in Parliament, Court and among London merchants—it was Penn's friendship with the Catholic Stuarts that got him his American colony—that set them apart from the First Publishers of Truth and measured the evolving character of the Quaker ministerial elite.[66]

Meetings changed too. In the early 1690's a few English monthly meetings requested the establishment of "retired" meetings for worship. In them everyone waited in silence for the Lord's blessing and wisdom,

[59] Arnold Lloyd, *Quaker Social History, 1669–1738* (London, 1950), pp. 12–13; N. C. Hunt, *Two Early Political Associations: The Quakers and the Dissenting Deputies in the Age of Sir Robert Walpole* (Oxford, 1961), pp. 1–4.

[60] George Fox, "To All who Love the Lord Jesus Christ...," [1654], in: *Gospel Truth Demonstrated, in a Collection of Doctrinal Books, Given forth by that Faithful Minister of Jesus Christ, George Fox* (London, 1706), p. 25; *The Memorable Works of a Son of Thunder and Consolation . . . Edward Burroughs* [sic] (London, 1672), pp. 689, 835, 844.

[61] The most thorough treatment of the activity of Public Friends still is William C. Braithwaite, *The Second Period of Quakerism* (2nd ed., Cambridge, Engl., 1961), Chaps. 1–4.

[62] See Geoffrey T. Nuttall, *The Holy Spirit in Puritan Faith and Experience* (New York, 1947), pp. 45–46.

[63] Quoted in William C. Braithwaite, *The Second Period of Quakerism* (2nd ed., Cambridge, Engl., 1961), p. 237.

[64] "Letters, &c., of Early Friends," A. R. Barclay, ed., *The Friends Library* (14 v., Philadelphia, 1837–1850) 11: pp. 422–424; Arnold Lloyd, *Quaker Social History, 1669–1738* (London, 1950), pp. 24–25; William C. Braithwaite, *The Second Period of Quakerism* (2nd ed., Cambridge, Engl., 1961), pp. 247–248.

[65] William C. Braithwaite, *The Second Period of Quakerism* (2nd ed., Cambridge, Engl., 1961), pp. 416–456; Arnold Lloyd, *Quaker Social History, 1669–1738* (London, 1950), pp. 157–165.

[66] See both Joseph E. Illick, *William Penn the Politician: His Relations with the English Government* (Ithaca, N.Y. 1965) and Alfred W. Braithwaite, "Thomas Rudyard, Early Friends 'Oracle of Law,'" *Jour. Friends Hist. Soc.*, suppl. 27 (1957).

while no one spoke, not even ministers, a quite different kind of worship from that which first distinguished the movement.[67] In addition, "weighty Friends" outside the ministry already had begun to share power with Public Friends. The first sign of their rise came in 1678 when the London Yearly Meeting admitted them to its gatherings. Thereafter the Yearly Meeting included all Public Friends who could attend it, as well as two weighty Friends from all the quarterly meetings except those in London and Bristol, which sent four weighty Friends to London.[68] In addition, outside England non-ministerial meetings began to look into the activity of the Public Friends for the first time. In 1692 and 1693 the Irish Half-Year's Meeting censured the behavior of some Public Friends and ordered weighty Friends from monthly and quarterly meetings to sit with local ministers in their previously private gatherings. By 1700 this practice had been adopted in two English counties, but not in others.[69] Then in 1697 the London Yearly Meeting institutionalized the weighty Friends' informal authority in the appointment of monthly meeting "overseers" or "elders" to help Friends enforce discipline at the local level and "keep to plainness, both to speech, habit and dealing." [70]

The renewed emphasis on discipline slowly cost Public Friends their independence. In 1703 the London Second Day Morning Meeting sent a twenty-point epistle to England's Quaker ministers that criticized their lengthy speeches, their occasional tendency to foster discord and even their ignorance of the Scriptures. These warnings had been heard before as part of the ministers' own efforts at internal discipline. But now they were part of the broader effort to guide further the behavior of all Friends, whether in meetings for worship, monthly meetings, or even among ministers. Thus, by 1710 what already had happened in Ireland also occurred in England, as weighty Friends outside the ministry gained admittance to nearly all the previously private ministerial gatherings.[71]

Had English Quakerism slowly become democratic on the eve of colonization in America? Clearly not. In 1680 and again in 1700 the movement remained oligarchic. The early emphasis on corporate ministerial authority begun by the First Publishers of Truth now manifested itself in a vast array of meetings and committees. By 1700 the Quaker denominational structure diffused more responsibility among more people in more meetings than ever before. Yet power in it still was held by the few rather than the many because only Public Friends and weighty Friends managed the movement. The tightly drawn meeting structure integrated the corporate authority of the Quaker leadership with the doctrine of the Inward Light in a way that fostered a solidness of purpose and leadership matched by few other religious groups in eighteenth-century England.

The Quaker achievement after 1660 is striking when we compare it to the fate of reforming Anglicans and Puritans in the same years. Negotiations that would have permitted their entrance into the restored Anglican Church were capped instead by the passage of the Act of Uniformity of 1664 and the Five Mile Act of 1665. These acts prohibited their activity and residence within five miles of any English town or city. The results were disastrous. Reformers who had leaned on state support for over a decade were forced to conform to the new Anglican Church—half those in Baxter's Worcestershire Association did, for example—or lose their parish pulpits. Communicants also faced this choice and a vast majority of them conformed, leaving old reforming clerics who rejected the new order with no congregations and no livings.[72]

Under these conditions the state-supported presbyteries and Baxter's ministerial associations collapsed. One minister believed that reform might still prosper if ministers preached to their congregations "by silence," which he thought would create "the most powerful and effectual sermon" the ministers had yet given.[73] But the silence that came was forcibly imposed by the state and had disastrous effects on reformed discipline. Congregations disappeared. Clergymen hid and only imitated their old reforming habits. Thomas Jollie and Oliver Heywood, two leading reformers, preached mainly in private homes. They re-emphasized catechizing and family worship, although both had originally been designed to supplement organized congregational activity. Jollie wrote often of his "retireings" in quiet meditation and

---

[67] William C. Braithwaite, *The Second Period of Quakerism* (2nd ed., Cambridge, Engl., 1961), p. 545; J. William Frost, *The Quaker Family in Colonial America: A Portrait of the Society of Friends* (New York, 1973), pp. 38–40. Frost suggests that retired meetings were uncommon in America, but warns that his conclusion is drawn from limited evidence. The fact of their existence, however, points to a new departure in Quaker worship after 1690.

[68] William C. Braithwaite, *The Second Period of Quakerism* (2nd ed., Cambridge, Engl., 1961), p. 276; Arnold Lloyd, *Quaker Social History, 1669–1738* (London, 1950), p. 27.

[69] William C. Braithwaite, *The Second Period of Quakerism* (2nd ed., Cambridge, Engl., 1961), p. 542.

[70] *A Collection of the Epistles of the Yearly Meeting of Friends in London ... 1675 to 1805* (Baltimore, Md., 1806), p. 71.

[71] William C. Braithwaite, *The Second Period of Quakerism* (2nd ed., Cambridge, Engl., 1961), pp. 541–543. The warning apparently was widely circulated and there are manuscript copies at both FHL and HSP.

[72] These are summarized in C. G. Bolam *et al.*, *English Presbyterians from Elizabethan Puritanism to Modern Unitarianism* (London, 1968), pp. 73–92, and in R. Tudor Jones, *Congregationalism in England, 1662–1962* (London, 1962), pp. 46–71.

[73] Quoted in C. G. Bolam *et al.*, *English Presbyterians from Elizabethan Puritanism to Modern Unitarianism* (London, 1968), p. 85.

thought.[74] At best the ministers gathered infrequently to perform an ordination. If they passed word to younger ministers of the old fraternal intercourse fostered by the associations, this probably happened most frequently in the schools or "dissenting academies" many of them were forced to organize to make their livings, since association or presbytery life disappeared altogether.[75]

By the mid-1680's, however, association activity reappeared. Thomas Jollie's diary reveals that the infrequent ministerial conferences occasionally held between 1660 and 1680 were replaced by more regular gatherings on the eve of the Glorious Revolution. Jollie recorded three ministerial gatherings in 1687, one in 1688 at which he circulated "papers of reformation and reunion" to ministers in his native Yorkshire, four in 1689 and two in 1690. In 1691 he helped turn these meetings into a new ministerial association, and similar associations were organized in Cheshire, Lancashire, Hampshire, Norfolk, Northamptonshire and Devon.[76]

Like Baxter's old associations, the new meetings did not test their members' doctrine and often contained both English Presbyterians and Congregationalists or Independents. They also were ministerial bodies. The "Heads of Agreement" that formed the basis for the association in London, for example, justified its organization with the familiar argument that congregational reform was a product of ministerial reform. It argued that "pastors ought to have frequent meetings together so that by Mutual Advise, Support[,] Encouragement, and Brotherly intercourse" their congregations could "strengthen the hearts and hands of each other in the ways of the Lord."[77] The Exeter Assembly formed in Devon in 1691 used the same model. Its ministers met to stimulate "mutual advice touching things pertaining to our Office, the right ordering of our Congregations, and the promoting of purity and unity in the Churches of Christ." They would uphold "the credit of the Ministry" by hearing sermons and by promoting other professional responsibilities—preaching, ministerial training, even by assisting "poor and aged Ministers" and "poor widdows and orphans of Dissenting Ministers."[78] Similarly, Thomas Jollie's Yorkshire association sponsored lectures to effect reform in negligent congregations. However, it wished to promote fellowship with only modest conviviality and ordered its treats "to be as little costly and as expensive as is convenient, viz: not above 2 dishes."[79]

Despite good beginnings the new associations proved fragile. In many places the doctrinal latitude permitted in them eased potentially damaging disputes about church government. But in London where some of the old rivalries continued they were heightened by arguments over theology. In particular, an obscure and bitter dispute about Antinomianism provoked by the republication of sermons written in the Commonwealth period shattered the association there. Since the association housed a fund to promote preaching in England and counted leading Independents and Presbyterians in its membership, its demise was a telling demonstration of the Restoration's devastating impact on the clerical cohesion of the Commonwealth years.[80]

Other associations also failed but usually for different reasons. Surveys of the Independent and Presbyterian congregations made in 1690 and again in 1715 revealed serious discrepancies in local church membership. Some congregations obviously were large and

---

[74] See *The Note Book of the Rev. Thomas Jolly . . .*, Henry Fishwick, ed., *Remains Hist. and Lit. Chetham Soc.*, n.s., **33** (Manchester, Engl., 1894) : pp. 1–15; Joseph Hunter, *The Rise of the Old Dissent Exemplified in the Life of Oliver Heywood, . . . 1630–1702* (London, 1842), pp. 143–169; *The Life of Adam Martindale . . .*, Richard Parkinson, ed., *Remains Hist. and Lit. Chetham Society*, 1st ser., **9** (Manchester, Engl., 1845) : pp. 169–174, 193. After his beloved associations had been destroyed, Richard Baxter spent much of his time in these years writing. See Geoffrey T. Nuttall, *Richard Baxter* (London, 1965), pp. 114–131.

[75] R. Tudor Jones, *Congregationalism in England, 1662–1962* (London, 1962), pp. 87–88. Although his comments on the effectiveness of the academies are exaggerated, see H. McLachlan, *English Education under the Test Acts* (Manchester, Engl., 1931).

[76] *The Note Book of the Rev. Thomas Jolly . . .*, Henry Fishwick, ed., *Remains Hist. and Lit. Chetham Soc.*, n.s., **33** (Manchester, Engl., 1894) : pp. 42, 44, 48–49, 52, 84, 85–86, 88, 91, 93, 95 f; R. Tudor Jones, *Congregationalism in England, 1662–1962* (London, 1962), p. 83. Most discussions of the post-1688 associations follow the difficulties of the ministers in London too closely and ignore developments elsewhere. See C. G. Bolam *et al.*, *English Presbyterians from Elizabethan Puritanism to Modern Unitarianism* (London, 1968), pp. 101–103, 113–123.

[77] See the copy printed in *Trans. Congregational Hist. Soc.* **8** (1920–1923) : pp. 38–48. The distinction between the legally established classes of the Commonwealth and the ministerial associations of the kind organized by Richard Baxter often was later blurred by even a great figure like Oliver Heywood, who in writing the life of John Angier interchangeably called the Manchester Presbyterian Classis a classis and a ministerial association. *Oliver Heywood's Life of John Angier of Denton*, Ernest Axon, ed., *Remains Hist. and Lit. Chetham Soc.*, n.s., **97** (Manchester, Engl., 1937) : pp. 66, 71.

[78] *The Exeter Assembly: The Minutes of the Assemblies of the United Brethren of Devon and Cornwall, 1691–1717*, Allan Brockett, ed., *Publ. Devon and Cornwall Record Soc.*, n.s., **6** (Exeter, Engl., 1963) : pp. 1–3.

[79] *Ibid.*, pp. 6, 56. The work of the association in Yorkshire can be glimpsed through the records of the church at Altham, printed in *The Note Book of the Rev. Thomas Jolly . . .*, Henry Fishwick, ed., *Remains Hist. and Lit. Chetham Soc.*, n.s., **33** (Manchester, Engl., 1894) : pp. 140 f.

[80] R. Tudor Jones, *Congregationalism in England, 1662–1962* (London, 1962), pp. 111–118; C. G. Bolam *et al.*, *English Presbyterians from Elizabethan Puritanism to Modern Unitarianism* (London, 1968), pp. 101–123; Roger Thomas, "The Break-up of Nonconformity," in: Geoffrey Nuttall *et al.*, *The Beginnings of Nonconformity* (London, 1964), pp. 33–60.

wealthy. But many were poor or small and scarcely able to support a minister.[81] Even more serious was the fact that some associations proved unable to sustain clerical order. In 1709 the Exeter Assembly heard complaints that ministerial candidates preaching in vacant congregations as part of their clerical training were refusing ordination. This produced "several inconveniencies," the Assembly worried, "namely that some children die unbaptiz'd" because the candidates were not qualified to administer the sacraments.[82]

The complaints were real, not imaginary. Of the ten ministerial candidates attending the Exeter Assembly in 1709, only four were ordained in less than three years after being granted candidate status. One was ordained in four years, three in five, and one in nine, while Thomas Hornabrook still was not ordained in 1719, although he had served a congregation since 1709. The situation was worse by 1717. Of seven candidates on whom reliable information can be gathered, only one had been a candidate for less than two years. Another had been a candidate for four years, one for five, two for eight and one for eleven years. In sum, the forty men accepted as ministerial candidates between 1691 and 1717 spent an average of four and a half years in their positions. Unfortunately, the "average" candidate was in the minority. Although ten men were ordained in three years, thirteen took between five and seven years to receive ordination, while three spent between eleven and twelve years as ministerial candidates—again, most of them serving congregations while unable to administer the sacraments.[83]

This difficulty with ministerial training epitomized the weaknesses of the reforming associations formed after 1690. On the one hand, they offered familiar forms of ministerial fellowship to their members— sermons, conferences, aid to aged clerics—and created denominational order by providing clergymen with a foundation for reform activity in congregations and sometimes by helping to settle local disputes. Yet their ministers too often held conflicting notions about church government and theology and proved strangely deficient in exerting order within their own ranks. If some ministerial candidates whom the Exeter As-

sembly "press'd to be ordain'd" in 1710 did so within the year, others, apparently backed by their congregations, resisted the pressure. Yet they were not expelled from the association.[84] This meant that the association did a better job promoting clerical fellowship than exercising power. Such inclinations presented no danger when ministers were agreeable and forgiving. But when, as happened in 1717 and 1718, ministers in many of the associations fell out over doctrine alone, ministerial fellowship shattered too. As happened in London, clerical union turned to hostility and in the process the tenuous denominational order that had been created after 1690 splintered, unable to withstand the destruction of the clerical order on which it had been based—certainly a difficult model on which to build a future in America.[85]

By nearly all accounts, of course, a more solid model for Calvinist cohesion existed to the north in the legally established Scottish Presbyterian system. Unfortunately, historians have so long treated the Scots system as unchanging and homogenous that they have obscured its real strengths and weaknesses. Its power also was founded on clerical cohesion and authority. Even after the 1660 Restoration, when bishops were imposed over the long evolving structure of kirks, presbyteries, synods, and assemblies, the concern for clerical cohesion and professional standards continued. Ministers alone supervised the training of ministerial candidates, heard sermons from fellow ministers in the presbyteries, and determined the policies that would guide both the congregations they served and the presbyteries and synods they controlled.[86]

But Scottish ministerial cohesion had to cut through much bitter argument. For example, the re-establishment of the Presbyterian system in 1690 caused intense debate among the Scottish clergymen. As before, ministers gathered in their presbyteries to test candidates, hear sermons, and discuss problems. But now they divided over issues of church polity. Thus the Barrier Act of 1697 that established rules for filling vacant parishes raised sharp questions about the rights of ministers, congregations, and presbyteries. About the same time doctrinal disputes similar to those dividing English Presbyterians and Independents began to infect northern clerics as well. And these disputes were further complicated by the fact that inevitably they always were immensely political, because Scottish Presbyterianism was a state Presby-

---

[81] The first list is printed in Alexander Gordon, *Freedom After Ejection: A Review of Presbyterian and Congregational Nonconformity in England and Wales* (Manchester, Engl., 1917), pp. 1–150.

[82] *The Exeter Assembly: The Minutes of the Assemblies of the United Brethren of Devon and Cornwall, 1691–1717*, Allan Brockett, ed., *Publ. Devon and Cornwall Record Soc.*, n.s., **6** (Exeter, Engl., 1963) : p. 73.

[83] The figures were compiled from information given in individual biographies in *ibid.*, appendix C, pp. 133–148. Some nineteen additional men also were candidates between 1691 and 1717 but their ordinations never were recorded. The association in Cheshire and Lancashire experienced similar difficulties. See *Cheshire Classis Minutes, 1691–1745*, Alexander Gordon, ed. (London, 1919), pp. 127–130.

[84] *The Exeter Assembly: The Minutes of the Assemblies of the United Brethren of Devon and Cornwall, 1691–1717*, Allan Brockett, ed., *Publ. Devon and Cornwall Record Soc.*, n.s., **6** (Exeter, Engl., 1963) : p. 73.

[85] Allan Brockett, *Nonconformity in Exeter, 1650–1875* (Manchester, Engl., 1962), pp. 74–95.

[86] James Meikle, "The Seventeenth Century Presbytery of Meigle," *Records Scottish Church History Soc.* **5** (1933–1935) : pp. 251–261; Walter R. Foster, *Bishop and Presbytery: The Church of Scotland, 1661–1688* (London, 1958), pp. 1–11, 89–95.

terianism. It was grounded in government coercion. When it established denominational order it did so not just because its clerics joined ministry with authority in voluntary denominational institutions, but also because the law supported them, a condition that did not exist for Presbyterians in either England or America.[87]

After 1660 England's Particular Baptists also marked retreat, although the effect may not have been as devastating as it was for English Presbyterians and Independents. The Particular Baptists abandoned their general meetings and many pastors were forced to operate "dissenting academies" to make their livings.[88] Still, the egalitarian conception of the ministry probably helped Baptists to continue their worship in private homes. When Charles II issued his Declaration of Indulgence in 1672 over two hundred Baptists applied for licenses as preachers while others preached without licenses, saying they should never have been restricted earlier. Indeed, even when the persecution was renewed Particular Baptists issued a *Confession of Faith* from London in 1677, showing that suppression did not imply extinction.[89]

After 1689 the Particular Baptist general meetings were revived as "associations" or "assemblies." But in even stronger terms than before they were held to promote the work of preaching ministers or pastors. The first national assembly of Particular Baptists was held specifically to repair the "great neglect in the present ministry" brought about by the difficulties of persecution.[90] While most congregations had many persons who served ministerial functions as elders and deacons, pastors who preached to others were in short supply. Worse, existing pastors were "so incumbered with worldly affairs, that they were not able to perform the duties of their holy calling." [91] To correct this, the 1689 Assembly established a general fund managed by seven men in London. It supported three types of ministerial labor: the work of pastors in poor congregations, that of men who would visit otherwise self-sufficient Particular Baptist congregations, and that of pastors who would preach to the general public.[92]

Particular Baptist support of the preaching ministry was not designed to centralize power in the associa-tions. The preaching ministers were still "to be approved of, and sent forth by two churches at the least," not by the associations. In this regard the 1689 assembly ratified a 1677 Particular Baptist *Confession of Faith* which stipulated that assemblies were "not entrusted with any Church-power properly so-called, or with any jurisdiction over the Churches themselves." In familiar phrases the 1677 *Confession* justified the assemblies because they brought the congregations "peace, increase of love, and mutual edification." [93] But as we have seen, when assemblies succeeded in these objectives they fashioned denominational order among Particular Baptists and implicitly gained power over congregations and individuals.

However, the national assembly that Particular Baptists established in London in 1689 proved short-lived. In 1692 the delegates divided it into two parts, half to gather in Bristol at Easter, the remaining half to meet in London during the Whitsuntide holiday. By 1694 the London gathering faltered as Particular Baptists in the east of England fell back upon the remaining county associations. For much of the early eighteenth century Baptists in London lacked any denominational gathering. A new association organized there in 1704 met for only a few years. In 1714 Particular Baptist pastors alone formed an association there with non-Calvinist General Baptist ministers. Since its membership was mixed, its main tasks were limited to the discussion of common ministerial problems. It seems not to have acted as an important agent of denominational order, and in another ten years it too collapsed when some of its members tried to provide financial aid for needy ministers and ministerial candidates, thus unsuccessfully turning it from fellowship to government.[94]

In rural areas Particular Baptist associations proved more enduring. Like the national assembly of 1689, they too accentuated the distinction between pastors and elders and deacons. Despite efforts to find pastors who would seek converts among the general public, Particular Baptist congregations decreased in number and size after 1700. Yet the associations still commanded the processes of church government by answering queries from their congregations and by offering financial help to hard-pressed pastors.[95] As we shall see, precisely because Particular Baptists

[87] A. Ian Dunlop, *William Carstares and the Kirk by Law Established* (Edinburgh, 1967), pp. 62–99.

[88] Alfred C. Underwood, *A History of the English Baptists* (London, 1947), pp. 89–101. Minutes of an assembly of General Baptists indicate that some kind of association still existed among these Arminian Baptists in 1668. See *Minutes of the General Assembly of General Baptist Churches in England,* W. T. Whitley, ed. (2 v., London, 1909) 1: pp. xvi, 23–24.

[89] Alfred C. Underwood, *A History of the English Baptists* (London, 1947), pp. 102–106.

[90] The call for the assembly is printed in Joseph Ivimey, *A History of the English Baptists* . . . (2 v., London, 1811) 2: p. 479.

[91] *Ibid.,* p. 483.

[92] *Ibid.,* pp. 491–493; Alfred C. Underwood, *A History of the English Baptists* (London, 1947), p. 129.

[93] Quoted in Joseph Ivimey, *A History of the English Baptists* . . . (2 v., London, 1811) 2: p. 492; *Baptist Confessions of Faith,* W. L. Lumpkin, ed. (Valley Forge, Pa., 1969), p. 289.

[94] Alfred C. Underwood, *A History of the English Baptists* (London, 1947), pp. 130–132; W. T. Whitley, *The Baptists of London, 1617–1928* (London, n.d.), pp. 47–48.

[95] Frank Buffard, *Kent and Sussex Baptist Associations* (Faversham, Engl., 1963), pp. 29–30; "Association Life to 1815," *Trans. Baptist Hist. Soc.* 5 (1961): pp. 24–28; H. Wheeler Robinson, "The Beginning of Association Life in Yorkshire and Lancashire," *Baptist Quart.* 23 (1970): pp. 208–211.

survived in the face of these problems, their associations ultimately furnished an important model for creating denominational order among Particular Baptists in the Delaware valley.

Paradoxically, the link between clerical reform and denominational order comes full circle in the last decade of the seventeenth century as it emerges again in the Church of England. This time, Anglican reformers stayed inside the Church to create institutions that quickly assumed responsibilities in both England and America. The movement itself was a response to widespread fears that a major social crisis was destroying the Anglican Church and English society simultaneously. Leading ministers worried that household education was faltering, that public morals were decaying, and that the Church could do little to stem growing immorality because so many of its own ministers scandalized parishes with their ignorance and degenerate behavior.[96] By the mid-1680's Anglicans attacked these conditions in several ways: in "religious societies" composed of young men worshiping under the guidance of pious Anglican ministers, in "Societies for the Reformation of Manners," also Anglican-led organizations that pressured Justices of the Peace to suppress lewdness and provided Christian education for lower-class children in "Charity Schools," and in the efforts of ministers like Thomas Bray, who wrote new Anglican catechisms designed as much for the Church's negligent, lackluster ministers as for its lay parishioners.[97] Far-sighted reforming bishops like Henry Compton, Bishop of London from 1675 to 1713, supported the religious societies, Charity Schools, and pastoral reform together, but worked especially hard to promote the latter as the basis of the other reform efforts. Compton did this through frequent parochial visitations, elimination of multiple benefices, by promoting higher standards in ministerial education, and by fostering clerical conferences where ministers discussed theological issues and common parish problems in a setting that paralleled the association meetings of English Presbyterians and Congregationalists.[98]

The institutional manifestation of the Anglican reform movement came in the formation of the Society for Promoting Christian Knowledge (the S.P.C.K.) in 1699, and in the Society for the Propagation of the Gospel in Foreign Parts (the S.P.G.) in 1701. Significantly, both societies were based on Dissenting models of ministerial activity—especially Quaker ones—at the same time that they were logical extensions of the Anglican reform movement. They were organized by the Anglican reformer Thomas Bray. Bray gained his appreciation of Dissenter and Quaker activity from different but compatible sources. Some of it came from contemporary literature. In the 1690's Charles Leslie and Francis Bugg, two popular anti-Quaker writers, warned that the real danger in Quakerism stemmed from its institutions, not its heresies. In his famous book, *The Snake in the Grass*, Leslie charged (wrongly) that because Fox controlled the Quaker treasury he had "more Money at his disposal, than any Bishop in England." Bugg called Quakerism England's "New Rome." He pointed to the parallel hierarchical structures of Quakerism and Catholicism and argued that Quakers followed the London Yearly Meeting as slavishly as Catholics followed the pope. Disputes within the movement gave the lie to Quaker claims that they rejected "forms" or human institutions. They revealed instead the power that their "church or Meetings do assume over the Infallibility of the Light within Particular Persons." [99]

Bray also learned first-hand about Dissenting organizational skill after his appointment as ecclesiastical "commissary" for Maryland in 1694. Dissenters scarcely caused all the Church's problems there. Its position often was undermined by Anglican laymen hoping to preserve their independent vestries. But the Church had especially effective opponents in the form of Dissenters, particularly from London Quakers who utilized their lobbyists in Court and Parliament to defeat new schemes that would solidify the Church's legal establishment in Maryland. Bray's Maryland experience also led him to appreciate the strength of the Dissenters in all the colonies. Thus in 1697 he ruefully told ministerial candidates going overseas that the relationship between Anglicans and Dissenters in England had been reversed in America. Only five Anglican ministers then resided in all the colonies north of Maryland. But Presbyterians, Baptists, and especially Quakers prospered everywhere.[100]

---

[96] J. H. Overton, *Life in the English Church, 1660–1714* (London, 1885), pp. 224–228, 232, 296–306; G. V. Bennett, *White Kennett, 1660–1728, Bishop of Peterborough* (London, 1957), pp. 184–190; Norman Sykes, *From Sheldon to Secker: Aspects of English Church History, 1660–1728* (Cambridge, Engl., 1959), pp. 9–10, 16–22.

[97] F. W. B. Bullock, *Voluntary Religious Societies, 1520–1799* (St. Leonards on Sea, Engl., 1963), pp. 125–150; J. H. Overton, *Life in the English Church, 1660–1714* (London, 1885), pp. 207–228; W. K. Lowther Clarke, *Eighteenth-Century Piety* (London, 1944), pp. 69–80; W. K. Lowther Clarke, *A History of the S.P.C.K.* (London, 1959), pp. 19–58; Norman Sykes, *Edmund Gibson, Bishop of London, 1669–1748* (London, 1926), pp. 193–209.

[98] Edward Carpenter, *The Protestant Bishop, being the Life of Henry Compton, 1632–1713, Bishop of London* (London, 1956), pp. 61–67, 208–232.

[99] Charles Leslie, *The Snake in the Grass: or Satan Transformed into an Angel of Light* . . . , (2nd ed., London, 1697), p. 81; Francis Bugg, *The Quakers Yearly Metting* [sic] *or Convocation Impeached on the Behalf of the Commons of England* ([London, 1976]), p. 1. For an earlier work that criticized Friends for their persecution of dissenters within their own ranks see Francis Bugg, *The Painted Harlot Both Stript and Whipt, Or the Second Part of Naked Truth,* . . . (London, 1683).

[100] H. P. Thompson, *Thomas Bray* (London, 1954), pp. 13–16; Thomas Bray, "Apostolick Charity, its Nature and Excellency Considered," in: *Rev. Thomas Bray, His Life and Selected Works Relating to Maryland*, Bernard C. Steiner, ed.,

All of Bray's disillusioning information played a part in his organization of the S.P.C.K. in 1699. His first draft setting forth the purposes of the Society specifically underlines his debt to Dissenting models. "Whilst the Papists, the Dissenters, and the very Quakers have such Societies for the carrying on [of] their Superstitious Blasphemies, Heresies and Fooleries[,] we have had nothing of this nature yet set up." Now he would create what he called "the intended Congregation *pro propaganda fide*," an obvious reference to the *Congregation pro Propaganda Fide* in Rome, the great agent of Catholic proselytization in Europe and an alleged model for Quaker organization in England.[101]

For reasons that are not clear, however, the charter granted to the S.P.C.K. limited its work to the publication and distribution of literature. Bray soon corrected this error. In *A Memorial Representing the Present State of Religion on the Continent of North America,* published in 1700, Bray again pointed to the Church's dismal condition there and to the poor prospects for establishing it by law, at least for the moment. Whether Anglicans liked it or not, most settlers were Dissenters, and as Bray coyly put it, "it will seem unreasonable to expect that a People, before they are converted . . . should be induc'd to maintain its Ministry." Instead, Bray proposed that forty missionaries should be supported by voluntary contributions raised among the "Noble Patrons of Religion" who already were supporting the English religious societies, Charity Schools and the S.P.C.K. Bray's suggestion was an instant success, and within the year another reforming society—the S.P.G.—had been chartered to maintain reforming Anglican ministers in the English colonies of North America.[102]

The S.P.G. epitomized late seventeenth-century English Protestant reform. It was organized on Dissenting models and its lay and clerical members accepted the leadership of reformers like Bray. By these standards the results in America should have been phenomenal. Where American Quakers had ridiculed Anglican ministers as thieves "come meerly for Bread," the S.P.G. would sponsor a new Anglican order in America. It would send the best and most pious ministers to the colonies and provide them with

travel funds, salaries for three years, and sometimes even glebes and houses to relieve them of their financial problems.[103] In this way Anglicans could use the kind of institutions Dissenters were using against them as a foundation to promote the growth of the Church of England in England's American colonies.

Our explication of S.P.G. origins brings us finally to America and the Delaware valley. How did the English tradition of ministerial dominance in church government fare where the first colonial Presbyterian and Baptist denominational meetings were organized, where the Philadelphia Yearly Meeting emerged as the most important Quaker gathering in all the colonies, and where the S.P.G. actively competed with these groups in the early years of the eighteenth century? As we have seen, English Christians of many kinds gave a special place to those who acted in the ministry. When they formed what we now call denominational bodies the effort was almost universally made by ministers, not by lay members of the congregations. And once formed, the denominations continued to be controlled by ministers, or by ministers and highly select groups of laymen. Thus in England each denomination propelled a general tradition of ministerial dominance into the future, yet defined the ministry and the minister's role in church government with sufficient flexibility to give each a special, even unique, place in the past.

The broad commitment to ministerial authority might be thought to demonstrate that the English past was static and unbending, and thus unsuited for successful transplantation in America. Yet Englishmen fashioned and manipulated the clerical reforming tradition to sustain denominational order for over a century because it produced effective solutions to difficult problems. They never committed themselves to narrow versions of that tradition. Within it each group altered its concepts of denominational order and ministerial authority as conditions themselves changed. These changes did not always prove successful. By the end of the seventeenth century the denominational cohesion of England's Particular Baptists, Congregationalists, and its few remaining Presbyterians was seriously strained, while Quakers were shaping theirs in significant new ways. But within the tradition clearly lay an enormous capacity for change, adjustment, and growth.

The very fact that English denominational institu-

Fund Publ. Maryland Hist. Soc. 37 (Baltimore, Md., 1901): pp. 71–97.

[101] *A General Plan of the Constitution of a Protestant Congregation or Society,* Bray Papers, Sion College MSS., pp. 62–63 (Library of Congress microfilm copy at University of California, Los Angeles); H. P. Thompson, *Thomas Bray* (London, 1954), pp. 36–37. Part of Bray's reference to Dissenters also pointed to the Heads of Agreement signed in London in 1691 and cited earlier in note 77.

[102] H. P. Thompson, *Thomas Bray* (London, 1954), pp. 44, 48–50; Thomas Bray, "A Memorial Representing the Present State of Religion on the Continent of North America," in: *Rev. Thomas Bray, His Life and Selected Works Relating to Maryland,* Bernard C. Steiner, ed., *Fund Publ. Maryland Hist. Soc.* 37 (Baltimore, Md., 1901): p. 169.

[103] H. P. Thompson, *Into All Lands, The History of the Society for the Propagation of the Gospel in Foreign Parts, 1701–1950* (London, 1951), p. 20; James S. M. Anderson, *The History of the Church of England in the Colonies and Foreign Dependencies of the British Empire* (3 v., London, 1856) 3: p. 33; the quotation is from Thomas Bray, "A Memorial Representing the Present State of Religion in the Continent of North America," in: *Rev. Thomas Bray, His Life and Selected Works Relating to Maryland,* Bernard C. Steiner, ed., *Fund Publ. Maryland Hist. Soc.* 37 (Baltimore, Md., 1901): p. 171.

tions were quietly dynamic and creative also meant that they often were in flux, however, and therefore subject to much disorder and argument. This condition created enough problems for Englishmen and Scots at home. It only added to their burdens in America. It meant that colonists looking eastward for help could not always find clear examples to follow. On the eve of colonization in the Delaware valley the authority of Quaker ministers was being impinged upon by weighty Friends while the Quaker institutional structure was expanding rapidly. Particular Baptists were elevating pastors or preaching ministers to a higher status than before while finding it difficult to hold denominational associations together. Those who inherited the name Presbyterian had to choose from conflicting organizational models that lacked unanimous support in either old or new England and caused dispute in Scotland. And Anglicans, or at least reforming Anglicans, worried that the Church of England lacked spiritual vigor at home and institutional support in America. In this sense then, the very dynamism and creativity that each of these groups knew in England as much provided a basis for discord and potential failure in America as remarkable tools to shape a successful future. But as we shall see, England's Dissenters returned to their English past constantly and profitably for nourishment. To their regret, only England's Anglicans escaped it.

III. BROADENING THE QUAKER HIERARCHY: THE FRIENDS IN THE DELAWARE VALLEY

For two centuries the rise and fall of William Penn's "Holy Experiment" in Pennsylvania has formed the centerpiece of American Quaker history. Penn's hopes for secular peace and religious toleration are seen as pragmatic extensions of his Quakerism, and the dynamic growth of the colony has helped eclipse the movement's history in other places in America. There are, of course, perfectly good reasons why these themes have been joined. Penn was one of the great leaders of late seventeenth-century English Quakerism and the sudden importance of Pennsylvania in Quaker affairs was recognized by contemporaries as well as later historians.[1]

Yet there is now need to approach the Delaware valley in different ways. Joseph Illick's study, *William Penn the Politician*, reveals how often non-Quaker considerations guided Penn's American doings. Penn was one of England's most skilled courtiers and he received—and later almost lost—his American property because of his high standing with England's

last Stuart monarchs, Charles II and his brother James II, the Duke of York.[2] In addition, Gary Nash has revealed a devastating gap between expectation and achievement in Pennsylvania's early spiritual and secular affairs. Agreement in religion implied no harmony in politics. Penn fought with his wealthy Quaker backers, then watched these men battle modest colonists seeking more equitable taxes and representation in Pennsylvania. By 1690 the political divisions in Pennsylvania were so bitter that Nash sees the colony as a model of instability in newly settled societies.[3]

Obviously such secular difficulties would have affected the course of Quaker development in the Delaware valley. Moreover, what we know of English Quaker development would have added to the potential problems there. Colonization began while Quaker institutional growth was accelerating and while challenges to those changes, such as the Wilkinson-Story dispute, still married Quaker unity. Yet the traditional emphasis on idealism in Penn's "Holy Experiment" and the obscuring of ministerial domination in seventeenth-century Quakerism has led to an essentially static conception of Quaker history in the Delaware valley.

In this view the crucial years for Friends were those of the 1680's, when Quaker meetings and the Quaker style in business and politics were established in the Delaware valley. Then Delaware valley Quakerism changed little until the great Quaker revival of the 1750's saw Friends withdraw from politics in Pennsylvania and strengthen their internal discipline. However, examining the developing Quaker institutional structure and the role Public Friends played in creating denominational order among Friends reveals a more dynamic and evolutionary process of Quaker history in the Delaware valley. It uncovers the background and special significance of the Keithian schism of 1691–1693, reveals a previously hidden disciplinary renascence that followed the schism, and for the first time allows us to observe a fundamental change in the structure of Quaker leadership, as weighty Friends outside the ministry began to share the management of Quaker affairs with Public Friends.

The ministerial discipline so important to Quaker growth in England proved to be equally useful in America. The Public Friends who first arrived in the New World in 1656 used it to develop what Frederick Tolles has since called the "transatlantic community of Friends."[4] Before 1680 they succeeded best where religious loyalties appeared to be in flux. In the north

---

[1] These views are best summarized in Frederick B. Tolles, *Meeting House and Counting House* (Chapel Hill, N.C., 1948), but see also Rufus Jones *et al., The Quakers in the American Colonies* (New York, 1911).

[2] Joseph E. Illick, *William Penn the Politician: His Relations with the English Government* (Ithaca, N.Y., 1965).

[3] Gary B. Nash, *Quakers and Politics, Pennsylvania, 1681–1726* (Princeton, N.J., 1968).

[4] Frederick B. Tolles, *Quakers and the Atlantic Culture* (New York, 1964), pp. 21–35; Rufus Jones *et al., The Quakers in the American Colonies* (New York, 1911), pp. 26–89.

Quakerism prospered especially well in Rhode Island. In the south, where ministers of any kind were scarce, Quakerism won a strong following in both Maryland and Virginia. Thus many of the same settlers who had tried unsuccessfully to secure Calvinist clergymen from New England in 1642 eagerly greeted the Public Friends who appeared among them in 1657, bringing news of a new ministry and a promise of spiritual renewal and stable local meetings.[5]

Yet disorder also prospered in America. In the late 1660's the schismatic John Perrot found attractive ground for his high-flown spirituality and individualist tendencies in some Maryland and Virginia Quaker meetings, while in Rhode Island Friends endured several outbrusts of extreme enthusiasm before 1680. Thus in 1671, when George Fox first came to America himself, he had to restore order there in addition to settling the new monthly, quarterly, and yearly meetings he also was establishing in England. Indeed, the two tasks were quickly coordinated. Yet if Quaker schismatics were "judged down and condemned" everywhere, Fox and the Public Friends clearly believed that order among American Quakers depended most on their acceptance of the new meeting system. Thus in Maryland, Fox measured his success not only in the fact that Perrot's followers were condemned but that during Fox's stay Friends there had a "glorious meeting . . . and an established and settled one."[6]

Quaker settlement in the Delaware valley stimulated new problems, however. Where in other colonies the Friends usually constituted only a minority of the population, they governed in Pennsylvania and West Jersey and dominated the population. These advantages made some English Friends bitter. To Quakers suffering from persecution at home those heading for Pennsylvania appeared to be cowardly. Some said they were leaving under a "fearfulness of suffering here for the testimony of Jesus." Yet other causes seemed to encourage the Quaker emigration since Friends departed for the Delaware valley in large numbers even as persecution in England decreased. Thus in 1698 the yearly meeting in Wales complained bitterly that "runnings to Pennsylvania" were stripping meetings of their members and that Public Friends, "meeting with discouragement, find cause to complain."[7]

In fact, enthusiasm for immigration stimulated the first major challenges to the denominational order Quakers had developed earlier in England. Even in West Jersey where settlement proceeded more slowly than in Pennsylvania, Friends found themselves confused and troubled by the great influx of settlers. The reason was simple. In England the Public Friends had established meetings in face-to-face communities. Now, however, the meetings were familiar but the faces were not. Mature Quakers arrived as strangers to each other in the New World. They were unable to confirm each other's standing in the truth. As early as 1681 West Jersey Friends complained that young Quakers who were "single and marriageable at their coming away," arrived with "no evidence of their clearness, or unclearness, from other parties."[8] "As there is frequent opportunities from London for doing it," they asked the London Yearly Meeting to insist that monthly meetings furnish departing emigrants with documents describing their standing and warned that without them immigrants in America would find it difficult to worship, marry, or even engage in business.[9] A year later Penn and the first arrivals in Pennsylvania put the matter even more strongly. Realizing that the Pennsylvania immigration would outstrip that in West Jersey, they told London Friends that they could "embrace and assist" only those Quakers who brought written certificates that guaranteed that they were "clear in life, credit, marriage engagements, and unity among God's people where they inhabit."[10]

The certificates were a clear response to the dislocations of large-scale colonization. Yet they were also innovative. Quakers had never before issued such documents in such wholesale fashion to serve such broad needs. In fact, their existence touched an important issue in Quakerism. As Richard Vann has argued, "membership" was a vague concept among seventeenth-century Friends. Although men and women might be disowned by a monthly meeting they never formally joined one. They simply attended meetings for worship that it supervised. Under these circumstances monthly meetings sometimes issued documents or certificates testifying to one's standing in a meeting. Usually these certificates were given to persons marrying someone from another such meeting or to persons who were moving and were addressed to particular meetings. Colonization pushed these old practices in new directions. The certificates sent to America were far broader in scope. They covered the whole of a person's life, even his credit, and were addressed to any colonial Quaker gathering, not to a specific meeting as had been the case in England.[11]

The existence of the certificates implied the existence

[5] "Two 1642 Letters from Virginia Puritans," Jon Butler, ed. *Proc. Mass. Hist. Soc.* **84** (1972): pp. 99–109.

[6] *The Journal of George Fox,* John L. Nickalls, ed. (Cambridge, Engl., 1952), pp. 617, 619, 653; Kenneth L. Carroll, "John Perrot, Early Quaker Schismatic," *Jour. Friends Hist. Soc.,* suppl. 33 (1971): pp. 65, 82.

[7] Quoted in William C. Braithwaite, *The Second Period of Quakerism* (2nd ed., Cambridge, Engl., 1961), pp. 408–409, 411.

[8] Quoted in James Bowden, *The History of the Society of Friends in America* (2 v., London, 1850–1854) **1**: pp. 402–404.

[9] *Ibid.*

[10] *Ibid.* **2**: p. 23.

[11] Arnold Lloyd, *Quaker Social History, 1669–1738* (London, 1950), pp. 56, 112; Richard T. Vann, *The Social Development of English Quakerism, 1655–1755* (Cambridge, Mass., 1969), pp. 122–143.

of meetings. Here too disorder lurked. Initial settlement in the Delaware valley produced a telescoping or contraction in the Quaker meeting system. This was first evident in West Jersey where it was reinforced by the relatively slow pace of immigration. Two monthly meetings, Salem in the south and Burlington in the north, were established in 1676 and 1678 and handled Quaker business alone. Creation of superior meetings lagged even though the population grew and new monthly meetings sprang up. A yearly meeting was not established in the colony until 1681.[12]

In Pennsylvania, rapid population expansion encouraged an earlier maturation of the meeting system than had been true in West Jersey. In January, 1683, a gathering of Quakers in Philadelphia—how many and who are not noted—established the first monthly meeting in Pennsylvania. These Friends moved quickly to reestablish the familiar institutions of Quaker denominational order. They appointed a committee to supervise the construction of a meeting house, agreed to purchase books for the keeping of records, ordered newly arriving Friends to register their certificates "according to the time of their arrival here," and named a two-part committee, "John Hart and Henry Waddy for the upper part of the county, and Thomas Bowman and Henry Lewis for the City and lower part of the County," to aid the sick and destitute. Thus within a month nine meetings for worship dotted the countryside and by February, 1683, a quarterly meeting had been established to supervise the several monthly meetings. Only a yearly meeting and a ministerial meeting remained to be formed.[13]

Responsibility for maintaining denominational order quickly fell to the Philadelphia Quarterly Meeting. In March and June, 1683, the meeting strengthened the institutional base laid out in January. It inspected the work of the newly established monthly meetings by having the certificates "brought in, and Read" and ordered the rural monthly meetings to establish permanent meeting times and locations. It approved a business meeting for women Friends—as in England their main task was to handle charity—and selected one Friend in each monthly meeting to explain "the Quarterly Meeting's Resolutions for the Service of Truth in these parts." Finally, it named a committee of six to "draw up a Brief (yet full) Account of the good Order of Truth as it is Practis'd in the Men and Women Meetings of Friends in England," an account that has not survived but which clearly was designed to justify its labors by reference to the work of such meetings in England.[14]

The Pennsylvania meeting system was not the luxuriant plant it seemed to be, however. A telescoping of meetings and compression of leadership also was occurring in Pennsylvania, but in a more subtle fashion than had been true in West Jersey. For example until July, 1686, Philadelphia Friends turned every third monthly meeting into a quarterly meeting by changing its title rather than hold separate quarterly and monthly meetings.[15] At the same time monthly meetings remained small despite great differences in the size of the meetings for worship that they supervised. The best indication of this comes by contrasting the Concord Monthly Meeting of Chester County with the Monthly Meeting in Philadelphia. The Concord minutes, rare for their lists of persons in attendance, reveal a monthly meeting membership of between seven and ten persons between 1682 and 1700.[16] Since the area covered by the meeting was sparsely settled, the discrepancy between the numbers of Quakers who attended meetings for worship there and those who sat in the monthly meeting may not have been large. But in Philadelphia the gulf was immense. Although the city's monthly meeting minutes do not contain attendance lists, an analysis of its records nonetheless suggests that, despite the size of the city, monthly meetings there probably were no larger than those at Concord, and may even have been smaller, with as few as five or six Friends gathering to accomplish its business.[17]

Philadelphia was unusual in another respect as well. The monthly meeting also seems largely to have contained only those Quakers who had served as Public Friends in England. Indeed, although they had not formed a separate ministerial meeting as would have been common in England, Public Friends moved into the Philadelphia Monthly Meeting (which also sometimes was the Philadelphia Quarterly Meeting) so

[12] The process is well summarized in John E. Pomfret, *The Province of West New Jersey, 1609–1702* (Princeton, N.J., 1956), pp. 216–223, 235–239.

[13] Minutes, Philadelphia Quarterly and Monthly Meeting, 9 January, 1682, FHL microfilm copy.

[14] *Ibid.*, 6 March, 1682/3; 5 June, 1683. One of the men named to the committee, Christopher Taylor, had been deeply

involved in combating divisions that the schismatic William Rogers was promoting in Bristol in the late 1670's and was the author of *An Epistle of Caution to Friends : . . .* (London, 1681), a tract directed against Rogers.

[15] Minutes, Philadelphia Quarterly and Monthly Meeting, 6 February, 1682/3; 5 June, 1683; FHL microfilm copy.

[16] The lists are found at the beginning of each monthly meeting entry. Minutes, Concord Monthly Meeting, 1684–1757, FHL microfilm copy.

[17] Thus in June, 1686, the clerk of the Philadelphia Quarterly Meeting, which had earlier agreed that it would be composed of six representatives from each constituent monthly meeting, listed the names of the representatives coming from the monthly meetings at Lower Dublin and near the Schuylkill River, but then described those coming from the city as "for Philadelphia the monthly meeting." This happening, and the manner in which the Philadelphia Monthly Meeting conducted its business and named committees to handle important matters, seems to indicate that between five and ten Friends usually attended its gatherings. However, these Friends may not always have been the same Friends and the total number of Quakers eligible to attend the Monthly Meeting may have been larger. Minutes, Philadelphia Quarterly and Monthly Meeting, 5 July, 1686, FHL microfilm copy.

thoroughly that the gatherings looked like ministerial ones.[18]

Despite the distortion of the Philadelphia meeting structure, which might have fostered discord itself, the first disagreement about denominational order in the Delaware valley occurred instead over attempts to organize a yearly meeting. Since 1681 West Jersey Friends had held their own yearly meeting at Burlington. Feeling a prior claim to leadership over Delaware valley Quakers, the Burlington Friends proposed in 1683 that a "General Yearly Meeting" be held in Burlington in 1684, and that its jurisdiction encompass all the American colonies "North-Ward as far as New England, and South-Ward, as far as Caroline." [19] The effort failed. Pennsylvania Friends never acceded to the proposal and two yearly meetings were held along the Delaware River in 1684, one in Burlington, another in Philadelphia. Pennsylvania Friends claimed that the two meetings "had such a blessed harmony together, that we may say that we know not that there was a jarring string amongst us." But the harmony obviously was fragile, since for their part Pennsylvania Quakers also tried to claim leadership of American Quakerism by inviting Quakers from New England, Virginia, and the Carolinas to attend their next yearly meeting in Philadelphia, "being," they said, "as a centre or middle place." [20]

Just how this contest was resolved never has been clear. But within the year the two yearly meetings had disappeared. Delaware valley Friends had agreed to establish a single yearly meeting that would gather alternately in Burlington and Philadelphia. At the same time the attempt to supervise all of American Quakerism waned. Representatives from Maryland attended the 1686 meeting but no Friends showed up from Virginia.[21] Thereafter, the Philadelphia Yearly Meeting exercised a formal authority only over Friends in the Delaware valley and older yearly meetings in Rhode Island and Virginia continued to command the loyalty of Quakers there. If the Philadelphia Yearly Meeting finally did emerge as the leading such gathering in the colonies, as in fact happened, this occurred largely because more Quakers lived there, and because those Quakers dominated affairs in a colony important in the eighteenth-century empire.

By 1685, then, Delaware valley Friends lacked only a separate ministerial meeting to finish replicating the institutional stucture of English Quakerism. Establish-ment of this gathering did not come easily, however, even though a need for it was painfully apparent by 1685. As Delaware valley settlements matured complaints about the ministers' behavior seemed to rise. In April, 1685, someone in Philadelphia accused two ministers of public drunkenness. The Philadelphia Monthly Meeting appointed a committee to investigate the charge but never placed the committee findings in its minutes, probably because monthly meetings did not yet discipline Friends in the ministry, even when those meetings might consist almost wholly of Public Friends, as was true in Philadelphia.[22] A second affair proved more serious. In May, 1685, the ministers received a bitter letter from George Fox written to eight Delaware valley Friends, who, he said, "use to minister." [23]

Fox had not heard of the charge of drunkenness; other failures led him to criticize Pennsylvania's leading Friends. "I know that some of You are but lately settled," he wrote, but where was their labor, their effort? He had received letters from Friends in Carolina, Virginia, and New England pleading for traveling ministers, yet he knew of none that had come from Pennsylvania. "They want visiting, and many would come in, as I understand, if they had some to visit them." Instead, Fox believed that the Public Friends were so entrenched in Philadelphia that their presence was harmful: "you being so many ministers there together at some meetings, itt is rather a stoppage to some of the tender Springs in others." Fox believed they should organize a ministerial meeting. "Then you might divide your selves to other meetings, and two by two to visit Friends, both in New England and Maryland Virginia and Carolina." He made many of the same points two months later when he again wrote to the Pennsylvania ministers to complain about their lethargy. In America they had "liberty to serve and worship God." But he still had heard nothing about their travel. "Improve your gifts and talents, and not hide them in a napkin, lest they be taken from you; . . . be not like the foolish virgins, which kept their name of virgins, but neglected having oil in their lamps." [24]

Under these circumstances the Yearly Meeting of 1685 asked for and won establishment of a ministerial meeting.[25] Public Friends now resumed their custom-

[18] The method used to identify Public Friends is described later in this chapter in note 37.

[19] Minutes, Philadelphia Yearly Meeting, 4 September, 1683, FHL microfilm copy.

[20] The epistle is printed in *The Friend* **18** (1884): p. 134. For the circumstances surrounding the establishment of the single yearly meeting, see John E. Pomfret, *The Province of West New Jersey, 1609–1702* (Princeton, N.J., 1956), pp. 221–223.

[21] Minutes, Philadelphia Yearly Meeting, 15 September, 1685; 8 September, 1686; FHL microfilm copy.

[22] Minutes, Philadelphia Quarterly and Monthly Meeting, 7 April, 1685, FHL microfilm copy. The entry was deleted in the version of these minutes printed in *Publ. Geneal. Soc. Penna.* **1** (1895–1898): pp. 286–288.

[23] George Fox to Christopher Taylor *et al.*, 20 May, 1685, in Etting Papers, **37**, HSP. The letter is printed in *Penna. Mag. History and Biography* **29** (1903): pp. 105–106.

[24] George Fox to Friends in the Ministry in Pennsylvania and New Jersey, 30 July, 1685, in: *Selections from the Epistles of George Fox*, Samuel Tuke, comp. (Cambridge, Mass., 1879), pp. 297–298.

[25] Minutes, Philadelphia Yearly Meeting, 15 September, 1685, FHL microfilm copy.

ary ministerial duties in their rightful place. They met four times a year. Most importantly, in their September meeting they forwarded recommendations to the Philadelphia Yearly Meeting which gathered a week or two later. By 1687 they had sent Friends on ministerial tours of Virginia, Maryland, and Carolina and had ordered one minister to stop his preaching until they resolved questions about his life and faith. They also began to edit and censor Quaker publications as the Second Day Morning Meeting did in London and decreed that "nothing be allowed to be printed . . . till first Examined and approved of by this Meeting." [26]

Thus five years after the colonization of Pennsylvania and a decade after the beginning of Quaker settlement in West Jersey, the denominational apparatus so patiently constructed in England since 1650 had been re-established in the Delaware valley. There was little conscious experimentalism in these proceedings. Friends settled monthly and quarterly meetings on the familiar English pattern, although in both West Jersey and Pennsylvania the meeting system evolved in response to immediate circumstances through sometimes peculiar processes. Monthly meetings sometimes became quarterly ones. A single yearly meeting was organized only after Delaware valley Friends settled conflicting claims to leadership. Public Friends formed the Philadelphia Meeting of Ministers after they had been embarrassed by charges of drunkenness and had been castigated by George Fox. Yet these circumstances were not unique. The rise of the Quaker meeting system in England also involved anomalies of order and discipline, and in this respect the American Friends offered no departure from the English pattern.

But now the American organization was to be tested. By the summer of 1691 order and peace that long had been absent from secular politics in the Delaware valley vanished in spiritual affairs as well. Anger, dissension, even physical brawling overran meetings for worship and business. By 1692 two Quaker movements competed for the loyalty of Delaware valley Friends. Significantly, much of the dispute centered on the work and place of the Public Friends. But where George Fox had found them lacking in their ministerial travel and neglectful of their institutional responsibilities in 1685, by 1691 others were finding them unsound in doctrine and authoritarian in manner, all in all unfit to provide leadership in a movement that had long countenanced hierarchical authority but not heresy.

Despite the failure to establish a separate ministerial meeting until 1686, Public Friends obviously dominated early Quaker discipline in the Delaware valley.

In 1684 it was Public Friends in the Yearly Meeting in Philadelphia who advised newly arrived immigrants to supplement the discipline of monthly meetings with family worship—a technique used by reforming Anglicans and Puritans earlier in the century—and warned against widening the divisions already visible in Pennsylvania politics. They hoped, they said, "that the World may not know of our Differences for the time to come Or that there is disunion amongst us." [27] They also stressed the importance of the meeting system. They encouraged monthly meetings "to Look and inspect into the Conversations of all such within their charge" and warned against disorder of the kind manifested by Commonwealth Ranters, "who cried up Liberty to their wicked Flesh when in the meane while they were become servants to their vile Lusts." These exhortations were summarized in an epistle written in 1691 by John Willsford, a Public Friend. Willsford delivered the usual cautions against marriage to non-Quakers, wedding feasts, and the celebration of Christmas, but reassured Friends that their discipline would not falter if they upheld the authority of the meetings. Indeed, Willsford eagerly quoted *Matthew*—"Whatsoever ye shall bind on Earth, shall be bound in Heaven"—to suggest that the Quaker meetings had been divinely established.[28]

However, serious problems relating to ministry and, hence, to authority, simmered underneath the pious warnings about marriages, weddings, and holidays. How far this discontent reached is not clear, in part because Quaker meeting clerks tended to ignore many disputes in the minutes they took. But the clerk of the Concord Monthly and Quarterly Meetings did not. Indeed, he found much to record. Between 1686 and 1690 these meetings discussed a good number of disputes, and these, it seemed, concerned more than the moral failings of individuals. In 1686 a meeting for worship was removed from the house of John and Margery Gibbons for their bad "behavior and carriage." Just what misbehavior might have been involved was demonstrated two years later, in 1688, when Margery Gibbons demanded the right to preach, disrupted meetings for worship with long and vile sermons, and circulated slanderous written attacks on the Friends among residents of Chester County. Then in 1690 another Quaker, Frances Harrison, tacked a paper to the door of the Chichester meeting house that charged Robert Pile, one of the most prominent non-ministering Friends in the meeting, "with the destruction of Thomas Ushers soul," after Pile disciplined Usher at the direction of the meeting, and argued that

[26] Minutes, Yearly Meeting and General Spring Meeting of Ministers, 5 March, 1686/7, FHL microfilm copy. Hereafter cited as Minutes, Philadelphia Meeting of Ministers.

[27] Thomas Janney *et al.* to Friends, undated, Pemberton Papers, Etting Collection, 2, HSP.

[28] John Willsford, *A Brief Exhortation to All Who Profess the Truth,* . . . (Philadelphia, 1691).

Pile "doth sway the meeting" out of proportion to his legitimate authority.[29]

By themselves the arguments in the Concord meetings revealed only that some of the bickering common in England had also come to America. But by 1691 the arguments assumed new significance as they were reshaped by the most urbane and sophisticated of the Public Friends to emigrate to America, George Keith. Keith fit them into a peculiar but comprehensive critique of the Quaker denominational order that challenged the power of his fellow Quaker ministers and led to a schism which threatened the very existence of orthodox Quakerism in the Delaware valley.

George Keith was born in Scotland in 1638, was raised as a Presbyterian, received an M.S. from the University of Aberdeen in 1658, and became a Quaker in 1664. After his convincement he joined the ranks of the Public Friends where he was a leading minister for the next three decades. He traveled through England and Scotland on preaching tours and in 1677 accompanied George Fox and William Penn on a ministerial tour of Holland and Germany. Keith was particularly skilled in public debate. But his greatest fame attached to his books. Together with his fellow Scot, Robert Barclay, Keith became a leading spokesman for the Friends. Before Barclay published his famous *Apology for the True Christian Divinity* in 1676, Keith's *Immediate Revelation not Ceased* (1668) and *Universal Free Grace of the Gospel Asserted* (1671) were widely acknowledged as among the most important treatments of Quaker thought yet published. Keith was more than an intellectual, however. Like his other ministerial colleagues, he spent considerable time in English jails, and it was following a year-long stay at Newgate prison in 1685 that he emigrated to America where Robert Barclay, then governor of East Jersey, had offered him a position as the colony's surveyor-general.[30]

In his first years in the colonies Keith's official duties occupied the greater part of his time, especially a project to lay out the boundary between East and West Jersey. But by the spring of 1688 he was active in the Philadelphia Meeting of Ministers, and when his boundary project was finished, he moved to Philadelphia to head the city's Latin school. There his ministerial activity increased. He was named to the committee that censored Quaker publications and traveled to New England to visit Friends' meetings. While there he debated leading Calvinist clergymen, including Cotton Mather, and after his return to Pennsylvania he published an attack on Mather as well as a book for Quaker families called *A Plain Short Catechism for Children and Youth*.[31]

Keith's work in the Delaware valley began to worry him, however. All was not well with American Friends. In the Philadelphia Yearly Meeting of either 1687 or 1688 (the date is not clear) Keith cautioned the Public Friends about misquoting the Bible in their sermons. Then in a letter of May, 1688, he told Fox and another English Friend, George Whitehead, that some American Quakers were drifting from their Christian moorings. While he had experienced many "precious Openings" in America himself, often he had been forced to emphasize the most rudimentary principles in his preaching: "My Great Work and Care hath been chiefly, and mainly, to declare and hold for the alone Foundation, . . . Jesus Christ." This was necessary because Quakers in surprising numbers slighted the Bible and ignored the historical Christ described in the New Testament. "They are but too little acquainted and known in the Holy Scriptures," he told Fox and Whitehead. Keith recommended that Quakers read the Scriptures regularly, "especially Friends Children and young People," and he tried to use the Scriptures often in his own work: "I find it most safe or sure in all Preaching or Writing to hold to Scripture Words; for the Scriptures are full enough and sufficient to furnish every Man of God and true Minister of Christ, with suitable Words in the hand of the Holy Spirit."[32]

In the letter of 1688 Keith also complained about those who twisted and disfigured the Christian tradition—"Ranters and airy Notionists, who teach and profess Faith in Christ within, as the Light and Word; but either deny or slight his outward Coming, and what he did and suffered for us in the Flesh." Clearly these people were in error, and just as clearly their error stemmed from their ignorance of the Scriptures. Keith stressed the same point in the *Plain Short Catechism* that he wrote for Quaker families in 1690, a work addressed to the problem on which he had written privately in 1688. He told the young Quakers that notions, or doctrines, never supplanted the spirit, that *"Doctrine and Words, without the Spirit of*

---

[29] Minutes, Concord Quarterly Meeting, 3 August, 1695; 2 August, 1696; 7 February, 1686/7; 6 August, 1688; 6 May, 1689; FHL microfilm copy; Minutes, Concord Monthly Meeting, 11 August, 1690, FHL microfilm copy. Margery Gibbons's support for Keith during the schism of the 1690's is mentioned in Minutes, Philadelphia Yearly Meeting, 23 September, 1702, FHL microfilm copy.

[30] Ethyn W. Kirby, *George Keith (1638–1716)* (New York, 1942), pp. 1–48. Many historians, including Kirby, have treated Keith as uncomfortable in his Quakerism. I have criticized this view in "'Gospel Order Improved': The Keithian Schism and the Exercise of Quaker Ministerial Authority in Pennsylvania," *William and Mary Quart.*, 3d ser., **31** (1974): pp. 431–452. A criticism of this interpretation can in turn be found in J. William Frost, "Unlikely Controversialists: Caleb Pusey and George Keith," *Quaker History* **64** (1975): pp. 16–36.

[31] Minutes, Philadelphia Meeting of Ministers, 4 September, 1688; 1 March, 1689/90; 9 March, 1689/90; FHL microfilm copy.

[32] George Keith to George Whitehead and George Fox, 23 May, 1688, in George Whitehead, *The Power of Christ Vindicated Against the Magick of Apostacy* (London, 1708), pp. 225–232.

Christ, is as Milk or Wine that is dead, and hath not the nourishing Virtue in it." But ignorance of the Scriptures also led to false doctrine and then to unsure, wavering convictions. And, Keith warned, *"where the Doctrine is not sound nor true, that pure and holy Spirit doth not joyn with it, to feed and nourish the Soul."* [33]

Keith's views easily remained within the boundaries of orthodox Quaker opinion. Despite assertions to the contrary, Quakers valued the Scriptures and the historical Christ as models through which they could understand the contemporary work of the Holy Spirit. Isaac Pennington, usually viewed as the most mystical of the early Friends, wrote that "we own Christ to be a Saviour; but we lay the main stress upon the life which took upon it the manhood." A strong Christological emphasis pervaded seventeenth-century Quaker writing. Penn, for example, rejected the notion that the Inner Light supplanted the Scriptures or Christ: "It is not our Way of Speaking to say the Light within is the Rule of the Christian Religion; but that the Light of Christ within us is the Rule of True Christians." As Robert Barclay put it, to Quakers the Scriptures were God's "looking glass." Without them Friends would drift toward an unchristian mysticism. But in them Friends could "see the conditions and experiences of the saints of old; that finding our experience answer to theirs, we might thereby be the more confirmed and comforted." [34]

Unfortunately, in neither the letter to Fox and Whitehead nor the *Plain Short Catechism* did Keith identify the individuals who appeared to be slipping off Quakerism's Christian foundations. But that his concern about them remained strong is revealed in yet a third document, a manuscript entitled "Gospel Order Improved," that he circulated among selected Pennsylvania Friends in March, 1690. Although this brief document is best known for its suggestion that Friends appoint elders and deacons to manage discipline in the Quaker monthly meetings, this proposal was not Keith's main point. [35] Instead, "Gospel Order Im-

proved" offered the Friends a rare critique that measured them by what Keith took to be incontestable standards—the goals and aims of the earliest Quakers, those whom Keith and his contemporaries had long called "the First Publishers of Truth."

"Gospel Order Improved" began with a simple assertion. The early Friends sought to develop a pure spiritual life, one that Keith likened to a "garden enclosed where no weeds nor tares should grow." To accomplish this end they separated from other men, "not only because of bad doctrine . . . but allso, and that especially, because of the vicious life and evill conversation and practices which were to be found among many of them." Yet this separation was imperfect. According to Keith, persons had "crept into the form and profession of friends' way, who are not really friends of Truth." How could Quakers rectify this fault? They could look to the first followers of Christ who sustained their purity "by feeling an inward knitting and uniting of th[ei]r hearts" and with "some open declaration and profession of their faith in the most principal and necessary Doctrines of Christian religion."

Confronted by weak, even hypocritical members, Keith asked the Quakers to emulate the discipline of the early Church. The movement should be reorganized. Friends who possessed a "good knowledge and discerning one of another" should declare themselves "one people and Societyee, in the Truth" and outline their doctrinal views in a creed. Gathered as Christ's Church they would then be ready to accept new members. But contrary to contemporary or even early Quaker practice, prospective members would be required to pass two tests. First they would be asked to assent to the newly drawn creed. Then they would be asked to give a more imposing demonstration of their orthodoxy by describing their experiences with God. They would have to relate their "convincement and what God hath wrought in them," a requirement that would raise even higher the wall between Quaker and non-Quaker.

Keith's proposed reforms carried as many implications for church government as for purity. In fact, the two were intimately connected. In apostolic times Christians used their discipline to build a dynamic cohesion among their members. As a result, government in the early Church was exercised through the whole membership, not by elders or selected representatives. As Keith described it, all the members were expected to "consult and resolve in the Wisdom and Spirit of God what was fitt to be done." Friends could do the same. They could make sure that new members would not drift into indifference and indo-

---

[33] George Keith, *A Plain Short Catechism for Children and Youth* (Philadelphia, 1690), unpaginated preface, p. 29.

[34] D. Elton Trueblood, *Robert Barclay* (New York, 1968), p. 137; William C. Braithwaite, *The Second Period of Quakerism* (2nd ed., Cambridge, Engl., 1961), p. 385; Geoffrey T. Nuttall, *The Holy Spirit in Puritan Faith and Experience* (New York, 1947), p. 44; Hugh Barbour, *The Quakers in Puritan England* (New Haven and London, 1964), pp. 145–146; Melvin B. Endy, Jr., *William Penn and Early Quakerism* (Princeton, N.J., 1973), pp. 281–292, 296–304.

[35] "Gospel Order and Discipline," *Jour. Friends Hist. Soc.* 10 (1913): pp. 70–76. Two manuscript copies of the document are in Box 572, Papers Relating to the Keithian Controversy, FHL. While the document is sometimes interpreted as having been written for Keith's followers after 1692, its style, together with a notable absence of the viciousness that marked the schism, makes it likely that this is the document Keith read to the Public Friends in March, 1690. Quotations in the next several paragraphs are from the printed version.

That Keith was not the only Delaware valley Friend thinking about Quaker discipline is evident from the 1691 epistle by John Willsford cited in note 28. However, unlike Keith, Willsford did not use his concerns to suggest that Friends create a new disciplinary system.

lence simply because there was no place for them in church affairs. By absorbing well-examined members in all church business the Friends could enhance their commitment to the Christian life. It was in this context that government by representatives was anachronistic, even dangerous. The church was not civil society, and, Keith wrote, "as the Church of God in other respects doth greatly differ from worldly Governments, so in this." True Christians should govern themselves. What was accomplished for the whole church "should have the consent of the whole church" and the best way to obtain that consent was through a government of and by the whole membership.

Still, Keith intended no revolt against the wise. He acknowledged complaints that older Quakers took "too much upon them and assume a rule over us without our consent." But he believed that maturity aided faith and readily asserted that older Quakers gave valuable help with discipline. Yet theirs was a capacity to advise, not to determine or order, and it was to preserve this distinction that Keith proposed that Friends appoint elders and deacons, the elders to oversee the "orderly walking of all under the profession of Truth," the deacons "partly to assist the Elders and partly to gather the collections of the Church." These officers were to serve, not govern, so that Keith stressed their duties rather than their powers. Elders would guide young Quakers "not by lording it over their consciences but watching over them," and deacons would distribute the church funds under the supervision of the membership.

Keith's suggestions flew in the face of Quaker practice. Never had the Friends adopted a creed, required a relation of spiritual experience, or so clearly formalized the handling of discipline and finances in local meetings as Keith proposed. Yet if Quakers hoped to end the "fair outward show" that disfigured their long-sought purity, Keith believed they needed "first to prove Men before they own them as fellow members of Christ's body." Would this effort presume to much? Not to Quakers who still aimed at the old Quakers goals. God Himself would help these Friends. He would "more and more endue the faithfull among us with a spirit of discerning . . . whereby to put a difference betwixt the faithful and the unfaithful." Assured of this help, Keith asked whether Quakers were not required to reform their discipline: "Ought we not therefore to do o[u]r utmost diligence to be a separate people still, and to purge out all the old leaven that we may be a wholly new lump?"

Keith's innocent title, "Gospel Order Improved," only thinly masked the dangers of his criticism. According to Keith, spiritual unity had been exchanged for institutional hierarchy. Instead it involved a synthesis of faith and discipline. Only by gathering the faithful in the communal experience of the church, and only by governing the church through assemblies of all its members, not by elders or representatives, could Friends achieve that synthesis. The challenge posed by these notions to Delaware valley Quakerism was obvious. Where ministers clearly dominated a hierarchical meeting system there, Keith's "Gospel Order Improved" emphasized a cohesion grounded in radical spiritual egalitarianism and strict doctrinal testing; he talked about monthly meetings as though they involved every Friend and did not even mention the quarterly and yearly meetings with their narrow and restricted membership.

It is precisely at this point that we can appreciate our knowledge of the Quaker denominational order. Most historians have treated the Keithian schism of 1692 as motivated largely by economic considerations, a revolt by small and modest Quaker settlers against the wealthy landowners and merchants who dominated Pennsylvania politics in the 1690's. Thus Gary Nash has well demonstrated that Keith's supporters were mostly modest farmers and small merchants and that his opponents often were the Delaware valley's richest and most powerful politicians.[36] But all of these people acted out of more than pecuniary interest. As we shall see, Keith's followers clearly were concerned for matters of the spirit. And so too were Keith's opponents, this for a very special and now understandable reason. Not only were they the rich politicians and merchants that political historians have described, but our study of Delaware valley Quakerism reveals that virtually all of Keith's vocal opponents were Public Friends as well. Their ranks included nearly everyone important in Pennsylvania's ruling clique: the deputy governor, Thomas Lloyd; his six principal supporters on the Pennsylvania council—Arthur Cooke, Samuel Jennings, John Delavall, Samuel Richardson, Anthony Morris, and Robert Ewer—and Lloyd's major supporters in Bucks and Chester counties—John Blunston, John Simcock, George Maris, Nicholas Waln, William Yardley, and Phineas Pemberton. Only in the case of some of Lloyd's supporters among the merchants does the ministerial association weaken. Three of them—Humphrey Morrey, John Day, and John Jones—probably were not Public Friends in this period, but two were—Samuel Carpenter and James Fox.[37]

It was before these ministers that Keith read his

---

[36] Gary B. Nash, *Quakers and Politics, Pennsylvania, 1681–1726* (Princeton, N.J., 1968), pp. 144–161.

[37] *Ibid.,* pp. 149, 155–156. The Philadelphia Meeting of Ministers did not maintain a list of active Public Friends in these years. This makes their exact identification difficult. However, their membership can be partially reconstructed by analyzing three ministerial activities—the proceedings of the Philadelphia Meeting of Ministers between 1685/6 and 1695, the ministerial epistle condemning Keith issued 20 June, 1692 and printed in James Bowden, *The History of the Society of Friends in America* (2 v., London, 1850–1854) **2**: pp. 86–90, and the ministerial letter to London of 9 June, 1693 in Box 572, Papers Relating to the Keithian Controversy, FHL.

"Gospel Order Improved" in March, 1690. Considering their history, both in England and in Pennsylvania, the Public Friends scarcely could be expected to accept Keith's criticisms, and not surprisingly they hesitated to discuss his work. "By reason of the great weight of the Things there treated on," they decided to read the manuscript and discuss it in one week.[38] When that week elapsed, however, the ministers postponed the discussion for six months, moving it to September, 1690. Even in the fall they were still apprehensive and with Keith's consent decided to study the manuscript for yet another year, this time to consider it at their meeting in September, 1691.[39]

As the ministers read and reread they maintained what appears to have been a harmonious relationship with Keith. They approved the publication of another book attacking Cotton Mather, and he engaged in much preaching. Although still in charge of the Philadelphia Latin School, he wrote later that he "kept an Usher and spent a great part of his time in Reading, Meditation, Visiting Meetings, and answering the Conscientious Doubts and Questions of many People." [40] The ministers aided him in this work and during the winter of 1690–1691 sent him on a ministerial tour of Maryland and Virginia. Upon his return Keith elaborated on his successes and reported that Public Friends would "be of good Service" in the southern colonies.[41]

It was Keith's preaching that brought about the first public breach between him and any of the ministers. His emphasis on the Scriptures and the historical Christ produced what Keith himself later described as "much whispering and back-biting," and in one of the Philadelphia meetings for worship (the date is not clear but it was sometime during the spring or summer of 1691) another minister, William Stockdale, disputed Keith's views.[42] Stockdale argued that the Inward Light alone brought salvation and that a belief in the body or historical existence of Christ was unnecessary, then accused Keith of preaching two Christs, one of the body, the other of the spirit.[43]

The accusation incensed Keith. Just as he had feared in 1688, Pennsylvania Quakers appeared to be slighting Christ and the scriptures. Worse, this behavior now was coming from a disturbing source, Stockdale, a Public Friend and a member of the Philadelphia Meeting of Ministers. Faced with the appearance of heresy among the ministers themselves, Keith moved beyond his "Gospel Order Improved," which still had not been discussed by them, to demand Stockdale's condemnation as a heretic.[44]

In the summer and fall of 1691 Keith kept up the pressure on Stockdale, who in turn rejected Keith's criticisms, and during the Yearly Meeting in September some half-dozen sessions were held in a fruitless effort to resolve their differences.[45] As the Friends discussed the charges against Keith and Stockdale, Keith became even more concerned about orthodoxy. Where in 1688 he had written only generally about "ranters and airy Notionists," now he found them throughout the highest levels of Pennsylvania Quakerism. In the September Yearly Meeting and at meetings held during the winter of 1691–1692 several Public Friends allegedly expressed views which Keith had long feared might be common in Pennsylvania and which he later recounted in a manuscript written in April, 1692. Thomas Fitzwater, he said, argued that Christ was "onely a Spirit in Heaven." Jacob Tillner, a minister who had emigrated from Holland, told listeners that "Christ mends Soules perfectly at once so as to have no Sin and that when we are Kings we are not to begg or pray to God." William Brought confirmed the worst of Keith's fears by asking "what good or profit can the name of Christ do us?" Finally, Keith quoted Samuel Jennings, one of the most prominent Public Friends in Pennsylvania and a leading Philadelphia merchant, as saying that spiritual values contributed little to daily work—that "to do God's business we need God's wisdom and power, but to do business as Men we needed not a supernatural power." Keith was appalled. Clearly heresy abounded in the Delaware valley.[46]

---

[38] Minutes, Philadelphia Meeting of Ministers, 1 March, 1689/90, FHL microfilm copy.

[39] *Ibid.*, 9 March, 1689/90, 6 September, 1690.

[40] George Keith, *New England's Spirit of Persecution Transmitted to Pennsylvania* . . . ([Philadelphia], 1693), p. 1.

[41] Minutes, Philadelphia Meeting of Ministers, 7 March, 1691, FHL microfilm copy. The approval of Keith's book, probably *A Serious Appeal to all the more Sober, Impartial and Judicious People in New England* (Philadelphia, 1692) was accomplished in the Philadelphia Monthly Meeting. See Minutes, Philadelphia Quarterly and Monthly Meeting, 26 February, 1691/2, FHL microfilm copy.

[42] George Keith, *New England's Spirit of Persecution Transmitted to Pennsylvania* . . . ([Philadelphia], 1693), p. 1. The first disagreement with Stockdale is mentioned vaguely in *An Appeal from the Twenty eight Judges* . . . (Philadelphia, 1692), p. 4, and in *The Plea of the Innocent Against the False Judgment of the Guilty* . . . (Philadelphia, 1692), pp. 2, 19.

[43] George Keith, *New England's Spirit of Persecution Trans-*

mitted to Pennsylvania . . . ([Philadelphia], 1693), p. 1; Ethyn W. Kirby, *George Keith (1638–1716)* (New York, 1942), pp. 60–63.

[44] John Gough, *History of the People Called Quakers* (3 v., Dublin, 1789) 3: p. 325. Gough charged that when members of the 1691 Philadelphia Yearly Meeting asked Keith whether he wanted his proposal sent to London, he answered, "Let it drop." The minutes of the Philadelphia Yearly Meeting do not even mention Keith's document and Keith's own discussion of the affair in *The Plea of the Innocent Against the False Judgment of the Guilty* . . . (Philadelphia, 1692), pp. 14–21, suggests that if such words ever were spoken they were most likely uttered in the ministers' meeting of September, 1691, or at the earlier ministerial gathering of March, 1691.

[45] Ethyn W. Kirby, *George Keith (1638–1716)* (New York, 1942), pp. 62–63.

[46] Some Propositions in Order to Heale the Breach that is amongst us, 8 April, 1692, in Box 572, Papers Relating to the Keithian Controversy, FHL.

In February, 1692, the Philadelphia Monthly Meeting drew such a large crowd that it was moved to Keith's school, where, taking advantage of the location, Keith's supporters won a condemnation of Stockdale. Their victory was short-lived. In March the Philadelphia Quarterly Meeting overturned the judgment and rebuked its sponsors. Keith and his followers then opened a separate meeting for worship in Philadelphia, or, as they later claimed, closed the regular meeting to heretics.[47]

Now the battle turned from questions of doctrine to issues relating to the locus and exercise of authority. No one resented Keith's behavior more than Philadelphia's Public Friends, and when Keith and his followers began their separate meetings the ministers reacted quickly. In an effort to contain the dispute several ministers visited Keith privately and urged him to discontinue the meetings. Keith rejected the advice, bluntly asserting that the ministers came only "to cloak Error and Heresie."[48] Startled by this rejection, the ministerial meeting named a formal committee to visit him again. This committee reported that Keith's mood had not changed: "He denied our Authority He denied [our] Judgment he did not value it a pin he would trample upon it as dirt under his feet . . . there was not any one of us all that did Preach Christ rightly." And when the ministers argued with him, Keith even ridiculed their anger: "See what Excessive passion thou art in look thy face in a glass see what a face thou hast."[49]

Keith's behavior tore at the heart of Quaker order. By his constant arguments and his support for the separate meetings he had made the dispute with Stockdale public and unseemly. But not until he insulted the ministers did Keith clearly assume the role of a schismatic. In visiting him the Public Friends had indicated their willingness to settle matters despite the harsh words about Stockdale or even the existence of the separate meetings. But when Keith rejected their authority as "rank popery" and demanded that the dispute be left to the "judgment of the Spirit of God," the ministers moved to protect Quaker order, a development that gave all the arguments a new and ominous character.[50]

Before dealing with Keith, however, the ministers first had to establish order in their own ranks. This was necessary because Keith had earlier received support from some Public Friends who also were distressed by Stockdale's views. But when the separate meetings for worship began, and especially after Keith had ridiculed the ministerial committee, only a few of those Friends continued to support him, namely John

Hart, George Hutcheson, and Thomas Budd. Other earlier supporters, including William and Jane Biles, Hugh Derborough, and John Delavall, a son-in-law of Pennsylvania deputy governor Lloyd, deserted him.[51]

In June, 1692, twenty-eight Public Friends sitting as the Philadelphia Meeting of Ministers condemned Keith's behavior. They also censured Stockdale, finding some of his notions "an Offence to many sound and tender Friends." Yet where Stockdale merely erred, Keith had been impudent, especially in his ridicule of the ministers. Keith, they said, had called them "fools, ignorant heathens, infidels, silly souls, lyars, hereticks, rotten ranters, m[u]ggletonians . . . thereby to our grief, foaming out his own shame." The Public Friends condemned this language and withdrew Keith's thirty-year standing in the ministry. They would, they said, "have him cease to offer his gift, as such among us, or elsewhere among Friends, till he be reconciled to his offended brethren."[52]

The condemnation caused Keith to renew his charge of ministerial "popery." He called the ministers' action an "encroachment upon our *Christian* Liberty [that] savours too much of the Church of Rome." Later he tried to split the orthodox ranks by pointing at the arrogance of the ministers. They claimed authority over other Friends merely, Keith wrote, "upon a pretence of their being ministers," and he quoted one Public Friend as saying that the ministerial meeting was infallible simply because it was "made up of such a Body of the Ministry."[53]

The ministers were not put off by Keith. Their condemnation never was withdrawn. Instead, it led directly to his disownment. It was communicated to monthly and quarterly meetings in Pennsylvania and the Jerseys wherever Keithian defectors might be found. As it passed through these meetings, ministerial authority passed with it. In Bucks County the Quarterly Meeting accepted and approved the condemnation, then added its own, calling Keith "Diotrepes-like, loving to have preeminence, [who] receiveth not them approved amongst us," meaning the ministers, "and yet doth publish to the world that he is in unity with

[47] Ethyn W. Kirby, *George Keith* (*1638–1716*) (New York, 1942), p. 65.

[48] Minutes, Philadelphia Meeting of Ministers, 5 March, 1691/2, FHL microfilm copy.

[49] *Ibid.*, 7 March, 1691/2.

[50] *Ibid.*, 17 June, 1692.

[51] *The Plea of the Innocent Against the False Judgment of the Guilty* . . . (Philadelphia, 1692), pp. 2–10.

[52] Quoted from the printed version in Samuel Smith, "History of the Province of Pennsylvania," *Register of Pennsylvania* 8 (1830): pp. 279–280. See also Ethyn W. Kirby, *George Keith* (*1638–1716*) (New York, 1942), p. 68.

[53] George Keith, *Some Reasons and Causes of the Late Separation that Hath come to pass at Philadelphia* . . . ([Philadelphia, 1692]), p. 12; George Keith, *An Expostulation with Thomas Lloyd* . . . ([Philadelphia, 1692]), p. 5.

[54] Quoted from the copy of the Bucks County Quarterly Meeting judgment inserted in the Minutes, Philadelphia Yearly Meeting, p. 32, FHL microfilm copy. See also *The Friend* 27 (1853–1854): p. 340. The judgment refers to III John 9–10, where the refusal of Diotrephes to hear the apostles is reported. In England in the 1680's the same text was used against William Rogers of Bristol, who supported John

the faithful brethren everywhere." [54]　At the Frankford Monthly Meeting where Keith reputedly had received much support, four ministers showed up to read the condemnation in person.　They were rebuffed, the meeting having fallen into Keith's hands, but they read their judgment anyway and then departed, leaving behind dire warnings about the consequences of following Keith.[55]

Clearly worried that Keith's support was increasing, in August, 1692, the Public Friends went beyond the familiar instruments of ministerial authority by hauling Keith to court on a charge of libel.　Ostensibly, Keith was arraigned for insulting the colony's leading officeholders, especially Thomas Lloyd, who Keith allegedly said "was not fit to be a Governor, and that his name would stink." [56]　More serious were his attacks on the union of politics and religion in early Pennsylvania. After the condemnation of June, 1692, Keith accused the Public Friends of acting more like magistrates than as ministers.　Government activity had corrupted their spiritual integrity.　This was true, he said, especially of Lloyd, Samuel Jennings, John Simcock, and Arthur Cooke, four ministers "concerned in Government and Magistracy . . . [who] exalt themselves, and lord it over G. K. and his friends, and seek to oppress and run [them] down, because of their worldly Power and Greatness." [57]　By midsummer, 1692, Keith was arguing that the Public Friends should be forbidden to sit as civil magistrates.　This was no mere academic charge because at least five of the six Quaker magistrates in Philadelphia were Public Friends and members of the Philadelphia Meeting of Ministers.[58]

Keith's new accusations came in the critical summer before the September Yearly Meeting.　Hearing them, the leading Friends panicked.　Having already split the Quaker meetings, Keith now seemed intent on destroying the Quakers' government.　Thus the minister-magistrates asserted that Keith's demands would "prostitute the Validity of every act of Government" in Pennsylvania, a clear indication that they, too, understood the closeness of politics and religion there. Hence, they ordered Keith and the printer, William Bradford, to cease publishing criticisms with a "tend-

ency to Sedition and Disturbance of the Peace." [59] By this, of course, they meant Keith to publish nothing, since everything he now wrote undermined orthodox Quaker conceptions of order and tranquility. More immediately, the order would stop some of Keith's activities during the two-week period that would elapse between their order and the beginning of the September Yearly Meeting.

The episode at Frankford revealed the seriousness of Keith's challenge, and in preparation for the Yearly Meeting in September, 1692, the Public Friends decided to leave nothing to chance.　In customary fashion they gathered a day prior to the Yearly Meeting itself.　This time they drew up a second judgment of Keith.　It listed more of his insults, reminded the yearly meeting of the ministers' own patient conduct— that the Public Friends had, for example, refrained from publishing the June condemnation until Keith had an opportunity to answer the charges against him—and asked the Yearly Meeting to condemn Keith.[60]

The September gathering confirmed the ministers' judgment.　About three-fourths of the representatives from the quarterly and monthly meetings condemned Keith.　The others followed him into yet another separation, this time a new Keithian yearly meeting. Appropriately enough, the majority at the orthodox meeting not only disowned Keith but upheld the action of the Public Friends.　They specifically supported their "dear and well esteemed friends and Labourers in the Gospel" and denounced the "spirit of Revileing, Raileing, Lying, Slandering and falsely accusing which hath risen up and acted notoriously in George Keith and his adherents." [61]

The ministers used their victory in the Yearly Meeting to press even harder on the loyalties of the Pennsylvania Quakers.　The judgment was circulated to meetings in Maryland, Virginia, and New England, and these gatherings in turn expressed their agreement with the Yearly Meeting verdict in Pennsylvania.[62] The consequence was inescapable.　Modest as well as prestigious Friends disavowed Keith.　Well-known Quakers sent apologetic papers to Philadelphia to

---

Wilkinson and John Story in their dispute with Fox.　See Richard Snead *et al., An Exalted Diotrephes Reprehended, or, the Spirit of Error and Envy in William Rogers against the Truth . . .* ([London], 1681), and *Minute Book of the Men's Meeting of the Society of Friends in Bristol, 1667–1686,* Russell Mortimer, ed., *Publ. Bristol Record Society* **26** (Bristol, Engl., 1971) : pp. xvii–xix.

[55] *The Plea of the Innocent Against the False Judgment of the Guilty . . .* (Philadelphia, 1692), p. 16.

[56] Quoted in Ethyn W. Kirby, *George Keith (1638–1716)* (New York, 1942), p. 78.

[57] *The Plea of the Innocent Against the False Judgment of the Guilty . . .* (Philadelphia, 1692), p. 9.

[58] The five were Samuel Jennings, Arthur Cooke, Robert Ewer, Samuel Richardson, and Anthony Morris.

[59] The order is printed in Ethyn W. Kirby, *George Keith (1638–1716)* (New York, 1942), pp. 78–79.

[60] The minutes of these ministerial meetings are missing, but the Public Friends' advice to the Philadelphia Yearly Meeting is printed in Samuel Smith, "History of the Province of Pennsylvania," *Register of Pennsylvania* **7** (1830) : p. 300.

[61] Quoted in *ibid.,* pp. 301–302; Ethyn W. Kirby, *George Keith (1638–1715)* (New York, 1942), pp. 75–77.

[62] Ethyn W. Kirby, *George Keith (1638–1716)* (New York, 1942), p. 77.　See also [George Keith], *The False Judgment of a Yearly Meeting of Quakers in Maryland* ([Philadelphia, 1693]).　For Delaware valley readings of judgments from other Quaker meetings see Minutes, Abington Monthly Meeting, 30 January, 1692/3, and Minutes, Burlington Monthly Meeting, 2 January, 1692/3; 6 February, 1692/3; FHL microfilm copies.

escape even the slightest association with the schism while many common Friends like James and Esther Cooper condemned the schism simply for "not proceeding from the meeke, and peaceable spirit of Jesus." [63]

In this context, the ministers' subsequent pursuit of Keith in the courts can only be regarded as an exercise in personal retribution. When, after September, Keith continued to talk and Bradford to print, the Philadelphia grand jury indicted them on charges of libel in October, 1692. Inevitably, Keith saw the indictment as but another ministerial maneuver and accused the magistrates of holding an inquisition. Nonetheless, the jury convicted him on the charge of libel. But when it refused to find a verdict against Bradford the magistrates became furious and, according to Keith, kept the jurors "without Meat, drink, fire or tobacco," behavior Keith gleefully found reminiscent of the Crown's threats to the jury during the famous trial of William Penn and William Meade in 1670. [64]

The lapse in ministerial judgment came too late for Keith, who soon fell into desperate acts of his own. After the 1692 Yearly Meeting he attacked the orthodox Quakers from anywhere and without warning. He would stop them on the streets, or he and his supporters would run into a meeting for worship, harangue the congregation, and run out. [65] Finally, condemned by the ministers and the Yearly Meeting, tried in the courts, and slowly losing ground in the countryside, Keith and his frustrated followers marched into Philadelphia's orthodox meetinghouse where they first built a gallery for their own leaders and then, in the midst of a scuffle, ripped down the ministerial gallery of their opponents. [66] The episode signaled defeat, not victory. Throughout 1693 Keith continued to tour Pennsylvania, kept up the separate meetings for worship (now called those of Christian Quakers), and issued a confession of faith. But his following dwindled, apparently never rising above the level of support he had received in the 1692 Yearly Meeting, and in February, 1694, Keith sailed home to take his case before the Quakers in London.

The reaction of the English Friends confirms, although in a peculiar way, the view that the Keithian dispute was essentially a contest involving ministerial authority. As early as September, 1691, several London ministers had tried to settle the Stockdale affair by letter, but their words excited everyone and solved nothing. [67] Later some of the London Quakers perceived too much ministerial conniving in Philadelphia and accused the Pennsylvania ministers of an overzealous prosecution of Keith. This charge angered the American Friends. "Did yu: there but see One Halfe of the trash he hath published: the notion of his former Services would never stay yu: from nauseating his disservice," Lloyd wrote. Hugh Roberts, another minister, complained to Penn that while the Public Friends in Philadelphia had expected help from London, all they heard were complaints that they had been "too hasty in judging G. K." Roberts was dismayed. Indeed, it was their bold condemnation of Keith that had saved orthodox Quakerism in Pennsylvania, and Roberts knew it. "If we did miss at all we did it becaus we had not pas it the sooner." The English Friends should not be fooled by Keith. "I shall tell thee plaenly that the sp[i]rit that G:K: is of is not oneley a tering devouring sp[i]rit but a cursed leing sp[i]rit also . . . think of him w[ha]t you will but at Last you will find it so." [68]

In the end London's Quakers discovered that the Philadelphia ministers had not been so wrong about Keith. In a letter to his Pennsylvania supporters in 1694, Keith reported that his preaching was "well owned and received by the Greatest Part of the People." But even Keith reported that it divided the English ministers, producing "contradictory testimonys in their public Meetings and frequent Disputes by Private Conferencys." [69] Fearing that such disputes marked the beginning of a second separation in England, in June, 1694, the London Second Day Morning Meeting reprimanded him for printing material on the Pennsylvania schism without its approval. But it also used the occasion to slap hands in Philadelphia. The Pennsylvania ministers should have been more patient. The legal action against Keith had been as embarrassing as it was wrong and, the London meeting wrote, "those Proceedings in Sessions against G.K. . . . we could not stand by . . . you may Remember that King David Patiently bore a greatter affront from Shimei than some Justices had from G.K." [70]

---

63 See the Testimony of Robert Owen, undated, and James and Esther Cooper, Acknowledgement for Having Followed George Keith, 9 January, 169[6], Miscellaneous Manuscripts, FHL. Four months earlier in September, 1695, James Cooper offered the Philadelphia Yearly Meeting a more elaborate recantation of his support for Keith. See *The Friend* **28** (1854–1855): p. 51.

64 Quoted in Ethyn W. Kirby, *George Keith (1638–1716)* (New York, 1942), p. 84.

65 *Ibid.*, pp. 90–94.

66 The act also betrayed Keith's acceptance of a legitimate ministry. *Ibid.*, p. 87; Gary B. Nash, *Quakers and Politics, Pennsylvania, 1681–1726* (Princeton, N.J., 1968), pp. 152–153.

67 George Whitehead *et al.* to Thomas Lloyd and Arthur Cooke, 28 September, 1691, in: Samuel Smith, "History of the Province of Pennsylvania," *Register of Pennsylvania* **7** (1830): pp. 242–245.

68 Hugh Roberts to William Penn, undated, in *Penna. Mag. History and Biography* **18** (1894): pp. 205–210; Thomas Lloyd to Philip Ford, [?] April, 1693, in *Bull. Friends Hist. Assoc.* **2** (1908): p. 19.

69 George Keith and Thomas Budd to Friends in Pennsylvania, 12 April, 1694, in Box 572, Papers Relating to the Keithian Controversy, FHL.

70 George Whitehead *et al.* to Thomas Lloyd *et al.*, 21 June, 1694, in *ibid.*; Ethyn W. Kirby, *George Keith (1638–1716)* (New York, 1942), pp. 95–100.

The London ministers set out to handle Keith in a model way. Despite a crabbed, defensive speech from him at the 1694 London Yearly Meeting, they lauded his professed desire for peace and unity and asked him to contain his bitterness toward the Public Friends. In turn, the ministers were ordered to forego assaults on Keith.[71] But Keith soon resumed his attacks, then accepted support from older separatists who had been condemned during the Wilkinson-Story dispute of the 1670's. Thus, by September, 1695, the London Yearly Meeting was able to record what to its mind had become an inescapable judgment: "That the said George Keith is Gone from the blessed unity of the peaceable spirit of our Lord . . . and hath separated himself from the holy fellowship of the Church of Christ." [72]

The Keithian schism was a watershed for Quaker development in the Delaware valley. On the one hand it demonstrated how effectively Public Friends controlled the Quaker ecclesiastical framework. Delaware valley Friends never became part of a wilderness experiment in spiritual or institutional democracy. Certainly they rejected the egalitarianism implicit in Keith's critique. But the schism also looked forward as it stimulated a renascence in disciplinary and institutional creativity that changed the leadership of Delaware valley Quakerism between 1695 and 1720.

Like the Keithian schism itself, the renewal that overtook Friends in the Delaware valley after 1693 also was rooted in a critique of the standing order. But it was developed first by Public Friends who feared that Keith indeed had exposed dangerous irregularities in their ranks. Thus they moved to cleanse their own membership after suppressing his challenge to their authority. In September, 1693, the Philadelphia Meeting of Ministers ordered Public Friends who had been accused of heresy to "clear themselves if they Can." Obviously worried that Keith had undermined confidence in their orthodoxy, the ministers also issued a statement of doctrinal beliefs in a pamphlet called *Our Antient Testimony Renewed*.[73] Although they never forced new Friends to sign such a statement, as Keith once demanded they do in his "Gospel Order Improved," its existence demonstrated that Keith still shaped Delaware valley Quakerism even after his disownment.

The search for orthodoxy also transcended ministerial bounds. Most important was the fact that it reinforced the concern for morality already evident in Pennsylvania and the Jerseys before 1692. As a result Friends moved toward a kind of moral casuistry in their affairs. This was expressed two ways. First, the number of behavioral prohibitions multiplied as Friends tried to identify themselves as a peculiar people in the world. Second, exceptions to these prohibitions were stated with increasing specificity so Friends could tell just what kind of behavior was disownable and what kind of behavior was not. An example is found in the epistle sent out from the 1694 Philadelphia Yearly Meeting. As usual it warned Friends to "keep out of the world's corrupt language, manners and vain, needless things . . . and to live soberly and godly in this present world." It then listed in detail some of the demands to be made on Friends. Quakers should not "ride, or go in the streets with pipes in their mouths." They should avoid ostentatious funerals. Monthly meetings should keep their "intire burying Place to themselves only." But Friends attending funerals, apparently Quaker and non-Quaker funerals alike, were told that they could "go orderly after the Corps[e] to the Grave not Exceeding four in breadth," since a procession of this size presumably was modest enough to be permitted.[74]

The new legalism also was prominent in advice about children. As was true for Keith, it was the behavior of the youngest Friends that attracted attention from Quaker moralists. According to the 1694 Yearly Meeting epistles, too many children indulged themselves with innocuous or hurtful games or answered their parents "forwardly and crossly." One remedy lay with parents "to be good examples in their families, and to watch over them for good." Another lay in describing the parental responsibilities with incredible precision. Thus a 1698 epistle from the women's meeting at Burlington warned that "over long scarfs" and "striped or gaudy flowered stuffs or silk" were inappropriate for children's clothes. It cautioned Friends that "little children's coats be pinned up behind, not in heaps or plaints," and warned that children's hair "be not cut, and left out on the brow, nor the head dressed high." Over the next several decades the Philadelphia Yearly Meeting and its subordinate meeting rotated these advices in their epistles so that nearly all important aspects of moral discipline had been discussed within a three- or four-year period.[75]

The renascence in disciplinary concern also explains the attention some Friends now gave to slavery. In

---

[71] These procedures are described in part in Francis E. Pollard *et al.*, *Democracy and the Quaker Method* (London, 1949), pp. 102–117, in a way that greatly exaggerates the democracy of the London Yearly Meeting and of Quaker affairs generally.

[72] Quoted in *ibid.*, p. 110.

[73] James Bowden, *The History of the Society of Friends in America* (2 v., London, 1850–1854) 2: pp. 28–33; Minutes, Philadelphia Meeting of Ministers, 2 September, 1693, FHL microfilm copy.

[74] Minutes, Philadelphia Monthly Meeting, 28 October, 1694, FHL microfilm copy.

[75] Epistle, Women's Meeting at Burlington to Friends, 21 September, 1698, Miscellaneous Epistles, FHL. Epistles sent out from the Philadelphia Yearly Meeting usually can be found in its manuscript meeting records. The epistle of 1701, for example, was concerned with seven items—humility, families, meetings, worldly interests, civil suits, and political activity —and that of 1706 with five worries—worship, apprenticeship, courtship, "Vain company," and charity.

1688 Friends in Germantown had attempted to encourage Delaware valley Quakers to renounce slave-keeping, but their effort was repulsed. Again prodded by Keith, whose Christian Quakers adopted an anti-slavery position in 1693, some orthodox Friends began a new attack on the institution. The 1694 Philadelphia Yearly Meeting decreed that Friends should be "Careful not to Encourage the bringing in of any more Negroes," meaning slaves. In 1696 Cadwallader Morgan, probably a weighty Friend and not a minister, urged the Philadelphia Yearly Meeting to condemn slavery outright. In 1698 Robert Pile, the man Frances Harrison had said unfairly dominated Quaker affairs in Chester County in 1690, proposed that quarterly meetings free slaves owned by Friends and compensate their owners for the loss. Nothing came of the suggestions made by Morgan and Pile. But the Yearly Meeting did condemn the sale of blacks in the public market in 1698 and started special worship services for Philadelphia blacks in 1700.[76]

As one might expect, the Quaker disciplinary renascence also led to a growth of new institutions. Between 1695 and about 1715 Pennsylvania and New Jersey Friends established new offices and meetings and altered the membership of old ones. In so doing they changed the contour of the denomination's institutional structure. This splurge began in 1695 when the Philadelphia Yearly Meeting ordered each monthly meeting to appoint two weighty Friends to inquire into the behavior of every Quaker in a meeting for worship. Such tasks had been undertaken casually by weighty Friends before, both in England and America. But this instruction formalized those duties and created a new office in monthly meetings, the "overseer," who, ironically, performed many of the tasks George Keith had given to "elders" in his "Gospel Order Improved."[77]

Other institutional developments followed quickly. In 1696 the Philadelphia Yearly Meeting established special quarterly meetings for youths where Quaker children could be drilled in their duties toward family, Friends, and society.[78] Monthly meetings also developed standardized questions to guide overseers in performing their duties. Those used in the Darby Monthly

Meeting probed many aspects of secular behavior, including attendance at meetings, dress, business affairs, the use of tobacco and alcohol, education, the apprenticeship of children, and "tattling, tale-bearing, back-biting, whispering, and meddling [oneself] in other men's business."[79]

The information gathered by the overseers also stimulated the creation of additional local meetings. Overseers' reports consumed much time in the monthly meetings and in 1698 the Philadelphia Yearly Meeting proposed that quarterly meetings allow weighty Friends to "prepare Matters before the monthly meetings" so the latter might proceed more smoothly. Although the Yearly Meeting did not order the quarterly meetings to organize the new meetings, what soon were called "preparative" meetings were begun at several places, including Chester County, where overseers prepared lists of subjects to be discussed at the monthly meetings, and they slowly became part of the eighteenth-century Quaker meeting structure.[80]

All of this activity led to the preparation of a formal written guide to discipline itself, a new departure for either English or American Friends. In 1705 the Philadelphia Yearly Meeting sent two papers, one on discipline, the other on its practice, to quarterly and monthly meetings for their use in local affairs. These documents, soon simply called the "Discipline" and revised between 1718 and 1719, codified Quaker norms and outlined procedures for their enforcement. The standards of behavior and the disciplinary procedures found there were old and differed from the more informal norms of twenty or thirty years before largely only in specificity. Marriage to non-Quaker still threatened disownment and uprightness in business and personal behavior remained a qualification for continued attendance in Quaker meetings. But these were now stated in a way they had not been before—formally and in a list—so that Friends could now look as easily at the circulating manuscript "Discipline" as they could at what might be found in the Light.[81]

The new disciplinary awareness did not prosper everywhere, of course. The Quaker concern for slaveholding remained little more than that. A forthright condemnation of the practice was not made until 1756 and even then many Friends continued to own slaves

[76] Sydney V. James, *A People Among People: Quaker Benevolence in Eighteenth-Century America* (Cambridge, Mass., 1963), pp. 103–127.

[77] Minutes, Philadelphia Yearly Meeting, 18 September, 1695, FHL microfilm copy; Ezra Michener, *Retrospect of Early Quakerism; Being Extracts from the Records of Philadelphia Yearly Meeting and the Meetings Composing It* (Philadelphia, 1860), p. 195.

[78] Minutes, Philadelphia Quarterly and Monthly Meeting, 25 September, 1696, FHL microfilm copy; Ezra Michener, *Retrospect of Early Quakerism; Being Extracts from the Records of Philadelphia Yearly Meeting and the Meetings Composing It* (Philadelphia, 1860), p. 143; Sydney V. James, *A People Among People: Quaker Benevolence in Eighteenth-Century America* (Cambridge, Mass., 1963), p. 69.

[79] Ezra Michener, *Retrospect of Early Quakerism; Being Extracts from the Records of Philadelphia Yearly Meeting and the Meetings Composing It* (Philadelphia, 1860), pp. 200–202; William C. Braithwaite, *The Second Period of Quakerism* (2nd ed., Cambridge, Engl., 1961), pp. 416–456.

[80] Minutes, Philadelphia Yearly Meeting, 21 September, 1698, Minutes, Concord Monthly Meeting, 9 September, 1700, FHL microfilm copies; Ezra Michener, *Retrospect of Early Quakerism; Being Extracts from the Records of Philadelphia Yearly Meeting and the Meetings Composing It* (Philadelphia, 1860), p. 196.

[81] Minutes, Philadelphia Yearly Meeting, 22–23 September, 1703, 19–20 September, 1718; 19–24 September, 1719; FHL microfilm copies.

despite the ruling of the Philadelphia Yearly Meeting.[82] Furthermore, some of the techniques used to enforce discipline also met resistance. In 1700 Radnor Monthly Meeting established a committee to visit Quaker families in their homes and in 1709 the procedure was endorsed by the Philadelphia Yearly Meeting. But many meetings ignored it. Thus Bucks Quarterly Meeting noted in 1721 that the committee had been "but slenderly managed for [some] time past" and most overseers in the monthly meetings proceeded with their work in less obtrusive ways.[83]

Paradoxically, the post-1695 disciplinary renewal also hastened the decay of the Public Friends' long-time domination of Quaker church government. However strong the ministers' defense of Quaker orthodoxy against Keith's attack—and some Friends in London thought the ministers had done their job too well— Public Friends in the Delaware valley experienced the same decline in authority known by their English counterparts. Signs of the decline appeared early. After 1693 the ministers failed to control the disciplinary renascence as firmly as they might have done earlier. The demands for the education of Quaker children incorporated in the 1694 Yearly Meeting epistle came from weighty Friends in the Philadelphia Monthly Meeting, not from the ministerial meeting. The ministers took no collective position on the slavery question, and in 1698 the Yearly Meeting sent the proposal for creation of preparative meetings to the quarterly meetings where ministers and weighty Friends considered it together.[84]

The institutional fruits of these developments were not long in coming. They occurred first in worship. In 1698 the Philadelphia Monthly Meeting moved to establish a "retired" meeting where Friends worshiped in silence without sermons from Public Friends.[85] In 1700 Middletown Monthly Meeting ordered ministers and weighty Friends to sit together in the galleries and ordered the remaining Friends "all to sit with their faces towards the galleries." [86] In 1712 the old method of admission to the ministry was partially re-versed. The ministerial meeting still remained the final judge of requests for ministerial status. But monthly meetings now began sending certificates to the ministerial meeting testifying to their prior approval of a candidate's request as the first step of the process.

By 1714 the Public Friends had lost their once solitary control of the Quaker institutional structure in the Delaware valley. This was dramatically symbolized by the incorporation of weighty Friends into the ministerial meetings. The process began in 1699 when Chesterfield Monthly Meeting ordered weighty Friends to accompany Public Friends to ministerial meetings "as need shall require," though the need was not explained and weighty Friends still could not attend the ministerial meetings. Then, first in the Bucks Quarterly Meeting in 1710 and later in the Concord Quarterly Meeting in 1714, requests were made to have weighty Friends join ministers in their previously exclusive meetings. Finally, in September, 1714, the Philadelphia Yearly Meeting created "Elders"— "prudent, solid Friends to sit with the ministers in their meetings." The erosion of the ministers' once unchallenged authority now had been completed and the old ministerial meetings were renamed Meetings of Ministers and Elders.[87]

Ministers and elders shared more than a meeting title. Weighty Friends gained important new responsibilities after 1714. They reported regularly on the state of the ministry and on its reception among the general membership.[88] They also shared directly in creating and sustaining ministerial activity. In 1723 the Philadelphia Yearly Meeting insisted that "both ministers and elders may be as nursing fathers and mothers to those that are young in the ministry" and a year later decreed that ministers and weighty Friends should work jointly to "watch over the flock of Christ, in their respective places and stations; always approving themselves, by their holy examples in conversation and conduct." [89]

The coalescence of ministers and weighty Friends in a single meeting, the creation of overseers, the establishment of preparative meetings and "retired" meet-

---

[82] Sydney V. James, *A People Among People: Quaker Benevolence in Eighteenth-Century America* (Cambridge, Mass., 1963).

[83] *The Friend* **70** (1896–1897): p. 67; Minutes, Bucks Quarterly Meeting, 24 September, 1715; 30 August, 1716; 30 November, 1721; FHL microfilm copy; Ezra Michener, *Retrospect of Early Quakerism; Being Extracts from the Records of Philadelphia Yearly Meeting and the Meetings Composing It* (Philadelphia, 1860), pp. 205–206.

[84] Minutes, Philadelphia Quarterly and Monthly Meeting, 23 February, 1693/4; Minutes, Philadelphia Meeting of Ministers, 2 March, 1694/5, FHL microfilm copies.

[85] Minutes, Philadelphia Quarterly and Monthly Meeting, 26 August, 1698; 30 September, 1698; FHL microfilm copies.

[86] Minutes, Middletown Monthly Meeting, 4 January, 1699/1700, FHL microfilm copy; Ezra Michener, *Retrospect of Early Quakerism; Being Extracts from the Records of Philadelphia Yearly Meeting and the Meetings Composing It* (Philadelphia, 1860), p. 178.

[87] Ezra Michener, *Retrospect of Early Quakerism; Being Extracts from the Records of Philadelphia Yearly Meeting and the Meetings Composing It* (Philadelphia, 1860), pp. 156–158, 169–171; Bucks Quarterly Meeting of Ministers and Elders, 22 February, 1709/10; 24 January, 1714/5; 23 February, 1714/5; Minutes, Concord Quarterly Meeting, 2 August, 1714; Minutes, Philadelphia Yearly Meeting, 18–22 September, 1714, FHL microfilm copies.

[88] For an example see Minutes, Bucks Quarterly Meeting of Ministers and Elders after 23 February, 1714/5, FHL microfilm copy.

[89] Minutes, Philadelphia Yearly Meeting, 18 September, 1722; 22 September, 1724; FHL microfilm copy; Ezra Michener, *Retrospect of Early Quakerism; Being Extracts from the Records of Philadelphia Yearly Meeting and the Meetings Composing It* (Philadelphia, 1860), pp. 159–160.

ings for worship, and the increasing trend toward moral casuistry marked a crucial change in the distribution of authority in Quakerism. With them the codification of Quaker disciplinary procedures in the manuscript "Discipline" first issued in 1705 assumed new importance. The swelling number of Quaker officials—and now they could indeed be called that—made it even more important for Friends to understand how all these new elements fit smoothly into the Quaker institutional structure. Thus a revised "Discipline" in 1719 took special care to specify that the line of authority in Quaker church government ran smoothly from overseers to the monthly meeting, then to the quarterly and yearly meeting. It also provided for a legalistic system of appeals. Decisions of the overseers could be challenged in the monthly and quarterly meetings. But since the hierarchical arrangement helped legitimate decisions made in all the meetings, especially local ones, appeals were discouraged. Friends contemplating them were urged to "weightily consider the Matter before they give the Meeting so much trouble." [90]

Understanding these changes is crucial to the task of uncovering the emerging pattern of colonial American denominationalism. Whatever the difficulties of establishing a separate ministerial meeting or in settling a single yearly meeting for Friends in the Delaware valley in the 1680's, immigrant Quakers were interested in re-establishing familiar English denominational institutions in America. A broad ecclesiastical experimentalism never figured in their settlement. When their denominational order finally was questioned—fitfully in the early protests in Chester County, and systematically by George Keith between 1690 and 1694—the critics proved a poor match for the established order and its defenders. Quakers may have fled the evils of state-coerced religion in England. But they never abandoned their own disciplinary institutions once in America.

The American experience also did little to democratize Quakerism. The post-1695 disciplinary renascence spread more work and responsibility among more people. But this probably strengthened the oligarchic tendencies of Quakerism rather than any democratic ones. After 1695 leadership still rested in the hands of small numbers of ministers and weighty Friends. In turn, these Friends now guided an even more complex meeting system than had existed before. They never shared their power with lesser Friends. Nor did they submit to elections, regular or irregular. In Bucks County, for example, weighty Friends named to sit in the ministerial meeting usually

did so for at least a decade. Although no one quite equalled his record, Adam Harker attended its sessions for over thirty years, from 1715 to at least 1749. At best, these Friends—"Elders"—shared power and responsibility with other weighty Friends who did not attend ministerial meetings. The Bucks County delegation to the Philadelphia Yearly Meeting between 1700 and 1740 contained only weighty Friends from the quarterly meetings and weighty Friends and ministers who sat in the meeting of ministers and elders. Some individuals alternated trips to the Yearly Meeting with others and attended only once every two or three years, while a few Friends went to the Yearly Meeting every year. But no one went to the Yearly Meeting as part of the Bucks County delegation who was not a weighty Friend or minister.[91]

The impact of this Quaker emphasis on hierarchical authority was not lost on contemporaries. In February, 1699, a minor Philadelphia merchant named Pentecost Teague addressed a petition to an unnamed Quaker meeting—probably the Philadelphia Quarterly Meeting—that revealed how thoroughly lesser Friends, especially poor ones, still were being kept from the center of Quaker denominational power. Teague complained that monthly meeting business was "continued from one month to another till some time [matters are] utterly lost or at least forgotten." Business was so often given over to "men of great business of their owne . . . that some times they have severall matters together from our meeting." The practice made business "long and tedious . . . and allsoe [made] a greate parte of the meeting useless in such matters."

Teague laced his criticism with numerous apologies. His complaint was not meant to foster discord. He "would desire friends to take itt as itt is Intended," with "noe false glory" and with no presumption that he would think himself "capable to be apointed by Friends in the management of such affares." But Teague did mean to defend the capabilities of Quakers like himself. "Some may say I am nott fitt to medle with such a matter because I am nott used to [illegible] accounts or I am a tradesman and have butt little skill in titles of land." Yet, Teague wrote, "lett noe man slight any of these because he doe nott see me to be soie [skilled] in such matters as others be: or because he is butt low in the world." Monthly meeting business ought to be conducted by Friends "that are nott Entangled with such great business of their owne" who could "end business that they are appointed to by the meeting with all Expedition." At the very least Friends could "make Choice of them whether poore or rich." For irrespective of their position in society, "if they are men fearing of god he will give them wisdom

---

[90] Friends Book of Discipline [1719], pp. 22–23, HSP. The revision was carefully done and suggestions were widely discussed, especially in the quarterly meetings. See the Minutes, Philadelphia Yearly Meeting, between 1717 and 1719, and Minutes, Bucks Quarterly Meeting, 27 February, 1717/8; 20 May, 1718; FHL microfilm copies.

[91] The long tenure of the elders is evident from the entry in the Minutes, Bucks Quarterly Meeting of Ministers and Elders, 28 May, 1746, FHL microfilm copy, that lists all the elders appointed from the monthly meetings since 1714.

and Sound Judgment and they will doe things Effectual." [92]

Leading Quakers ignored Teague's petition. The minutes of Pennsylvania Quaker meetings do not mention it. Yet its existence testifies eloquently to the emerging characteristics of Delaware valley Quakerism. Above all, Teague's petition, the Keithian schism, the post-1695 disciplinary renascence demonstrate that the Quaker denominational order did not remain static between 1680 and 1730. Quaker church government evolved in complex ways in those years. Although this evolution was affected by American conditions—even by the "American experience"—it was not the product of it. Colonization exposed weaknesses of ministerial endeavor, for example. But similar weaknesses were known in England too and Quaker clerical authority there was on the wane as well. Thus in both places Friends profoundly altered the early practice that gave Public Friends the exclusive right to manage church business by admitting weighty Friends into Quaker governing councils at the end of the seventeenth century.

The broadening of the Quaker governing hierarchy that occurred in both England and America reveals a supple malleability in Quaker institutions that served the transatlantic experience well. In the Delaware valley, Friends first immersed themselves in secular battles that nearly cost Penn his colony, then engaged in a bitter religious schism that almost destroyed Delaware valley Quakerism. Yet Friends prospered nonetheless. Contrary to the myths created in the nineteenth century about early American development, this success never depended on a democratization of church government or a rejection of European or English institutions. Indeed, Friends sustained themselves through a strong non-democratic leadership that fostered corporate unity and denominational order in well-structured disciplinary institutions despite the fact that important changes significantly altered the structure of that leadership after 1695.

IV. IN THE TWILIGHT OF AN EGALITARIAN MINISTRY: BAPTISTS IN THE DELAWARE VALLEY

Understanding the history of Baptists in the Delaware valley never has been easy. Although Baptist congregations existed there as early as 1685, they always were small. Even by 1761, when Baptists first took a census of their congregations, they counted only 1,318 members in a total population of over 200,000.[1] Moreover, Baptist congregational records

are scarce. Few covering the years before 1730 have survived and those that have been printed provide relatively little information for the historian. Thus, despite the fact that the Philadelphia Baptist Association, which was organized in 1707, was the first such body in the American colonies, Baptists in the Delaware valley have received little modern attention from scholars. Even local histories are scarce and major studies in American religious history give these colonists little more than passing attention.[2]

Still, we can know more than we do. The manuscript records of the Pennepek Baptist congregation, which was located north of Philadelphia, probably contain the fullest set of minutes available for any colonial congregation before 1730.[3] As we shall see, they will greatly increase our knowledge of Delaware valley Baptist activity. Moreover, our excursion into English history will allow us to compare American and English experiences in the one major Dissenting denomination whose church government ever fostered egalitarian tendencies of some kind. Of course, by 1690 Particular or Calvinist Baptists gave more attention to pastors or preaching ministers than they had earlier and they shared power in congregations and associations less widely on the eve of settlement in Pennsylvania than they had during the Commonwealth period. Since these patterns were associated with a general decline in membership and decay in English association life between 1690 and 1720, the history of the Baptists in the Delaware valley should provide us with an especially good test of the adapt-

---

women, and children associated with the congregations by family ties, not to the number of adult members. See Thomas Crosby, *History of the English Baptists* (2 v., London, 1738) 1: pp. 122–123.

[2] An association of Six Principle Baptist Churches was formed in New England in 1692, but since its records have not survived its activities and even its status as an association never have been clear. See William McLoughlin, *New England Dissent, 1630–1833: The Baptists and the Separation of Church and State* (2 v., Cambridge, Mass., 1972) 1: p. 267. The most useful modern history of Delaware valley Baptists is Norman H. Maring, *Baptists in New Jersey: A Study in Transition* (Valley Forge, Pa., 1964). Two small sets of Baptist records have been printed: *Records of the Welsh Tract Baptist Meeting, Pencader Hundred, New Castle County, Delaware, 1701 to 1828, Papers of the Historical Society of Delaware* 42 (Wilmington, Del., 1904), and "Record of the Baptist Church, Middletown, N.J.," in: John E. Stillwell, ed., *Historical and Genealogical Miscellany* (5 v., New York, 1903–1932) 2: pp. 256–275. The early Middletown records printed here appear only in digest form.

[3] The manuscript minutes covering the years 1687 to 1730 and 1745 to 1894 are at the American Baptist Historical Society, Rochester, N.Y. and are hereafter cited as Minutes, Pennepek Baptist Church, ABHS. A smaller volume containing lists of baptisms, admissions, births, deaths, and a few miscellaneous notes is at the Historical Society of Pennsylvania. Some of the birth records in this volume have been printed: "Records of the Lower Dublin or Pennypack Baptist Church," *Penna. Mag. History and Biography* 11 (1887): pp. 58–62.

---

[92] Pentecost Teague to Friends, 27 February, 1698/9, Parish Collection, HSP.

[1] *MPBA*, p. 85. In 1714 Abel Morgan claimed that the Delaware valley congregations contained some 500 persons, but his figure probably refers to the total number of men,

ability of English denominational forms to New World conditions.

We begin with congregations of course. Before 1700 five were formed in the Delaware valley, each one organized by a pastor or preaching minister of the kind being encouraged by the reorganized English associations of the 1690's. Thomas Dungan organized the congregation at Cold Spring north of Philadelphia in 1685 but died in the early 1690's, after which the congregation apparently disbanded. Elias Keach, son of Benjamin Keach, one of England's most distinguished Particular Baptists, organized groups of worshipers at Pennepek and in West Jersey, and Thomas Killingsworth, whose background is obscure, helped establish congregations at Middletown and Piscataway in East Jersey between 1688 and 1690 and served as the preaching minister at Cohansey until his death in 1709.[4] Unfortunately, the early minutes of all but the Pennepek congregation have disappeared. But the Pennepek records tell us a good deal about Delaware valley Baptists because of the special nature of the congregation there. As sometimes happened in England, this was a congregation of many parts. At times it comprised members who worshiped separately at Pennepek, in Philadelphia, and in Burlington and Cohansey, New Jersey. The members seemed to agree that those who gathered at Pennepek were more important to the group's existence than were the others. But they never stipulated that the Pennepek worshipers made up the home or parent congregation while the others remained "branches."[5] In any case, its activities extended into both Pennsylvania and the Jerseys, and until 1701 it was the only Baptist congregation in Pennsylvania of any kind.

The Pennepek records also reveal how thoroughly seventeenth-century English Baptist practices were carried to the New World. Even the organization of the congregation reflected the familiar English concern for proper form in the creation of a congregation of saints. Elias Keach, who had arrived in Pennsylvania in 1687, sought the sanction of Thomas Dungan of Cold Spring before he first baptized four persons at Pennepek in November, 1687. Then with others he set a day apart "to seek god by fasting and prayer in order to form ourselves in A church state," a day in which Keach was accepted as the congregation's preaching minister and Samuel Vaus as a deacon.[6]

Keach's work at Pennepek reflected the presence of both old and new elements in Baptist worship in America. Although he was a preaching minister, Keach wove his work around the potential ministry of others. "With the advice and consent of our said pastor," the congregations held a "meeting for Conference" every Thursday to stimulate spiritual awareness among their members and to give each member "opportunity to Exercise what gifts god had been pleased to bestow upon them for the Edification of one another."[7] Linked closely with this was the exercise of a strong congregational discipline. In their first two years when their membership was very small, Pennepek Baptists excommunicated one member for his "disorderly walkings," then were chagrined to discover that their deacon, Samuel Vaus, had never been baptized as an adult, "no, nor so much as Sprinkled in his Infancy." They excommunicated him too, then looked more warily at potential new members.[8]

Keach's work as a preaching minister extended this Baptist worship elsewhere. Under his guidance groups of Baptist worshipers were gathered at Burlington and Salem in West Jersey, Cohansey in East Jersey and at Philadelphia and Chester County in Pennsylvania. Unfortunately, the spiritual intensity Keach encouraged in these groups also stimulated disagreement. Some of the argument may even have been formented by Keach himself. For example, three or four months after the congregation at Pennepek had been organized Keach began to argue for the use of the rite of "laying on of hands" in the administration of baptism. The practice had long engendered controversy among English and Welsh Baptists. But it was used by Thomas Dungan at Cold Spring and according to the Pennepek minutes Keach "did accordingly press it upon others."[9] Tension over this episode was further aggravated when unnamed persons criticized Keach's demeanor, saying that Keach "did not walk so circumspectly, as became a minister of the gospel of Christ." Then, according to the Pennepek minutes, "this unhappy breach was

---

[4] Norman H. Maring, *Baptists in New Jersey, A Study in Transition* (Valley Forge, Pa., 1964), pp. 11–17; David Spencer, *The Early Baptists of Philadelphia* (Philadelphia, 1877), pp. 17–26. Descriptions of the founding of the congregations written between 1746 and 1749 are in *MPBA*, pp. 11–15.

[5] Such congregations were not unheard of in Baptist circles. In the 1680's the Baptist congregation in Boston contained a group of worshipers at Woburn, and in the late 1690's the Seventh Day Baptist congregation at Newport, Rhode Island, contained worshipers at Westerly. William McLoughlin, *New England Dissent, 1630–1833: The Baptists and the Separation of Church and State* (2 v., Cambridge, Mass., 1972) 1: pp. 74–75; "The Seventh Day Baptist Church in Newport, R.I.," *Seventh-Day Baptist Memorial* 1 (1852): pp. 172–173.

[6] Minutes, Pennepek Baptist Church, p. 144, ABHS; David Spencer, *The Early Baptists of Philadelphia* (Philadelphia, 1877), pp. 21–24.

[7] Minutes, Pennepek Baptist Church, p. 4, ABHS.

[8] *Ibid.*, p. 6. For an important discussion of discipline in Baptist congregations during the Commonwealth period see Michael Walzer, *The Revolution of the Saints: A Study in the Origins of Radical Politics* (Cambridge, Mass., 1965), pp. 219–224, and for disciplinary proceedings in the Delaware valley in later years see Norman H. Maring, *Baptists in New Jersey, A Study in Transition* (Valley Forge, Pa., 1964), pp. 28–31.

[9] Minutes, Pennepek Baptist Church, p. 4, ABHS.

helpt to be made wider, by means of some difference in Judgment, conceived to be made about predistination betwixt him and Some Brethren," Keach most likely, then as later, a Particular Baptist who accepted the notion of predestination.[10]

The disputes over Keach's person and doctrine were complicated by an inability to define the character of the Pennepek congregation. In the fall of 1688 the Pennepek Baptists refused to record the names of twelve persons baptized by Keach at Burlington and Salem in their record book "because they were not received members of this Church, Considered as a particular church." This problem centered directly on the thrust of Elias Keach's work. As the Pennepek group put it, "wee [knew] not in what relation we stood . . . whether we were a particular Church at Dublin, or whether all the Brethren in the two provinces, made but one body, or particular church, who had been Baptized and received into Communion by Elias Keach." [11] In fact these newly settled Baptists were caught in the dilemma of transition—not between Old World and New—but between old and new concepts of church and congregation. The older one dated from the Commonwealth period and tied all those persons sharing a dynamic and decentralized ministry into a single universal church. The more recent one identified Baptist congregations closely with the presence of a preaching minister or pastor.[12]

Both notions existed side by side in the Delaware valley. When Keach preached at Pennepek the records noted that "we commonly acted as a particular church." At meetings held in the spring and fall "all the Brethren from all parts of the provinces were desired generally to Come together, to hear the word, etc., and to Communicat[e] at the Lords table." This implied that Keach served several groups of worshipers who together formed a single congregation or "particular" church. Yet the minutes also record that "in those times of beginning we had not opportunity to be formed into particular Churches for want of persons fittly qualified to oversee a Church, or to carry on the work of the ministry," a reference to the perceived need for a pastor and to Keach's frequent absences from Pennepek while serving the other places of worship.[13]

In the fall of 1689 Baptists from the groups gathered by Keach at Pennepek, Philadelphia, Chester, Salem, Cohansey, and Burlington held a meeting at Burlington to resolve these arguments. They were only partially successful. Their efforts to still the personal and doctrinal criticisms leveled against Keach proved unsuccessful.[14] And their decision that remaining

meetings would be "kept up and maintained by gifted brethren" when Keach was preaching at one location, yet leave the administration of the Lord's Supper to Keach "as his proper work," hinted that these worshipers now viewed themselves as a single particular congregation. But it scarcely solved the problem of congregational identity.[15]

The compromise failed to keep Keach in Pennepek, however, and in 1690 he left to become preaching minister of the congregation at Middletown in East Jersey. He stayed in Middletown for only one year, then moved to Burlington, in West Jersey, in 1691. Finally, in 1692 he returned to England to serve as the preaching minister in a Particular Baptist congregation in London until his early death in 1699.[16]

Keach's departure forced a crucial shift in the practice of the ministry at Pennepek. In the aftermath of his exit only the worshipers at Cohansey succeeded in finding a replacement, this being Thomas Killingsworth who had worked with Keach earlier.[17] The remaining worshipers associated with the Pennepek congregations now were forced either to tolerate each other or to maintain their worship independently. Sometime in 1691 the Baptists at Pennepek, Burlington, and Philadelphia (the group at Salem apparently had disbanded) agreed to stop their bickering. They decided, for example, that "the difference in Judgment between some of us about Singing of psalms, and Laying on of hands"—the former apparently a new argument—"should break no Bonds of Communion, but that we should bear with one another Leaving Each other to their Liberty." They also apparently agreed to share ministerial responsibilities.[18] They were, however, extraordinarily careful to follow the forms Keach had used. Indeed, Keach would have been amazed at how clearly he had set norms for the practice of the ministry among the Pennepek congregations. After his departure the Pennepek minutes note carefully how, "as touching the Lords Supper, we observed the same order which we had done before," or that how, before the baptism and admission of new members "our usual Custom now (as also when Elias Keach was with us) was, that when wee were to break Bread upon the Lords day we would Come together upon the 7th day before, in order to [prepare ourselves]." [19]

Despite these agreements, the issue of the ministry still brought trouble. Before his departure for Eng-

---

[10] *Ibid.*, p. 5.
[11] *Ibid.*
[12] See the discussion in chap. I, pp. 15–17, 24–25.
[13] Minutes, Pennepek Baptist Church, p. 5, ABHS.
[14] *Ibid.*, pp. 5–6.

[15] *Ibid.*, p. 6.
[16] *Ibid.*
[17] The event was reported by Nathaniel Jenkins in his brief narrative of the congregation's founding sent to the Philadelphia Baptist Association in 1746. Jenkins cited as evidence "a paragraph in Pennpek Church Book [*sic*], page the 7th." This, and page 8, now are missing from the Pennepek records. *MPBA*, p. 14.
[18] Minutes, Pennepek Baptist Church, p. 9, ABHS.
[19] MS: "to preparation." *Ibid.*

land Keach "was willing to have ordained John Watts to be an Elder, or pastor, by Laying on of Hands," probably because Watts had done much of the speaking in the Thursday conferences.[20] But others objected. Although the case is far from clear, the action hints at a reluctance to install another preaching minister like Keach and a desire to hold to the ministry of their fellow members. The congregation insisted that Watts was not ordained because there was "no presbitery, Eldership or Elder to give him ordination"—the use of the term "presbitery" meaning only that these Baptists understood one crucial function of this non-Baptist body.[21] But the reasoning was specious because Keach was himself a preaching minister, had been ordained by Thomas Dungan at Cold Spring in 1687 or 1688, and could have ordained Watts if the Pennepek congregations had been willing to ask for his help.

In any event, Watts remained "pastor onely by Election," meaning that he could serve those associated with the Pennepek congregations but was not authorized to extend his ministry elsewhere.[22] This arrangement appears to have worked well for the next half-decade. The Pennepek congregations maintained a strict discipline. In 1692, for example, a woman was excommunicated for engaging in illicit sexual activity and a couple was readmitted to the congregations after a brief sojourn among Pennsylvania's Quakers. In 1695 Watts began to preach twice a month in Philadelphia, thus giving sermons only once a month at Pennepek and Burlington. If this work implicitly increased Watts's power in the congregations, he carefully pursued old ways. He introduced no known novelties in worship but "usually (as Elias Keach before did) sung a psalm, or part of a psalm, in the publick assembly, before his sermon, and also Sometimes after, and also before [the] Sermon he usually Expounded in a brief manner what was to be Sung."[23]

With their congregations at peace again the Pennepek Baptists in Pennsylvania hued to old ways. They eschewed the associations then being reorganized in England and rested group order on the sharing of worship among small local populations; certainly they felt little need to create broad denominational institutions to sustain group discipline or to maintain pastors as was being done in England.

Yet trouble from new sources now disturbed these Baptists. Until 1697 they had lived in relative isolation from the other religious groups in the Delaware valley. No evidence points even to significant formal contact between Baptists and the Delaware valley's dominant Quakers, for example. Yet the Baptist openness to preaching by persons other than pastors, and their failure to create an association that could aid and protect troubled congregations helped sustain three years of argument over authority and doctrine, as old supporters of the Quaker schismatic, George Keith, moved to new spiritual homes.

As early as 1692 Philadelphia's Public Friends claimed that George Keith was associating with Baptists. Baptists "say he is coming to them," the Quaker ministers wrote: "he lately said he had now much less against Water Baptism than he had formerly."[24] Although it would be true later, the statement was false when it was made. Keith only accepted the rite of baptism when he became an Anglican in London in the late 1690's. And in Pennsylvania, few of Keith's followers became Baptists until 1697, when a congregation of Keith's old followers in Chester County independently adopted the rites of baptism and the Lord's Supper, then asked the Baptists worshiping in Philadelphia to help them form a Calvinist Baptist congregation.[25] For unknown reasons, however, the Philadelphia Baptists rejected the request. According to a Keithian narrative, the latter simply "left us to our Liberty to chuse an Administrator to baptize."[26] Acting on their own, between 1697 and 1700 the ex-Keithians sustained a congregation that combined Baptist theology with Quaker pacifism but which continued to be ignored by Pennsylvania's Particular Baptists.[27]

Similarly, sometime in 1696 a part of a Keithian congregation led by a man named William Davis sought union with the Pennepek Baptists. The latter hesitated. Some members feared that the Keithians "retained still some of the Quaker principles." Others worried about Keith's attacks on Pennsylvania's

[20] *Ibid.*, pp. 4, 9.

[21] *Ibid.*, p. 9. The Particular Baptist Confession of 1677 Fasting and Prayer, with imposition of hands of the Eldership provided that church officers would be "Solemnly set apart by of the Church if there be any before constituted therein." However, Particular Baptist associations did not ordain ministers themselves. This was done only among General Baptists. *Baptist Confessions of Faith*, W. L. Lumpkin, ed. (Valley Forge, Pa., 1969), p. 287; *Minutes of the General Assembly of the General Baptist Churches in England* [1654–1811] (2 v., London, 1908) 1: pp. 110, 116.

[22] Minutes, Pennepek Baptist Church, p. 9, ABHS.

[23] *Ibid.*, pp. 9–10, 20.

[24] Meeting of the Ministering Friends at Philadelphia to George Whitehead, *et al.*, 17 June, 1692, in Minutes, Philadelphia Meeting of Ministers, p. 25, FHL microfilm copy.

[25] I have described the history of these groups separately in an article, "Into Pennsylvania's Spiritual Abyss: The Rise and Fall of the Later Keithians, 1693–1703," *Penna. Mag. History and Biography* 101 (1977): pp. 151–170.

[26] Things transacted by a Congregation usually met at Powell's house . . ., in Records, Brandywine Baptist Church (microfilm copy from the Southern Baptist Historical Society, Nashville, Tenn.) A portion of this document has been printed in R. E. E. Harkness, "Early Relations of Baptists and Quakers," *Church History* 2 (1933): p. 228.

[27] Things transacted by a Congregation usually met at Powell's house, in Records, Brandywine Baptist Church (microfilm copy from the Southern Baptist Historical Society, Nashville, Tenn.)

Quaker politicians and ministers. In all their opinions "seemed to be of very Ill tendency, as to destroy Christian Civil government and [were] very offensive to the Christian Civil magistrate." Thus when the Keithians continued to pursue their quest for membership the Pennepek Baptists sought the advice of their former preaching minister in London, Elias Keach.[28]

Keach's response was as direct as it could have been. After conferring with other London ministers he advised the congregation to reject the Keithian overtures. "It is all our Judgments that you by no means Baptize them, much Less Admitt them to your Communion: seeing we are assured of the Ill Consequences of such an Act, Especially they holding against the authority of the Civil Magistrate, etc." Yet inexplicably, Davis and several other Keithians were admitted to the congregation.[29] Perhaps the Pennepek Baptists were fearful of the new congregation forming among the disaffected Keithians of Chester County and sought to contain the growth of this "Baptist" opinion in Pennsylvania. Perhaps some still resented Elias Keach and admitted Davis and the Keithians to demonstrate their independence. Whatever their reasoning, they came to regret the decision. By January, 1698, the congregation was embroiled in a dispute that destroyed the Thursday conferences, that crippled the special form of the ministry still being used there, and that forced the reorganization of the congregations themselves.

Most of the trouble came from William Davis. Davis was an English Quaker who already had left the movement at least once before coming to America. He had supported George Keith in 1692, but by the fall of 1694 had fallen out with some of Keith's remaining supporters.[30] He apparently listened to Keith's argument that Friends paid insufficient attention to the outer or historical Christ with considerable interest. In Davis, Keith's notions took unusual turns, however, since soon after his admission at Pennepek he began to regale the congregation with what the latter termed "divers strange opinions." According to the congregation's minutes Davis argued that it was impossible to separate Christ's human and divine natures. Christ was "godman, and not humane and Divine; but human divine, or divine-human." Christ also "was Inferious to his father . . . and is no otherways Equal with God the father, than Joseph was to pharoah, or as a man's son can be to his father." Indeed, Davis believed that there were "two gods in heaven, A greater, and an Inferious god,

and that the greater sent the Inferious or Lesser god to dye, and the Inferious god didd." [31]

The Pennepek Baptists' sensitivity to the spiritual concerns of their members forced them to listen carefully to Davis. They were both "willing to know what his doctrine was [and] to use the best method to preserve the meeting in peace." They asked John Watts to confer with him. But when Watt's efforts accomplished little the congregation twice warned Davis about his views and ordered him to accept its advice and counsel. Davis refused. He would confer with Watts, who had "much tedious discourse with him," but would not accept the judgment of the congregation. Finally, when the congregation "could perceive no appearance of any grounds to hope for his recovery," Watts expelled Davis from the meetings "in the name of our Lord Jesus Christ, and in the behalfe of the Church." [32]

Davis continued to agitate at Pennepek. Finally he forced the congregation to hold an extra-legal trial that produced some short-lived interdenominational communication in the Delaware valley. During the winter of 1698–1699 the Pennepek Baptists watched Davis "Rage, and Raile against us," and in March, 1699, Davis challenged John Watts to debate Davis's excommunication of 1698. Watts refused but agreed to put the issue before a panel of "either presbiterians, Independents, or of the Church of England." Within a month Davis forwarded a different proposal to Watts. Astutely quoting Elias Keach's *Glory and Ornament of a True Gospel-Constituted Church*, a small work on discipline Keach had published in London in 1697, Davis proposed a hearing before a "sister church . . . at German town at the house of Isaac Jacobs" that would follow rules formulated by the London Baptist assembly of 1692 and elucidated by Keach.[33]

The Pennepek Baptists rejected Davis's proposal. They saw the congregation at Germantown as little more than a melange of mystics and disaffected, heretical Keithians who "made up a kinde of Society, did Break bread, Lay on hands, washed one anothers feet, and were about haveing A Community of goods." [34] And since these people were as heretical as Davis, the Pennepek Baptists accused Davis of sponsoring a hearing where he and his friends were "both accuser, and judge." Instead, since they had "as good authority, and as much reason to appoint a

[28] Minutes, Pennepek Baptist Church, p. 10, ABHS.

[29] Keach's reply was dated 1 October, 1687, but the Pennepek records do not give the date of its receipt in Pennsylvania. Neither do they record the date of Davis's admission to the congregation.

[30] William Davis, *Jesus the Crucified Man, the Eternal Son of God* . . . [Philadelphia, 1700], unpaginated preface.

[31] Minutes, Pennepek Baptist Church, p. 12, ABHS.

[32] *Ibid*, pp. 13–15.

[33] Davis to Pennepek Baptist Church, 29 April, 1699, in *Ibid.*, p. 21. His references to Keach's work was to material on pp. 38–39.

[34] Minutes, Pennepek Baptist Church, pp. 25–26, ABHS. Little is known about this group, but see Julius F. Sachse, *The German Pietists of Provincial Pennsylvania* (Philadelphia, 1895), pp. 67–68, and Harold S. Bender, "The Founding of the Mennonite Church in America at Germantown, 1683–1708," *Mennonite Quart. Rev.* 7 (1933): pp. 247–248.

meeting as he," and knew that Davis's supporters "were of restles Spirits and bent for Contention," they moved to settle the affair by appointing three non-Baptist judges from Philadelphia to hear Davis's complaints—Thomas Revel, "by Profession an Independent," Samuel Richardson, a member of Philadelphia's new Presbyterian congregation, and the Presbyterian minister in Philadelphia, Jedidiah Andrews. They then invited Davis to appoint three judges of his own liking. Realizing that his opponents would probably never appear at Germantown, Davis named the city's Anglican clergyman, Thomas Clayton, and two members of Clayton's congregation to compose his portion of the ecclesiastical jury.[35] Although the Anglican minister, Thomas Clayton, allegedly "did not handle the matter in so fair a method, and manner as was proposed," the six man ecclesiastical jury finally upheld Davis's excommunication, thus removing him as a serious threat to stability in the Pennepek congregations.[36]

The Davis affair again demonstrated how thoroughly Baptist denominational order in the Delaware valley hinged on the local practice of the ministry. It also changed some of those practices. Most important, it helped destroy the diffusion of ministerial responsibilities among the membership and strengthened John Watts's position in the congregation. This change was rooted in the circumstances of Davis's disputing. During the argument with Davis, attendance at the Thursday conferences established in 1688 to encourage individual members to develop their spiritual gifts, declined sharply. As a result, the congregations decided to hold the sessions for the "Encouragement, and benefit of young gifted brethren" only twice each month. But since Davis had misused them they found it "expedient and necessary" to restrict preaching there. In the future no one would be allowed to preach "unless he were a member known to be sound in faith," or had been "allowed by some other Church or Churches, for such Publick work."[37]

The Pennepek congregations also reorganized themselves. This occurred after John Watts appointed a meeting in March, 1699, "to Conferr about the Discipline, order, and government of the Church." At it, the congregations decided to administer the Lord's Supper in each place on a rotating basis and to appoint ruling elders in their gatherings. This was an important point because it acknowledged an increasing separation of duties between elders and the preaching minister. At the same time John Watts was named to serve as pastor and Samuel Jones and Joseph Wood to serve as deacons. Business meetings were to be held the day after the administration of the Lord's

Supper so the members might better "examine and order matters relating to the discipline and government of the Church" and the same members were warned that those who absented themselves from the Lord's Supper would be expected to "give an account of their reasons for so doeing, . . . so sloath and negligence may be prevented, and order, Love, and unity preserved."[38]

For two years events at Pennepek proceeded smoothly. In 1700 the congregation claimed forty full members—forty-six a year later—and voted to publish a catechism written by John Watts to counter William Davis, who still was "going under the denomination of Baptist."[39] (No copies of the catechism have survived.) Then in 1701 a group of Welsh Baptists settled near Pennepek. They added both numbers and a new particular church in Pennsylvania, making it the first time that two such congregations had existed in Pennsylvania since Thomas Dungan ministered to the long defunct congregation at Cold Spring. In 1702, however, John Watts died of smallpox. Although initially disruptive, his death and the arrival of the Welsh Baptists firmly turned Delaware valley Baptists in new directions and led ultimately to the formation of the Philadelphia Baptist Association in 1707.[40]

The death of John Watts sparked a ten-year search for a new pastor. The congregations' first response was to return to their old pattern of a shared ministry by naming three persons to preach—Samuel Jones, who had been named deacon in 1699, and two former Keithians, Evan Morgan and John Swift. They also asked another old Keithian, John Hart, and the Welsh minister, Thomas Griffiths, to administer baptism.[41] These nominations were temporary, however. Watts's death left the congregations "like a flock of sheep deprived of there Shepherd," and in 1703 they wrote Benjamin Keach, father of Elias Keach, to ask his help in finding a new preaching minister. They were "in a destitute condition for want of an able man" and implored London's Particular Baptists "to find one well qualified with "grace and gifts requisite for a gospell minister to come over to us."[42] After

---

[35] Minutes, Pennepek Baptist Church, pp. 26–27, ABHS; William Davis, *Jesus the Crucified Man, the Eternal Son of God* . . . [Philadelphia, 1700], unpaginated preface.

[36] Minutes, Pennepek Baptist Church, p. 28, ABHS.

[37] *Ibid.,* p. 16.

[38] The meeting also had been called to ease the threat made by Baptists at Burlington to call their own pastor. *Ibid.,* pp. 19–20, 30–31.

[39] *Ibid.,* pp. 33, 34–35, 37. Watts also wrote another tract directed specifically at Davis which the congregation voted to publish in 1706 but which apparently never was printed. Some of Watts's writings are mentioned by Davis in *Jesus the Crucified Man, the Eternal Son of God* . . . [Philadelphia, 1700], unpaginated preface.

[40] Minutes, Pennepek Baptist Church, p. 38, ABHS; William Davis, *Jesus the Crucified Man, the Eternal Son of God* . . . [Philadelphia, 1700], unpaginated preface.

[41] Minutes, Pennepek Baptist Church, pp. 38, 39, ABHS. Thomas Griffiths also administered the Lord's Supper on some occasions between 1702 and 1705.

[42] *Ibid.,* p. 40.

waiting two years to hear from Keach the congregations turned to a controversial, perhaps desperate, method to solve their problem. In 1705 they agreed to nominate two members for the position of pastor—Evan Morgan and Samuel Jones—and then, "to see which god would Chuse to be our pastor," to cast lots at a meeting in September, 1706. Although the practice had been approved by some reformers a century earlier—William Perkins wrote that casting lots was "an act of religion in which we refer unto God the determination of things of moment that can no other way be determined"—as early as the 1650's most clerics had come to reject it, at least as a means of choosing church officers.[43] Such aversions finally prevailed in Pennsylvania too. By October, 1706, the congregations dropped the plan and authorized Morgan and Jones to preach jointly. At the same time they decided to continue to search for a pastor to replace Watts.[44]

In the same period the Pennepek congregations healed an unfortunate break that had created tension between them and the new Welsh congregations in Pennsylvania. Many Welsh settlers first stayed at Pennepek in their early years of settlement between 1701 and 1703. There, however, the two groups maintained separate congregations. The Welsh Baptists used the rite of "laying on of hands" in the baptismal ceremony administered to all members. But the Pennepek congregations used the rite only to confirm church officers. Although the Pennepek congregations agreed to "walk in brotherly love and Church fellowship" with the Welshmen, the Pennepek minutes insist that the Welsh stubbornly "kept by themselves."[45] After the latter moved to the so-called "Welsh Tract" south and west of Philadelphia in 1703, tension between the two groups remained high, and in June, 1706, representatives from them met at Radnor to discuss their relationship. Noting that they were "all of the same faith in Religion" except for their views regarding the "imposition of hands on every believer," they agreed to respect each other's views on the latter point "within the bounds of brotherly Love." This resolution carried with it pragmatic results. From now on the congregations could not refuse to administer the Lord's Supper to each other's members. Persons "cast in Either Place" now would "freely enjoy occasional or transient comunion with either of the afore Said congregations."[46]

The Radnor meeting can be seen as an important step in forming the first Baptist association in America. Further groundwork for this move came in September, 1706, when the congregations at Pennepek and Middletown agreed to hold a joint yearly meeting in May, 1707, that they hoped all the remaining congregations in the Delaware valley also would attend. Although the evidence is vague, the meeting apparently took place, since according to the Pennepek minutes the Pennepek congregations as well as those in Middletown, Welsh Tract, and Cohansey agreed to choose representatives "such as they thought most capable in every congregation" to meet each September in Philadelphia. There they would "consult about such things as were wanting in the Church and set them in order." In short, they had agreed to form what became the Philadelphia Baptist Association.[47]

The new association closely resembled its contemporary English counterparts. Meetings were thought to manifest ministerial labor, and while some of their records are fragmentary and difficult to interpret, before 1730 the meetings seem to have been attended by pastors, deacons, and elders who still were viewed as partaking in ministerial tasks. Thus the Association agreement stipulated that meetings would begin on the Sabbath and "be continued till the third day of the week in the work of the public ministry and by whom the public ministry of the word should be carried on." Understandably, one of the Association's most important tasks was to determine who could and could not preach in Delaware valley Baptist congregations. At its first meeting, the gathered representatives hit hard at persons who preached without proper credentials. Henceforth, a stranger with no letter of recommendation from a Particular Baptist congregation in England or America and not "known to be a person gifted and of a good conversation" was forbidden to preach in any of the Association's congregations.[48]

At its first meeting the Association also established criteria for healing disputes within congregations and between them. The Association would hear these disputes only if the disputants agreed to accept its findings; then it would appoint a committee to hear the case and issue a verdict, principles that established the Association's jurisdiction in such affairs but left initiatives for bringing it into a dispute in the hands of the disputing parties.[49]

Problems concerning pastors and preachers quickly involved the Association in local affairs. These problems usually concerned the older congregations in the

[43] *Ibid.* The quotation from Perkins is in Keith Thomas, *Religion and the Decline of Magic* (New York, [1971]), p. 120.

[44] Minutes, Pennepek Baptist Church, p. 42, ABHS.

[45] *Ibid.*

[46] *Ibid.*, p. 41; David Spencer, *The Early Baptists of Philadelphia* (Philadelphia, 1877), p. 41; *Records of the Welsh Tract Baptist Meeting, Pencader Hundred, New Castle County, Delaware, 1701 to 1828, Papers of the Historical Society of Delaware* 42 (Wilmington, Del., 1904): pp. 8–10.

[47] Minutes, Pennepek Baptist Church, pp. 42, 44, ABHS; *MPBA*, p. 4. Maring discusses what he calls "yearly meetings" before 1707, but these were the yearly gatherings of the Pennepek congregations, not those of an association. Norman H. Maring, *Baptists in New Jersey, A Study in Transition* (Valley Forge, Pa., 1964), p. 32.

[48] Minutes, Pennepek Baptist Church, p. 43, ABHS.

[49] *Ibid.*

Delaware valley. The newer Welsh groups, namely those organized at Welsh Tract in 1703, in Chester County in 1711, and in Montgomery County in 1719, were well staffed with preaching ministers and were populated with many elders who had long served their old congregations in Wales.[50] But the congregations at Pennepek and Middletown enjoyed no such stability. Instead, they were rescued from self-destructive disputes only by the efforts of the newly organized Association.

The Pennepek case involved a classic combination of mismanagement among sometimes vain and self-seeking persons. After the ordination of Evan Morgan and Samuel Jones in 1706 the congregations pressed hard to find a permanent preaching minister. They again wrote to London but with no success.[51] In 1708 the congregations asked Thomas Killingsworth, the preaching minister at Cohansey, "to sell of[f] his plantation and give himself wholly to the ministry of the gospel." But Killingsworth died in 1709 and apparently never accepted the offer anyway.[52] Then between 1710 and 1711 the congregations secured not one preaching minister, but three, and turned their search into a brawl.

In August, 1710, the Pennepek congregations hired a Welshman named Abel Morgan for their post, even though Morgan was still in Wales and had advised them that his departure would be delayed. Then they hired John Barrows of Somersetshire in England to preach to them until Morgan arrived. But before Barrows arrived two other newly arrived pastors announced their readiness to preach to the Pennepek congregations—Nathaniel Jenkins, another Welshman, and Thomas Selby, an Irish Baptist most recently living in Rhode Island. Although Jenkins moved quickly to New Jersey, Selby was paid to preach at Pennepek at least temporarily. But he argued with Jenkins, led some members to complain about his "traducing of other ministers" (perhaps deacons and elders), and refused to leave after Barrows arrived from England in the fall of 1711 and Morgan arrived from Wales in the spring of 1712. Now "the whole broke out into a flame." The congregation had three ministers and Selby's supporters threatened to secede from it if he were not retained as its pastor.[53]

The Association healed the affair in a quiet demonstration of its authority in the Delaware valley. First, the dispute was reduced to one involving only Selby and Morgan because Barrows quickly surrendered his position. Then, supporters of Selby and Morgan agreed to choose persons from other Baptist congregations to hear and adjudicate the matter during the Association meeting in September, 1712.[54] Although this was not quite the procedure outlined in 1707, which called for the Association to name the committee, it probably was used simply because it brought the disputing parties together. Whatever its origins, the committee emphatically decided in Morgan's favor. It asked the congregation to pay Selby any funds due him, ordered the parties to "freely forgive each other all personal and other offences" and asked that Selby's supporters be allowed to resume their places in the congregation.

But the committee also sought to protect all the Delaware valley congregations from Selby. It recommended that Selby be "discharged from any further service in the work of the ministry." He was "a person, in our judgment, not likely for the promotion of the Gospel in these parts of the country." Indeed, the committee suggested that all Delaware valley congregations refuse to administer the Lord's Supper to him under any circumstances. As a result, Abel Morgan retained his position as pastor at Pennepek (he remained there until his death in the 1720's) and Selby departed for the Carolinas where, according to the Pennepek minutes, he "created destraction . . . and within a 12 month after dyed."[55]

In another dispute at Middletown the Association healed an argument over preaching and found a permanent place for John Barrows, the man who had been left without a post during the Selby dispute at Pennepek. Between 1709 and 1711, the congregation at Middletown lacked a pastor. For a time two of its members—John Bray and John Okison—preached and administered the sacraments. But in 1711 their work apparently generated antagonism in the congregation. One group demanded that Bray and Okison stop their work while another insisted that they continue. In May, 1712, the dispute was heard by an Association committee that included Abel Morgan, the new minister at Pennepek. The committee ordered the congregation to "bury their proceedings in oblivion," silenced Bray and Okison, and asked the congregation to write a new church covenant. At the same time it suggested that Morgan and John Barrows should preach there alternately so members would "keep their places and not wander to other societies." The congregation complied. Bray and Okison apparently

---

[50] See the lists of ministers and elders scattered through J. Davis, *History of the Welsh Baptists* (Philadelphia, 1835).

[51] Minutes, Pennepek Baptist Church, p. 44, ABHS.

[52] *Ibid.* Maring reports that Killingsworth left his wife an estate of £297, including a black slave. Norman H. Maring, *Baptists in New Jersey, A Study in Transition* (Valley Forge, Pa., 1964), p. 39.

[53] The Pennepek congregation inserted these details in their minutes in 1715, apparently to justify the final exclusion of some of Thomas Selby's supporters. Minutes, Pennepek Baptist Church, pp. 56–58, ABHS.

[54] *Ibid.*, p. 47. There is some evidence that the affair betrayed tension between former Keithians and other members of the congregation, since Selby was supported by John Swift, a Keithian admitted in 1701, and who was admonished in 1724, when reference was made to the 1712 affair. *Ibid.*, pp. 47, 73.

[55] *Ibid.*, pp. 47, 57; *MPBA*, p. 26

stopped their work and about two-thirds of the congregation signed a new covenant, the remainder signing over the next few years.[56] Most important, the congregation acquired a pastor as a result of the committee's recommendation about preaching. At the special urging of the Pennepek congregation, Middletown Baptists offered John Barrows the position and Barrows served there from 1713 until his death in the 1720's.[57]

How thoroughly the Association continued its intimate concern for ministerial problems in the years between 1713 and 1720 is difficult to determine because most of its records have been lost. However, the records that do survive clearly indicate that such a concern remained important. A special gathering of preaching ministers at Cape May in August, 1714, called for a fast so Baptists could pray for ministerial success in the existing congregations, and so they might obtain additional men to "spread abroad the gospel, through out the Dark Corners of the Country." [58] Yet a year later Abel Morgan wrote to London that despite recent growth American Baptists still were "greatly scattered on this mainland." "Our ministers are necessitated to labour with both hands" because congregations remained small and often were unable to support them, although "if it pleases God to supply us with more help, we shall be more churches in a little time." [59]

The reappearance of some Association records after 1722 makes it clear how thoroughly problems of authority and ministry remained its principal business in the next decade. First, however, and as a measure of its growing importance and power, the Association became increasingly concerned with its own internal procedures. In 1724 it asked congregations to submit their concerns in differing forms. "Salutations, contemplations, congratulations, etc." might be sent on a single sheet. But "complaints, queries or grievances, etc." were to be "written apart." The first would be read publicly, while "the latter, the church's doubts, fears, or disorders, etc." would "be opened and read to the Association only." Three years later, in 1727, the Association lengthened its meetings by asking "messengers" or representatives to arrive a day earlier than usual, on Saturday, "in order to prepare for the affairs of the churches," and requested the congregations to free messengers "from their businesses at home and assist them with money to bear their expenses in that affair." [60]

The Association also increased its effort to promote the preaching ministry. In 1722 it tried to sponsor clerical education in England for promising Delaware valley youths. Each congregation was asked to "make inquiry among themselves, if they have any young persons hopeful for the ministry, and inclinable for learning." If so, they would be sent to England where Thomas Hollis, a rich and well-known London Baptist, would finance their stay at a Baptist academy. Unfortunately the plan met no known success.[61]

A year later the Association laid down additional rules for preaching when no pastor was present. These rules were given out in advice offered to a new congregation meeting near the Brandywine River. Lacking a preaching minister, its members asked "which way they might improve their vacant days of worship." The answer was simple. They were to read from the scriptures, "sing a psalm, . . . go to prayer and beg of God to increase their grace and comfort," but "not to suffer any to exercise their gifts in a mixed multitude until tried and approved of first by the church," meaning that not everyone was to be allowed to preach.[62]

In the same meeting the Association also approved rules for receiving ministers from England and Wales. These rules were "drawn by the several ministers," probably meaning pastors, and "signed by many others," but have since been lost. The Association minutes which discuss them, however, make it clear that Delaware valley Baptists no longer intended to accept pastors merely because they had exercised the office elsewhere. The representatives agreed that the rules governing "examination of all gifted brethren and ministers that come in here from other places, be duly put in practice, we having found the evil of neglecting a true and previous scrutiny in those affairs." Seven years later the concern for ministerial problems still dominated Association business. In 1730 the Brandywine congregation again asked about the conduct of worship. It was referred to the answer given in 1723 and advised to "read some sound, profitable, approved sermon books, in the absence of the ministers that visit them." Significantly it was not told to cultivate a broadly shared ministry among its own members on a permanent basis. Likewise the congregation in the Great Valley, also in need of a preaching minister, was told to "encourage the gifts they have among them," but also to send to nearby churches "for helps and supplies" in the absence of one. And the congregation at Piscataway, which lacked a pastor and had asked preaching ministers from other congregations to attend its yearly meeting, was promised that pastors would appear there in the future.[63]

Such discussions at Association meetings did not

---

[56] Details of the Middletown affairs are found in documents printed in David Benedict, *General History of the Baptist Denomination in America* (New York, 1855), pp. 562–563.

[57] *Ibid.;* Minutes, Pennepek Baptist Church, p. 58, ABHS.

[58] Minutes, Pennepek Baptist Church, p. 50, ABHS.

[59] Quoted in Joshua Thomas, *A History of the English Baptists* . . . (2 v., London, 1738–1741) 1: p. 123.

[60] *MPBA,* pp. 27–29.

[61] *Ibid.,* p. 27.

[62] *Ibid.*

[63] *Ibid.*

mean that congregations always heeded the Association's advice. In 1728 or 1729 the Piscataway congregation ordained one Henry Loveall as its preaching minister despite a suggestion from the Association that they hear Loveall for a trial period before committing themselves to his ministry. Within a year trouble developed. Some members discovered that Loveall's past was replete with moral failings and, indeed, that he was not Henry Loveall at all but Desolate Baker, who had changed his name to disguise a bigamous marriage, sexual relations with blacks and Indians, and an apparent case of syphilis.

All of this was discussed in a letter sent out by Nathaniel Jenkins, pastor at Cape May, to the Piscataway congregation in December, 1730. Apparently writing in response to a request from Piscataway for help from the Association, Jenkins averred that Baker's use of the name "Loveall" was well suited to one who "loves so well the Black, the swarthy and the white." Little more could be expected of him. But more indeed was expected of the congregation. "As persons Infatuated you have Rushed on without rule or presidence to Ordain a Man for the Ministry that is hardly fit to be a Common or private member." The congregation had succeeded in having Baker ordained by a South Carolina minister named Paul Palmer, who was only visiting in New Jersey. But Jenkins observed that there had been other, more profitable, sources of wisdom and ordination available nearby. "What right had *Paul Palmer* to be employed by you in that work? Were there no ministers belonging to your own Association? . . . Consider that reproach you have brought on your profession hereby. I am ashamed of it. I could have told you." [64]

Even the proceedings at Piscataway illustrate how the existence of the Association encouraged middle colony Baptists to act differently in 1730 from the way they had in 1700. In contrast to the years when the Pennepek congregation sought William Davis's condemnation from a jury of Anglicans and Presbyterians, now Baptists received help and occasional censure from the Association. Sometimes, as at Piscataway, the aid was rejected. Sometimes the Association was unable to offer a solution. Difficulties in finding pastors continued well into the 1740's. But solutions were not necessarily the principal achievement of the Association. The Association's main strength lay instead in the hegemony of discussion and expectation that it came to exercise over Baptist affairs. Far smaller than other groups and exercising a worship that still seemed relatively egalitarian—the problems

in securing preaching ministers alone encouraged them to sustain some shared ministerial responsibilities that had grown up in the Commonwealth period—by 1730 Baptist denominational order in the Delaware valley was supervised by an Association organized in 1707 whose existence belied a significant shift in the practice of the ministry among some of the oldest Delaware valley Baptists. Whatever their earlier behavior, congregations now joined together to share their searches for pastors, to establish rules for the reception and behaviour of preachers and to adjudicate internal disputes that usually centered on arguments about the ministry. This Baptist denominational structure was less complex and certainly less oligarchic than that found among Friends. Yet it easily remained within the broader tradition from which it came, a tradition that saw denominational order focused around problems of the ministry and controlled by persons in the ministry. Baptists handled those problems differently from the Quakers. But they also found them as persistent in the Delaware valley as in England.

V. TOWARD TENSION AND DISORDER: THE AMBIVALENT MAKING OF PRESBYTERIAN DENOMINATIONAL ORDER

On nearly all accounts the history of Delaware valley Presbyterianism has seemed clearer than that of other groups. The clean lines of Presbyterian ecclesiology with its linear channels of authority running from Synod to presbytery to congregation seemingly make its development less convoluted than that of the Friends. Its history has not been ignored either. Leonard Trinterud's *The Forming of an American Tradition* and Guy S. Klett's *Presbyterians in Colonial Pennsylvania* have cleared away the kind of factual underbrush that has hindered our view of Delaware valley Baptists.[1]

Yet a strange disquiet pervades this Presbyterian history. Nowhere before 1728 did Delaware valley Presbyterians define their Presbyterianism, even though presbyteries existed and men and women obeyed them. This fact has induced both Trinterud and Klett, as it did their predecessors, to try to describe early Delaware valley Presbyterian principles by determining the geographical origins of the presbyteries' ministers. In this formula the number of clerics from Scotland or New England tells us whether the Presbytery or Synod of Philadelphia really were Presbyterian in the Scottish sense or Presbyterian in a less rigorous New England fashion. Unfortunately, the success of this method depends on a homogeneity of thinking among New England and Scottish clerics.

[64] Jenkins to the Congregation at Piscataway, 30 December, 1730, in *The Diary of John Comer,* C. Edwin Barrows, ed., in: *Collections of the Rhode Island Historical Society* **8** (1893): pp. 117–118. Details about Baker's offenses were omitted from the printed version but can be found in the manuscript diary at the Rhode Island Historical Society, Providence, R. I.

[1] For a summary of this debate see Leonard J. Trinterud, *The Forming of an American Tradition: A Re-examination of Colonial Presbyterianism* (Philadelphia, 1949), p. 332n.

And as we saw in our second chapter, such unity of opinion on church government scarcely existed in those places. Saying that a minister was from Scotland or from New England tells us less about their concept of denominational order than we need to know. Instead, here we shall explore the common clerical roots of early Presbyterianism in the Delaware valley as a way of understanding how the ministers who formed the first presbytery in America could come together at all, and how that original foundation also proved to be increasingly inadequate to unite the growing number of people who claimed the Presbyterian label in the two decades before the Great Awakening.

Before 1700 any possible Presbyterian presence in the Delaware valley was minor. The first congregations that seem likely candidates for the label Presbyterian rejected it instead. For example, a congregation formed at Newark in East Jersey whose first minister was Abraham Pierson, a strict Congregationalist from Bradford, Connecticut, turned against Pierson's son, who succeeded his father in the pulpit, because the son allegedly had become some sort of Presbyterian, although of what kind is not clear. Another congregation at Woodbridge contained a mixed group of settlers, Scots, and older New England immigrants, whose first minister, Archibald Riddell, was a Scottish Presbyterian. However, Riddell's ecclesiastical principles had little meaning in Woodbridge because no presbytery then existed in America, and after his return to Scotland in 1689 the congregation simply hired a minister from New England who rejected Presbyterianism.[2]

The experiences in Woodbridge and Newark did not typify later developments in the Delaware valley, however. Instead, events in Philadelphia soon demonstrated the potential force of ministerial authority among Delaware valley Calvinists when a newly arrived minister ended an early ecumenical experiment in the colonies and created the city's first Presbyterian-inclined congregation. Records of the Pennepek Baptist congregation reveal that in Philadelphia Presbyterians worshiped with Baptists there "because they had no minister of their own." Baptists even listened to visiting Presbyterian clergymen in these services "if at any time they Came amongst us to pray and preach in our Assemblys."[3]

Sometime in 1698, however, the Presbyterians acquired a clergyman named Jedidiah Andrews, a recent graduate of Harvard who remained in Philadelphia until his death in 1741. His arrival changed the Philadelphia services. "Being now provided with a minister from New England," the Baptists observed that the Presbyterians "appeared to [have] some Scruple on their Side as not being willing to Con-

descent so far to us, or to allow our Ministers Like Liberty." "Being desirous of your Company heavenward as farr as may bee," the Baptists offered to continue the joint services if ministers from both groups might be allowed to preach there. But Andrews asked for "some friendly Conference concerning those Affairs, before we give you A direct Answer to your proposition." Yet when the conference was appointed Andrews "excused himself that he knew not that it was the day." The Baptists "tarried there till near sunset, and thus understood how the matter was . . . whereupon the next day following being the Lords day, we mett apart from them, by ourselves and so have since continued to do."[4]

Just as professional ministerial interests ended ecumenical worship in Philadelphia in 1699, so professional ministers, not laymen, created the Presbytery of Philadelphia in 1706. They could not do so without numerical strength, of course, and this came to them slowly. In 1698 or 1699 an Irish Presbyterian minister settled in Lewes, Delaware, and a New England minister settled in New Castle. At about the same time the New England clergymen at Elizabethtown and Newark in New Jersey added several outlying groups of worshipers to their listeners. Then in 1705 two Scottish clergymen, George McNish and John Hampton, settled in Maryland, their voyage to America having been financed by a remnant of the United Brethren, the short-lived association of English Presbyterians and Independents formed in London in 1691. After McNish and Hampton became acquainted with ministers already located to the north—Jedidiah Andrews in Philadelphia, John Wilson at New Castle, Samuel Davis at Lewes, Nathaniel Taylor at Pautuxet in Maryland, and an important itinerant named Francis Makemie, whose influence we shall examine shortly—they agreed to form a presbytery in Philadelphia in the fall of 1706.[5]

But what kind of presbytery? Here history takes a difficult turn. Beyond a broad belief in Calvinism and a commitment to ministerial authority of the kind demonstrated by Jedidiah Andrews in Philadelphia, those who called themselves Presbyterians elsewhere in Scotland, England, and America argued over doctrine, ministerial rights, congregational authority, and the power of presbyteries and synods. The English ministerial associations formed after 1688 were vic-

---

[2] *Ibid.*, p. 24.

[3] Minutes, Pennepek Baptist Church, p. 16, ABHS.

[4] *Ibid.*, pp. 16–19; David Spencer, *The Early Baptists of Philadelphia* (Philadelphia, 1877), pp. 33–34.

[5] Leonard J. Trinterud, *The Forming of an American Tradition: A Re-examination of Colonial Presbyterianism* (Philadelphia, 1949), pp. 24–26. In contrast to this growth, the Anglican minister in Philadelphia, Thomas Clayton, predicted in 1698 that the city would be a "quiet place" for Andrews and reported that "he is so far from growing upon us that he threatens to go home in the Spring." Thomas Clayton to William Markham, 29 November, 1688, in: *Historical Collections Relating to the American Colonial Church*, William S. Perry, ed. (5 v., Hartford, Conn., 1871) 2: p. 15.

timized by these disagreements. As we saw in Chapter II, some of them found it difficult even to force ministerial candidates to accept ordination. In New England the term Presbyterian remained an epithet or was described in terms so diverse as to defy definition. Ministers in eastern Massachusetts organized an English style association at Cambridge under the leadership of Increase Mather in 1690. But they never called it a presbytery and failed in efforts to increase its authority in 1705, although the new proposals fell far short of the norms for Scotch Presbyterianism. Even in Scotland where much Presbyterian debate centered on church-state problems not at issue in the Delaware valley, other problems raised divisive questions about church government among persons who almost universally accepted the label "Presbyterian."[6]

It is possible, of course, that such questions were settled at the opening meeting of the Presbytery in 1706. The first two pages of the Presbytery's minutes are lost and historians have long wondered whether they contained agreements now unavailable to us. This is unlikely. No entry in any of the Presbytery's eighteenth-century minutes makes even the most oblique reference to an agreement, "constitution," or list of principles that the founding ministers might have adopted. Instead, the ministers who later worried about the subject were distraught because they knew no written agreement ever had existed at all.[7]

In this context it is difficult to know what ecclesiastical principles the Presbytery's original members believed they were upholding. In 1706 to be a Presbyterian could mean that one was a Calvinist of some sort but not a Baptist, that one believed in some sort of casual ministerial cooperation and union as in New England, that one accepted the authority of a clerical association as in old England, or as in Scotland that one accepted a union of church and state in which the church was governed through a clerically dominated synod and its constituent presbyteries and received the protection and aid of the state in pursuing its religious aims. What then underwrote the organization and early activity of the Philadelphia Presbytery?

In fact, what united the Presbytery's first members was the tradition of clerical association that served as the basis for the differing forms of Presbyterian denominational order in both England and Scotland. This interpretation is supported both by the circumstances of the Presbytery's formation and by an analysis of its early activities.

The only contemporary document that describes the Presbytery's first meeting links it directly to the tradition of clerical cohesion we have been discussing. This is a 1707 letter from the itinerant preacher Francis Makemie, who was one of the Presbytery's original seven members. Precisely because of his itinerant travels, Makemie came into frequent contact with other clerical organizations.[8] He had been ordained by a presbytery in Ireland, knew of the English associations—he was in London in 1691 just after the United Brethren had been formed and later helped secure funds from its old members to send George McNish and John Hampton to Maryland in 1704 and 1705—and was well acquainted with members of the Cambridge Association in Boston, including Cotton and Increase Mather and Benjamin Colman.

Thus when Makemie described the origins of the Philadelphia Presbytery he wrote of ministers meeting to improve clerical discipline, the same concern that provided denominational order among English and American Quakers and Baptists. Makemie noted that the ministers intended to hold their yearly meetings "to consult the most proper measures, for advancing religion, and propagating Christianity, in our Various Stations," and to improve "our Ministeriall ability by prescribing Texts to be preached on by two of our number at every meeting, which performance is Subjected to the censure of our Brethren."[9] The concern for propagating Christianity and improving ministerial talents was connected, of course, and could have been lifted straight from Richard Baxter's associations of the 1650's. But more pertinent is the fact that Makemie's words uncannily paralleled a formula laid out in 1705 by Benjamin Colman of

[6] Williston Walker, *The Creeds and Platforms of Congregationalism* (Boston, 1960), pp. 463–495; Robert F. Scholz, "Clerical Consociation in Massachusetts Bay: Reassessing the New England Way and Its Origins," *William and Mary Quart.,* 3d ser., 29 (1972): pp. 391–414. A direct connection between the Cambridge Association and the English associations of the Commonwealth existed for at least one person. After 1686 Charles Morton kept the Cambridge minutes in the book he had used between 1655 and 1659 to keep the minutes of the association in Cornwall. The minutes of both groups are printed in *Proc. Mass. Hist. Soc.* 17 (1879–1880): pp. 254–281. For the situation in Connecticut and western Massachusetts see Paul R. Lucas, *Valley of Discord: Church and Society along the Connecticut River, 1636–1725* (Hanover, N.H., 1976), and for the history of clerical organization in eighteenth-century New England see J. William T. Youngs, Jr., *God's Messengers: Religious Leadership in Colonial New England, 1700–1750* (Baltimore, Md., 1976). Unfortunately, Youngs's study came to my attention only after this work was in press. Although Youngs does not discuss his subject in a comparative context, the clerical professionalism he finds new and significant among eighteenth-century New England ministers appears to have been far less imposing than that which characterized Delaware valley Dissenters three or more decades earlier. Indeed, it scarcely approaches that attained in Richard Baxter's English ministerial associations in the Commonwealth period.

[7] Leonard J. Trinterud, *The Forming of an American Tradition: A Re-examination of Colonial Presbyterianism* (Philadelphia, 1949), p. 30.

[8] His life is best summarized by Boyd S. Schlenther, *The Life and Writings of Francis Makemie* (Philadelphia, 1971), pp. 11–28.

[9] Makemie to Benjamin Colman, 28 March, 1707, in *ibid.,* pp. 252–253.

Presbytery of Philadelphia, 1707–1716

	1707	1708	1709	1710	1711	1712	1713	1714	1715	1716
Ministers absent						3	2	3	3	9
Ministers attending	4	6	6	4	6	6	7	7	11	8
Elders attending	4	3	5	4	5	4	5	8	9	4

Synod of Philadelphia, 1717–1730

	1717	1718	1719	1720	1721	1722	1723	1724	1725	1726	1727	1728*	1729	1730*
Ministers absent		3	17	10	4	7	12	6	2	4	4		7	11
Ministers attending	13	18	9	17	21	19	15	18	16	13	23	17	20	17
Elders attending	6	6	6	12	9	9	6	7	7	8	14	12	13	10

* Not a full Synod.   Delegates selected from presbyteries.
Source: *RPC*.

FIG. 1.   Ministers and elders attending yearly meetings of the Presbytery and Synod of Philadelphia.

Boston as part of the effort to broaden the authority of the Cambridge Association. Coleman's plans were spelled out more clearly than Makemie's. Colman was, after all, outlining a new scheme of ecclesiastical organization to wary New England clerics. But he too proposed meetings "for the Increase and Improvement of Ministerial Gifts," and suggested that "two or more Ministers be apointed [illeg.] to Preach During said meeting, on texts Prescribed by the Proceedings [sic] Meeting and they submit to the opinion of the said meeting for aprobation and Censure." And it was to Benjamin Colman that Francis Makemie was writing two years later in 1707.[10]

Still, the Philadelphia organization was called a presbytery, not an association. Thus, while its members hesitated to define their Presbyterianism, their choice of labels made it clear that they intended the institution to govern congregational affairs in some fashion, not merely to serve as a casual meeting where like-minded persons could engage in pleasant conversation or receive advice they might freely accept or decline. Indeed, the commitment to governance is emphasized by the fact that like the Scottish Presbyteries, the one in Philadelphia admitted lay elders to its sessions. Here the situation paralleled the origins of European parliaments. Just as late medieval kings used the gatherings of representatives in parliamentary institutions to increase public taxes and win new monarchical powers from the people, so the Presbytery's admission of lay elders permitted it to establish rules for the congregations from which they came. Thus, elders and ministers did not share power in the

Presbytery; rather, the elders' presence in presbytery meetings reinforced clerical domination.[11]

Theoretically, elders could outnumber ministers in the Philadelphia Presbytery meetings because each congregation was allowed to send two elders to attend the meetings, while each congregation had only a single minister. But elders outnumbered ministers at only one such meeting—eight elders and seven ministers attending the 1714 sessions—and only twice, in 1707 and 1710, did the number of elders equal the number of ministers. Furthermore, as congregations multiplied the gap between the number of ministers and elders attending Presbytery meetings widened. As figure 1 illustrates, until 1715 ministers and elders attended Presbytery sessions in fairly equal numbers. But after 1716 more than twice as many ministers usually attended the Synod meetings than did elders, while in the New Castle Presbytery after 1716, the only one for which early attendance records are available, ministers continued to outnumber elders through the 1730's. Finally in these meetings only ministers were given the dignity of having their names recorded as absent, and on several occasions the ministers clearly excluded elders until matters relating to ordination and the admission of new clerical members had been resolved. However, in no case did elders hold a meeting of the Presbytery or Synod while excluding ministers.[12]

The elders' presence also hinged on the admission and attendance of the ministers of their congregations. In 1710, for example, the Presbytery admitted three

[10] Proposals for promoting an Universal Correspondence among Protestant Dissenters, undated, Benjamin Colman Papers, Massachusetts Historical Society, Boston.

[11] Lists of persons attending the meetings of the Presbytery and Synod are found at the beginning of each session's minutes in *RPC*.

[12] *RPC*, p. 17.

new ministers to its membership and noted in its minutes that "upon the admission of these ministers . . . three elders more sat in the Presbytery." In 1716 the Presbytery recorded the absence of nine ministers "and their elders" from the year's sessions, again suggesting that elders attended only when their ministers did, then dealt with the unusual problem of an elder who had come to Philadelphia without his minister. Noting that a Mr. Edmundson had arrived "as a representative of the congregation at Patuxtent," in Maryland, and that its minister was absent, the Presbytery had to decide whether he could "act here as a representative notwithstanding the minister's absence." The ministers decided that Edmundson could remain. But the discussion reveals how unusual and undesirable the attendance of laymen without ministers was thought to be.[13]

The clerical roots of Delaware valley Presbyterianism are further illustrated in the character of the Presbytery's early business. Church government and denominational order require obedience from laymen as well as ministers and the Presbytery worked for two decades to maintain the kind of discipline that would encourage both. In the most elementary way this meant, of course, that the ministers were obliged to maintain order in their own ranks. They did so with consistency and diligence. Most importantly, they controlled access to the ministry by supervising the ordination of ministers. At the second meeting of the Presbytery in 1706 one John Boyd appeared to be tested as a ministerial candidate. The ministers examined Boyd for two days. On the first, Boyd delivered a lecture on church government and presented them with a written treatise on a Biblical passage selected earlier. On the second, he delivered a "popular sermon" designed for a lay audience and defended the written treatise on the selected scriptural passage. Finally, after he had also given "satisfaction as to his skill in the languages and answered to extemporary questions" the ministers agreed to ordain him two days later "in the public meeting house . . . before a numerous assembly." Only then was the ceremony opened to the public.[14]

Even in the early years the ministers tolerated no challenge to their authority in ordinations. Clergymen were always in short supply in the Delaware valley. Yet the Presbytery encouraged colonial laymen to enter the ministry only with the greatest caution. The result of such caution is illustrated in the example of David Evans, a member of a Presbyterian congregation at Welsh Tract in Chester County. In

1710 the Presbytery indignantly cited Evans for "invading the work of the ministry" because he preached and offered scripture lessons to the congregation without ordination and without the Presbytery's consent. But knowing of Evans's inclinations the ministers also outlined a plan whereby Evans would "lay aside all other business" for a year to prepare for the ministry. Under the direction of Philadelphia's Jedidiah Andrews he would "apply himself closely to learning and study."[15] In 1711 a presbytery committee took note of his "hopeful proficiency" in ministerial studies and in a most unusual development in 1712 he was elected clerk of the Presbytery's session meetings. Yet when Evans's Chester County congregation asked for his ordination, the ministers refused. Apparently they had other plans for him. The same year Evans traveled north to enroll at Yale. After receiving a master of arts degree in 1713, the Presbytery allowed him to preach at Welsh Tract, received the congregation's call for him to become its minister, and ordained him in November, 1714.[16]

If Evans's experience instilled any bitterness in him, such feelings receded over the next sixteen years. In December, 1731, Evans preached an ordination sermon for Robert Treat that was a model of clerical orthodoxy and a rebuff even to those laymen who had exerted pressure on Evans's behalf years before. For Evans, a minister had to be theologically orthodox, learned, able to preach, and capable of faithful and unspotted Christian service.[17] Two steps created such men. First, one was "called by God, and by him put into the Ministry." Second, "a Minister must also be solemnly called and set in this Office, by the Steward's of God's House," meaning, of course, by "the laying on of Hands by the Presbytery."[18] What were the rights of congregations and laymen in such matters? Notably few. Congregations had duties, not rights. They were obliged to support their clergymen, to "take great Delight and Pleasure in them" and to "hear their discourses with great Pleasure and Satisfaction." True, it was their "duty and Privilege, to hear any lawful, sound and faithful minister of Christ." But Evans placed enormous emphasis on the meaning of "lawful, sound and faithful." "Some are, and will be, so diseased with itching ears as to loathe their own Ministers, and to wander about to hear others," Evans wrote. But Christ had sent orthodox men to most congregations which laymen were obliged to obey. "Your spiritual Lusts and Wantonness may indeed be better tricked and fed, by gadding up and down to hear others, but your Souls

13 *Ibid.*, pp. 17, 42; "The Records of the Presbytery of New Castle upon Delaware," *Jour. Dept. of History* 14 (1931): pp. 299–300.

14 *RPC*, p. 9; Walter R. Foster, *Bishop and Presbytery: The Church of Scotland, 1661–1688* (London, 1958), pp. 93–96; Horton Davies, *The Worship of the English Puritans* (London, 1948), pp. 228–231.

15 *RPC*, pp. 17–18.
16 *Ibid.*, pp. 23, 25, 28, 34, 36, 38; Franklin B. Dexter, *Biographical Sketches of the Graduates of Yale College . . .* (6 v., New York, 1885–1912) 1: pp. 111–113.
17 David Evans, *The Minister of Christ and the Duties of his Flock* (Philadelphia, 1732), pp. 7–14.
18 *Ibid.*, pp. 16–20.

will not be edified in true Faith and real Holiness."
If ministers erred the Presbytery provided for their
discipline. "If your own minister be not gifted and
sent of God, or is unfaithful in his Place and Office,
then endeavour in a regular way to be rid of him,"
Evans wrote, thus reminding his listeners that the
Presbytery also controlled the instruments of clerical
discipline.[19]

As we shall see, by 1731 Evans's allusions to discipline touched a long-developing controversy over the
strictness of the ministers' standards. But however
troubling later, the ministers' early exercise of authority in clerical affairs was a major cause of the
Presbytery's expansion between 1706 and 1720. Not
only did the ministers determine who would and who
would not be ordained in the Delaware valley, but
they continued to watch their colleagues through the
many years of a man's ministerial life. In 1707, for
example, the ministers adopted suggestions for worship and congregational activity. Each minister was
asked to read portions of the Scriptures in every
church service as far as "discretion and circumstances
of time, place, etc., will admit." He was asked to
"set on foot and encourage private Christian societies"
which probably resembled those promoted by reforming Anglicans in the 1690's. And he should preach in
"neighbouring desolate places where a minister is
wanting, and opportunity of good offers." Added to
this advice was a continuing inspection of the ministers' preaching. At the Presbytery's annual meetings
at least one and usually two clergymen delivered
"presbyterial exercises" designed to test their preaching style and doctrinal orthodoxy and which were
subjected to the criticism of the membership.[20]

Of course, discipline sometimes involved punishment. When moral problems appeared the Presbytery asserted a broad right to punish those on which it
had conferred membership. The case of Paulus Van
Vleck, minister of a congregation at Neshaminy,
north of Philadelphia, offers one example of its
methods. In 1711 rumors began to circulate that
Van Vleck was a bigamist. When the case was
brought before the Presbytery in 1712 the ministers
determined that Van Vleck's defense was "not sufficient to take off the scandal wholly" and they suspended
him from his ministerial functions until he could resolve their doubts. After the Presbytery meetings
ended a group of ministers still in Philadelphia acquired a letter from Van Vleck's mother that confirmed the charges made against him. When this
fact was announced at the Presbytery's meeting in
1713 the ministers continued his suspension. In 1714,
however, the Presbytery appointed another committee
to investigate the affair when Van Vleck insisted that
the charges were false. But a year later, the com-

mittee reported that it had received no replies to its
inquiries and that Van Vleck had "run out of the
country." Thus the ministers were rid of an embarrassing member. Then they warned Van Vleck's old
congregation "not to encourage such a person, under
such grievous scandals, in the work of the holy ministry among you, but rather to study and endeavour to
supply other ways, by such Christian means as providence may direct you"—these, of course, coming
through the Presbytery.[21]

The ministers also used the Presbytery as a vehicle
to increase their numbers and to improve their financial condition. In 1708 they ordered Francis
Makemie to write to Scotland to secure a minister for
a congregation in Delaware and in 1709 pleaded for
help from Sir Edmund Harrison, an influential London layman with wide connections in English Dissenting circles. They reminded Harrison of the
advantages Anglicans held "from the settled fund of
their church," meaning the S.P.G., and told him that
raising a two hundred pound contribution to support
the Delaware valley ministers "would enable ministers
and people to erect eight congregations" there and
put them all "in better circumstances than hitherto
we have been." [22] Yet despite these and other pleas
no institutional mechanisms ever were developed to
transfer ministers or funds regularly from Scotland
and England to America. Most ministers traveled to
the New World in much the same way that their ulti-
mate parishioners did—out of individual volition.
Only a few made the journey because they had been
asked to leave a Scottish congregation to serve a new
congregation in America. Similarly, after 1712 even
irregular gifts of money from Scotland or England
appear to have stopped altogether.

The Presbytery's acquisition of power over ministers also gave it power over laymen. Precisely because the Presbytery monopolized access to the ministry and guaranteed clerical orthodoxy and behavior,
worshipers began asking for ministers as soon as the
Presbytery had been formed. When none were
available the Presbytery asked neighboring clergymen
to preach to the supplicants until a permanent minister
could be found. The Presbytery also accepted and
forwarded "calls" for the services of a specific minister in ways that strengthened its authority and made
it more than a mere conduit for messages. Thus in
1707 residents of Snow Hill in Maryland sent letters
to Philadelphia asking for the ministers' "joynt con-
currence, and assistance in prosecuting their call to
Mr. John Hampton," a member of the Presbytery.
Although Hampton rejected the offer, the ministers
decided that he should "have the call and the paper

19 *Ibid.*, pp. 58–59.
20 *RPC*, p. 10.

21 The Presbytery discussed the case numerous times. See
RPC, pp. 17–40.
22 *Ibid.*, pp. 11, 15, 16. The ministers sent additional requests for help to the presbyteries in Dublin and Glasgow in
1710. *Ibid.*, pp. 19–20.

of subscription continued in his hands for his further perusal." Sometime thereafter Hampton changed his mind and moved to Snow Hill. But the congregation failed to support him and in 1708 the Presbytery sent a letter "requiring their faithfulness and care in collecting the tobacco promised by subscription to Mr. Hampton," since it had aided the congregation in securing Hampton as its minister.

By 1712 the Presbytery had established general rules for calling ministers. The Presbytery tied its willingness to supply clerics for new congregations to a guarantee of financial support for them. It ruled that in the congregations "none should be allowed to vote for the calling of a minister, but those that shall contribute for the maintenance of him." It also attempted to diminish the role rich parishioners might have played in such affairs by demanding that "the major vote" of all contributors "shall be determinative" in selecting ministers, thus giving the choice to a majority of those willing to support him, not to the wealthiest.[23]

Before 1716 the Presbytery even inspected relations between ministers and their congregations. In 1710 it ordered both ministers and elders attending the next Presbytery "to give a true and impartial account how matters are mutually betwixt them, both with regard to spirituals and temporals." Ministers reported on "the state of their congregations and of themselves," and elders told "not only of the doctrine taken to support the ministry, but of the life, conversation, and doctrine of their several ministers." But the practice continued only until 1716 when it apparently was dropped after the creation of the Synod.[24]

The usefulness of these techniques in extending the Presbytery's authority is well illustrated by three episodes involving congregations in Cohansey, New Castle, and Woodbridge. The Cohansey congregation came under the Presbytery's scrutiny after the ministers negotiated with it to settle Joseph Smith there in 1708 after it had ordained him. Unfortunately, the congregation failed to pay Smith regularly and in 1709 the Presbytery had to ask Cohansey's settlers "to perform their obligations to Mr. Smith." The effort apparently met with little success, since Smith soon left the congregation. It then hired another minister (his name is not known) without consulting the Presbytery.

The man proved so disappointing that the Cohansey congregation soon complained to the Presbytery about him. The ministers scarcely could have been more pleased. "We could have wished you had taken better advised steps for your provision" they told the Cohansey worshipers and despite the congregation's negligence the Presbytery already had tried to improve the situation, although without success. "He

was invited to be present at our meeting, but he neither came nor sent [a reply.]" Worse, the ministers found his sermons riddled with errors "so far as they are intelligible." The implications were obvious. Although they still offered their assistance for "your comfortable settlement," they reminded the Cohansey congregation that it had created its own problem when it hired a minister the Presbytery had not approved. Obviously others who acted similarly could expect no better results.[25]

Some situations required stronger words. Between 1708 and 1709 Presbyterians living in New Castle, Delaware, decided to dismiss their old minister, John Wilson, so they could call George McNish to their pulpit, while rural members voted to support Wilson and to form a separate congregation to do so. When New Castle's call to McNish reached the Presbytery in 1709 the result was a stern lecture on the implications of local disputing. "We would be glad to fall upon a healing method to remedy these unhappy divisions," the ministers wrote. But calling McNish to New Castle would only cement the division. Could not Wilson "continue in his pastoral charge and function among you as formerly?" Still, "out of tender respect to you," they presented McNish with their call, knowing that he would reject it, which he did. Then, telling the New Castle congregation to "put favourable constructions upon what we do," the ministers warned them that they would have to patch up their quarrel with Wilson or go without a minister. McNish would not move there and no other clergyman was available to them. "Therefore," they wrote, "we entreat, nay require you in the Lord, to concur with us; lay aside all prejudices, struggle not too much with providential, unavoidable difficulties; be submissive, which is a truly Christian temper; trust in God, use patient endeavors, and expect without doubting a comfortable issue, which we hope for and shall constantly endeavour." Their rhetoric proved futile, however. The New Castle congregation refused to obey the Presbytery's command and the dispute apparently was healed only when the Presbytery named another minister to serve it, with Wilson ministering in the countryside until his death in 1712.[26]

The most outrageous example of the Presbytery's method in expanding its authority occurred in Woodbridge, New Jersey, between 1708 and 1712. Here, the Presbytery gained the allegiance of a congregation by winning over its minister, then later used that power to censure him and finally remove him from the congregation's pulpit. The affair began in 1707 when the Woodbridge worshipers, who had never before had any dealings with the Presbytery, sought a new minister in New England. As a result of their

---

[23] *Ibid.*, pp. 10, 12, 14, 15, 24, 36.
[24] *Ibid.*, pp. 21–22.

[25] *Ibid.*, pp. 11, 14, 22–23.
[26] *Ibid.*, pp. 11–12, 15; Richard Webster, *A History of the Presbyterian Church in America* (Philadelphia, 1857), p. 312.

inquiries the ministerial association in Fairfield County, Connecticut, sent Nathaniel Wade to them. When he arrived he found the congregation badly split, with only some of its members supporting his candidacy. As a consequence, he was not inducted into the position. Wade then discovered that his opponents were appealing to the Presbytery for help. However, the Philadelphia Presbytery was reluctant to enter the dispute because the congregation never had accepted its authority. It only suggested that perhaps the Presbyterian minister at Freehold, John Boyd, might preach in Woodbridge every three weeks. At the same time the ministers informed members of the association in Connecticut of the advice they had given to the Woodbridge dissidents and asked for the New Englanders' "charitable constructions upon what we have directed unto, in so difficult a matter." [27]

In 1710 the character of the affair changed completely when Nathaniel Wade joined the Philadelphia Presbytery in a move obviously designed to appease his opponents. With Wade's membership in hand, the Philadelphia ministers now sought to end the dispute. First they wrote to Wade's early supporters, most of whom probably were not well inclined toward the Presbyterian order, to inform them of Wade's admission to the Philadelphia Presbytery and to ask them to study "unity, peace, and holiness . . . that all divisions and animosity by-past may be entirely buried." Then, in quite different terms, they wrote to Wade's early opponents, who had previously asked the Presbytery to supply them with a minister. They reminded them that "you do professedly own this judicatory," announced that they would not countenance "anything that looks like dissenison or separation" from Wade and his original supporters, and made special note of the "exhoratory letter to your neighbours . . . [which] we hope may be of a cementing use." [28]

Any peace prevailing in Woodbridge lasted for less than a year. By the summer of 1711 the congregation was again divided, this time by Wade's behavior. For reasons now lost Wade dismissed two members of the congregation from full communion. In September the Presbytery not only reversed Wade's order—in itself an important precedent—but drew up "a form of words, which Mr. Wade is to use in the public reversing the sentence." This action, which took place at the Presbytery's session of September 22, 1711, failed to heal the division. Four days later, on September 26, Wade offered to resign his position at Woodbridge, "heartily wishing that they may unite in calling another minister, that the Presbytery shall ap-

prove of." The Presbytery accepted Wade's resignation, voted to allow the congregation to secure a replacement as "shall be offered" by the Presbytery, and ordered Wade to continue preaching there until the new minister had been installed. At the same time the ministers reminded the congregation of the "fault on all hands" and expressed hope that the Woodbridge worshipers would "not utterly neglect our Brother Wade, who is to be your present supply," even while they were trying to replace him. [29]

With the help of the Presbytery, the Woodbridge congregation soon hired one George Gillespie, who was recently arrived from Scotland, to replace Wade. Now, however, complications increased. Wade suddenly refused to leave Woodbridge. He began to criticize the Presbytery for helping to secure Gillespie and despite his earlier promise, pursued what the Presbytery called a "pastoral relation to some of the people in Woodbridge" by withdrawing his resignation and naming new church officers for the congregation. In response the Presbytery ordered him to stop preaching without its permission and demanded that he surrender the Woodbridge pulpit to Gillespie.

The Presbytery also was forced to deal with other disturbing aspects of Wade's behavior, namely its effect on the ministers' relations with New England clergymen. Not only had Wade first arrived under an agreement reached between the Woodbridge congregation and Connecticut ministers, but Gillespie came to the middle colonies with a recommendation from none other than Cotton Mather. These potential strains were even further complicated when Wade went to Boston after Gillespie's arrival in Woodbridge and got Mather to send yet a third minister to Woodbridge—presumably as Wade's own replacement—yet not telling Mather that the Philadelphia Presbytery had already selected Gillespie for the post. When the poor man arrived—who he was is not known—he found himself a pawn in the dispute between Wade, Gillespie, and their supporters, and apparently returned to Boston. Thus, the Presbytery was forced to write Mather an apology because one of its members had involved him in a dispute of which he had no knowledge. [30]

Having tried to salvage their reputation in the north, the Philadelphia ministers turned once more to Woodbridge. Again they told Wade to stop opposing Gillespie and to act "as becomes a minister of the Prince of Peace." Now, however, the Presbytery faced problems with Gillespie. The dispute had "produced thoughts in him, that his abiding there will make him very uncomfortable." These thoughts apparently were engendered not only by the continued hostility of Wade's backers, but by some erosion in Gillespie's

[27] RPC, p. 13; Richard Webster, A History of the Presbyterian Church in America (Philadelphia, 1857), p. 333. Fragmentary materials from these years are found in a manuscript volume, A Record for the Church of Christ at Woodbridge, in the Presbyterian Historical Society, Philadelphia.
[28] RPC, pp. 10, 18–19.

[29] Ibid., pp. 22–24.
[30] Ibid., pp. 27–29; Richard Webster, A History of the Presbyterian Church in America (Philadelphia, 1857), p. 339.

own support, so that while the Presbytery bolstered Gillespie's resolve it also warned the congregation that his departure would complicate matters and "prove a vast discouragement to another from venturing among you." But should Gillespie leave Woodbridge the ministers reassured the congregation that they would "not be wanting, both by our prayers and other endeavours, to promote your happiness in the enjoyment of so great a blessing." [31]

Since Gillespie did in fact leave, the dispute reveals as much about limitations in the Presbytery's power as its tactics. In addition, after nearly five years of such bickering one group of settlers finally abandoned the congregation altogether and asked the S.P.G. to provide "the true worship of our Lord Jesus Christ here amongst a poor deluded people." [32] But the Presbytery, having gained followers there in so intricate and difficult a manner, did not abandon its prize. Rather, it delayed any additional assistance until 1715, when the ministers tried to bridge what probably was the cause of the original dispute in 1709 —disagreement between those who wanted a New England trained minister and others willing to accept leadership of the Philadelphia Presbytery. "Taking into consideration that the people of Woodbridge have not had the sealing ordinance administered among them," the Presbytery asked Philadelphia's Jedidiah Andrews to write to John Pierson in Connecticut, informing him of the Woodbridge vacancy and urging him to move south. The tactic worked. Pierson moved to Woodbridge, and after settling a small disagreement about his salary, was ordained and installed as the congregation's minister. In this way Woodbridge obtained a long-lived New England clergyman—Pierson remained there until 1753—while the Presbytery obtained a new member and sustained its authority. [33]

By 1716 the Presbytery's pursuit of power and increase in members strained its geographical boundaries. As a result the ministers reorganized themselves into a synod, the Synod of Philadelphia, and three subordinate presbyteries, those of Long Island, New Castle, and Philadelphia. To some extent creation of the Synod of Philadelphia signaled a loss of clerical intimacy among Delaware valley Presbyterians. After 1716 elders and ministers no longer reported on each other's performance—such reports were perhaps too personal to continue in a gathering whose membership was steadily rising—and after 1724 some Synod meetings were only attended by delegates from the presbyteries rather than by all Presbyterian ministers in the Delaware valley. [34]

The ministers scarcely abandoned interest in the exercise of power, however. Now they had added to the set of hierarchical denominational institutions being created in the Delaware valley. The Synod's command of its prebyteries, for example, was illustrated when every year it inspected the minutes of each presbytery, with the Synod clerk writing his name in the presbytery minutes when they were approved. [35] And the authority of the Synod and its presbyteries over congregations was illustrated in the congregations' continued willingness to submit disputes to the ministerial bodies for adjudication, as well as in their steady requests for ministers. The Synod and its presbyteries used these tendencies to extend their power. Thus after 1716 the New Castle Presbytery routinely required a statement from laymen pledging financial support and submission to the Presbytery's decisions before it would send clergymen into the countryside. [36]

The Synod and presbyteries also continued to protect clerical ranks both before and after ordination. In 1721 the Synod rejected the membership application of James Morehead, a recent immigrant from Scotland who had become minister of the congregation at Pilesgrove, New Jersey, without its supervision. It criticized Morehead's "irregular and factious carriage in his own country, . . . together with his scandalous and disorderly behaviour since he came into America" and ordered its members "to give him no encouragement as a minister, but to advertise all as they have opportunity, and occasion to beware of him." Similarly, in 1723 the Synod told a layman, George Williamson, that he was unqualified for ordination, although they were "satisfied as to his piety and godly life," and hoped he would "endeavour to be useful as a private Christian." [37]

Unfortunately, the growth in the number of ministers and the formation of the Synod and its presbyteries also strained the old denominational order. Some ministers—not laymen—demanded a more precise formulation of Presbyterianism than earlier practice and mere remembrance provided. Thus the 1720's were marked by a new tension. In order to justify and rationalize the authority they had long been accumulating, these ministers pressed the adoption of a written document that would outline polity in the Presbyterian denominational order of the Deleware valley. They not only ran afoul of past evasiveness— many ministers obviously preferred to continue following the comfortable and silent clerical tradition they already knew—but also wandered into a thicket of controversy about ecclesiastical authority, the character of the ministry, and doctrine. The result was a

[31] RPC, p. 30.
[32] Quoted in Richard Webster, A History of the Presbyterian Church in America (Philadelphia, 1857), p. 334.
[33] RPC, p. 41.
[34] Ibid., p. 80.

[35] "The Records of the Presbytery of New Castle upon Delaware," Jour. Dept. of History 14 (1931) : pp. 301, 307.
[36] Ibid., pp. 296, 297, 306, 384.
[37] RPC, p. 60.

decade of growing controversy among ministers who had known relatively little internal dissension for almost twenty years. Of course, the two themes were related. The peace and even the prosperity of the earlier years had come at the expense of discussion about the nature of Presbyterian church government, while the debate of the 1720's was greatly affected by the realization that the ministers had exercised power without ever having to define its limits or source. The result was a stand-off. Between 1716 and 1728 a majority of ministers rebuffed attempts to define synodical authority and fashion a clear definition of Presbyterianism. And when they "subscribed" the Westminister Confession of Faith in 1729, their act signaled no victory for any party. Instead it solidified a long-developing pattern of evasion and even procrastination that set the stage for the next two decades of Presbyterian history in the Delaware valley.

Three events served as catalysts of efforts to solidify the Synod's ecclesiastical foundation in the 1720's— the censure of Robert Cross, a long dispute in the Presbyterian congregation of New York City, and the problems of adopting the Westminster Confession. The case surrounding Robert Cross was a simple one involving immorality. In 1720 members of Cross's congregation—Cross a young Scotch-Irish minister who had been ordained in Philadelphia in 1719— accused him of committing fornication. The charge was first made before the New Castle Presbytery. Then it was referred to the Synod of Philadelphia where Cross, "with great seriousness, humility, and signs of true repentance confessed the charge laid against him." As punishment the Synod suspended him from his ministerial functions for four weeks, after which the congregation was allowed to decide whether it wished him to continue as its minister.[38]

The proceedings angered some members. As the last item of business in 1720 George Gillespie, the man who had been involved earlier in the complex Woodbridge affair, "entered his protest and dissent against the procedure of the Synod" and in 1721 he asked the Synod to alter or annul their proceedings. The Synod refused, whereupon Gillespie offered an "overture" or resolution to the ministers designed to permit a tightening of discipline. It having "been for many years in the exercise of Presbyterian government and Church discipline as far as the nature and constitution of this country will allow"—this probably a double reference to the fact that the American ministers had some Presbyterian procedures but had not defined them, and that in the Delaware valley Presbyterian ministers were not supported by the state, as they were in Scotland—Gillespie asked that anyone with a sug-

gestion "for the better carrying on in the matter of our government" should be allowed to offer it to the whole Synod. Although the Synod passed Gillespie's resolution, it did so only "by a majority of votes," and six ministers, two Welsh immigrants and four New Englanders, entered a protest against the act.[39]

Unfortunately some of the principal points in the Cross dispute are not readily distinguishable. It is not clear, for example, just what Gillespie opposed in the Cross affair. He may have thought that the matter should first have been considered by the New Castle Presbytery. Moreover, his later resolution seemed only vaguely connected to the Cross affair. Yet the intent of Gillespie's protest is clarified by other events. For example, Gillespie was a strict disciplinarian in his own congregation. Between 1716 and 1730 several of its members appeared before the New Castle Presbytery to protest their exclusion from the sacraments after Gillespie accused them of commiting moral offenses.[40] His inclination to judge ministers as harshly is further supported by a letter written in 1723 to Robert Wodrow, one of the most powerful Scot Presbyterians. It is one of the few letters surviving from Delaware valley Presbyterian ministers and in it Gillespie bemoaned conditions in the colonial churches. Although ministers and congregations had increased in number, "yet alas," he wrote, "there is little of the power and life of Religion with either." Little clerical discipline existed in the middle colonies. "There are not above 30 ministers and probationer preachers in our Synod, and yet six of the said number have been grossly scandalous; Suspension for 4 Sabbaths hath been the greatest censure inflicted as yet," an obvious reference to the Synod's proceeding with Cross.[41]

Although Gillespie's resolution probably was designed to introduce more stringent rules for disciplining ministers like Cross, it was Gillespie's assertion that the ministers had "been for many years in the exercise of Presbyterian government and Church discipline" that may have posed the greatest obstacle to its passage. The reason was simple. It could be used to push the ministers to a more formal Presbyterianism than they had ever practiced before. Such fears clearly were on the mind of Jonathan Dickinson, one of those who protested against the adoption of Gillespie's resolution in 1721. Preaching the opening

---

[38] *Ibid.*, p. 63; Leonard J. Trinterud, *The Forming of an American Tradition: A Re-examination of Colonial Presbyterianism* (Philadelphia, 1949), pp. 38–39.

[39] *RPC*, pp. 64, 67, 68.

[40] "The Records of the Presbytery of New Castle upon Delaware," *Jour. Dept. of History* 14 (1931): pp. 302, 308, 378–379, 381–382. These difficulties probably made Gillespie's congregation at Christiana Creek ripe for itinerant ministers. Thus the James Morehead who was censured by the Synod in 1721 reportedly preached there, much to Gillespie's chagrin. *Ibid.*, p. 382.

[41] The letter of 16 July, 1723 is printed in Charles A. Briggs, *American Presbyterianism: Its Origins and Early History* (New York, 1885), pp. lxxxiv–lxxxv of the appendix.

sermon at the Synod's sessions in 1722, Dickinson cautioned against imposing complex schemes of church government on the Delaware valley Presbyterians. If a model for such a venture existed it was a Scottish one, of course. But Dickinson turned the Scottish example on its head. In 1698 the Commission of the Scottish Presbyterian General Assembly issued a *Seasonable Admonition* to both laymen and ministers by which it tried to calm fears that the reestablished Presbyterian system was too authoritarian and too much weighed down in secular politics. The Commission reminded Scots that "Jesus Christ is the only Head and King of His Church and that He hath instituted in his Church officers and ordinances, order and government, and not left it to the will of man, magistrate or Church to alter at their pleasure." [42]

Of course, the *Admonition* was an apology for a church government that was, in fact, authoritarian and clerically dominated. But Dickinson ignored this fact and instead followed the rhetoric of the *Admonition*. He reminded the Synod that church government of any sort "must be either of a Religious Nature or meerly Humane Politics" and protested that "any authoritative obligatory *Interpretation* of the Laws of Christ, is a *Law-making Faculty* that we are not entitled to." Thus while the ministers might condemn heretics and uphold orthodox doctrine, "yet even these essential Articles of Christianity, may not be imposed by Civil Coercions, temporal Penalties, or any other way whatsoever." [43]

Having made his point, Dickinson then offered a compromise. Together with three other ministers who had also protested against the passage of Gillespie's resolution of 1721, Dickinson submitted a proposal to the Synod "testifying in writing their sentiments and judgment concerning church government." [44] The statement tried to please too many sides in the Synod, however. On the one hand it asserted that the Synod and its presbyteries held "full executive power of church government," that those bodies might "use the keys of discipline to all proper intents and purpose" and that those keys were "committed to the church officers and them only." Yet Dickinson then diluted this authority. "Ecclesiastical judicatories" determined only "the mere circumstantials of church discipline, such as the time, place, and mode, of carrying on in the government of the Church." Worse, Dickinson insisted that such acts "be not imposed upon such as conscientiously dissent from them." Thus any book of discipline the Synod might write could only be used "provided that all subordinate judica-

tories may decline from such directories when they conscientiously think they have just reason so to do."

The 1722 agreement understandably inspired more questions than it answered. Exactly which "keys" were possessed by the Synod and its presbyteries? What particular procedures were "conformable to the general rules in the word of God"? How was conscientious dissent to be defined? Which church officers held powers of government—ministers meeting together in the Synod and presbyteries, minister and elder together in the congregation, or simply ministers acting as individuals?

Even though the 1722 Synod adopted Dickinson's resolution, the new agreement on church government failed to sharpen the ministers' attitude toward erring colleagues. In the case of Henry Hook, for example, their punishment seemed particularly lenient. Hook had fallen into a bitter controversy with his congregation at Cohansey in New Jersey, had performed "sham marriages" at a shooting match, and falsely accused one worshiper of saying that Hook's "fingers and toes were cut off in Ireland for stealing." In addition, Hook slept during his own church services. According to the Synod he was "chargeable with folly and levity unbecoming a gospel minister," and was suspended from his ministerial functions. Yet the Synod agreed to lift the suspension if Hook would "make his publick acknowledgment viva voce or in writing, as he thinks fit." Since Hook apparently made such an acknowledgment immediately, he was quickly restored to his post.[45]

A second case brought an even milder response from the Synod and another protest from Gillespie. According to Joseph Morgan, the minister at Freehold in New Jersey, a ministerial candidate preaching at Maidenhead, one John Walton, bore a "lustful carriage to some young women." Although Walton was censured by the Synod and forced to make a public acknowledgment of his sin, the Synod suspended him from preaching for only three weeks, even after he also derided the Synod's authority. Thus Morgan informed Cotton Mather that at the end of the Synod meeting "pious Mr. Galespie with some of 'em entered their Dissent"—Morgan himself shocked by the leniency shown Walton but scarcely surprised by Gillespie's response.[46]

A dispute among New York City Presbyterians revealed how hesitantly the Synod approached local congregational problems when those problems edged toward the tension about defining Presbyterianism itself. Essentially, the dispute occurred in two stages. The first lasted from 1719 to 1723 and was motivated by efforts to shift blame for the high cost of a new meeting house from several prominent laymen in the

---

[42] Quoted in *ibid*.
[43] Jonathan Dickinson, *A Sermon Preached Before the Opening of the Synod at Philadelphia, September 19, 1722* (Boston, 1723), pp. 17–18.
[44] *RPC*, pp. 73–74.

[45] *Ibid*., pp. 72–73.
[46] Joseph Morgan to Cotton Mather, 31 October, 1722, in the Simon Gratz Manuscript Collection, HSP.

congregation to the minister, James Anderson, who had arrived there in 1718. Ultimately, it involved suggestions that the congregation's eclectic membership—this only partly symbolized by the members' geographical origins, some from New England, some from Scotland, some long-settled New Yorkers—crippled prospects for peace there, then raised complaints to the Synod about the propriety of Anderson's settlement at New York, the orthodoxy of his sermons, and the power of the Long Island Presbytery to intrude into local affairs. It finally led to a brief division of the membership in which the dissidents secured the services of a young and unknown Jonathan Edwards in 1722 and 1723 using financial support furnished by New England ministers. Although the Synod and the Long Island Presbytery struggled with the matter each year between 1720 and 1723, peace arrived only when Dr. John Nicoll, a New York physician, raised nearly £600 in Scotland to ease the congregation's building debt.

By 1725, however, the congregation was again divided and the dispute entered its second stage. Nicoll apparently refused to surrender bonds owned or inherited by the congregation. Later he fell into arguments with the minister, James Anderson, who, in turn, fell to arguing with yet other members of the congregation. Part of the tension was relieved when Anderson left New York for Philadelphia in 1727, a move probably made with the help of the Philadelphia Synod. Yet as late as 1730 some of its members still were complaining that Anderson had absconded with a piece of communion linen, a complaint the Synod wisely refused to consider.[47]

The New York dispute was significant for two reasons. First, it demonstrated a disturbing inability of the Philadelphia Synod and the Long Island Presbytery to settle a congregational dispute presented to them for nearly a decade. Second, even when settling it the Synod remained as interested in its own authority as in healing local discord. After James Anderson left the New York congregation it called a man ordained by Boston ministers—Ebenezer Pemberton—to its pulpit without consulting the Long Island Presbytery or the Philadelphia Synod. In 1727 the Synod declared that in doing so "the rules of our Presbyterian constitution were not observed"—the constitution, of course, being defined by custom—and delayed seating Pemberton in the Philadelphia Synod, not from "any fault objected against him," but because of the congregation's behavior.[48] Then in 1728, when one of the Synod's own committees virtually guaranteed that Pemberton would be admitted to the Synod, the whole Synod ruled that the committee

never should have made such a promise. The action intruded on the Synod's right to examine each candidate for membership. Instead, the Synod admitted Pemberton in a separate vote, at which time it again grumbled about the "irregularity" of his call to New York City.[49]

The New York City episode fed a widening stream of discontent in the Synod. After 1720 disputes increasingly endangered harmony in individual congregations and strained the presbyteries' capacities for healing them, although they probably only grew as the number of congregations themselves multiplied. Between 1726 and 1729, for example, the Synod adjudicated disputes in the congregations at Elk River, Maryland, and Newark, New Jersey, and heard complaints against three ministers, Joseph Morgan, Malachi Jones, and John Boyd, the latter the first minister ordained in the Presbytery of Philadelphia.[50] Although these squabbles were serious in themselves, they became even more significant because they renewed the efforts of some ministers to adopt a written statement about church government and denominational order in the Synod. In 1727 and again in 1729 John Thomson, a member of the New Castle Presbytery, proposed that the ministers officially endorse the *Westminster Confession* of 1649, which was the formal basis of Presbyterian church government in Scotland. Thomson's arguments went directly to the anomoly of middle colony Presbyterianism. Although a true church existed there, it was "a church without a confession," he said. "We all generally acknowledge and look upon the Westminster Confession and Catechisms to be our confession," Thomson observed, but the ministers refused to acknowledge their practice by formally adopting the document. The result was a paralysis of denominational government. Without a confession "there is no bar provided to keep out of the ministry those who are corrupt in doctrinals." Corrupt men could not be censured effectively "because (supposito ut supra) the truth was never publicly received among us." Possessing no seminary where they might prepare ministerial candidates, and surrounded by heretics, imposters, and other Dissenters, ministers like Thomson felt the lack of a foundation in the disciplinary system of Delaware valley Presbyterians more painfully than did ministers elsewhere. Thomson proposed that the Synod, "as an ecclesiastical judicature of Christ" and a body "cloathed with ministerial authority," should adopt the *Westminster Confession* as the standard of religious orthodoxy for Presbyterians in the Delaware valley. After much debate the Synod agreed. It required its current and future members to subscribe to the *Westminster Confession* "as being in all the

[47] Boyd Schlenther, ed., "The Presbyterian Church of New York vs. John Nicoll, M.D.," *Jour. Presbyterian History* **42** (1964): pp. 198–215, 272–285; *RPC*, p. 99.
[48] *RPC*, pp. 88–90.

[49] *Ibid.*, p. 86.
[50] *Ibid.*, pp. 85, 86–87, 90–91, 92, 95.

essential and necessary articles" the exemplar "of sound words and systems of Christian doctrine." [51]

Here again appearances belied reality. The Synod's action did not necessarily reflect a new ministerial consensus. First, the six or seven men who had long opposed such declarations were not well represented at the 1729 Synod. Malachi Jones of Welsh Tract had died in March, 1729, and Joseph Morgan, Joseph Webb, and Nathaniel Hubbell were absent from the 1729 sessions. [52] More important, the resolution itself was weak. Like the 1722 agreement, it was riddled with so many qualifications that it gave the appearance more of veneer than of substance. The text began with a crucial qualification—"Although the Synod do not claim or pretend to any authority of imposing our faith upon other men's consciences . . . and do utterly disclaim all legislative power and authority in the Church"—then was filled with the parenthetical expression of others. The *Westminster Confession* was described as being correct in "all the essential and necessary articles," but this phrase invited dispute over what might be thought unessential. Those who had "any scruple" about such articles had only to inform their presbyteries, "who shall, notwithstanding, admit [them] to the exercise of the ministry within our bounds, and to ministerial communion." Only if the objections concerned "essential and necessary articles of faith," which the Synod still refused to define, was the presbytery authorized to reject the candidate's membership. [53]

The ambivalent "subscription" of the *Westminster Confession* well summarized the informal processes by which a distinctly Presbyterian denominational order emerged in the Delaware valley. That order was first sustained by a clerical fraternalism whose roots were as deep as they were broad and vague. Before 1720 the ministers who dominated the Philadelphia Presbytery used this fraternalism to nourish institutions that moved from event to event, supplying a minister here, healing a dispute there, and increasing the authority and prestige of the Presbytery in the process. To some, this experience offered precedents that were sufficient to carry them safely into the future. But to others, simple experience was not sufficient. These persons—ministers like George Gillespie, for example—believed that authority was compromised when those who claimed it also refused to define it and they pushed hard to develop a clear intellectual foundation for the powerful institutions they were creating in the Delaware valley.

In this context the agreement of 1729 signaled a victory for no one. The document evaded so many major points that neither side could use it effectively. And it was not a compromise, as historians often have suggested, because it only marked a pause in a confrontation that had been developing since 1720. As we shall see in the final chapter, it instead connected early Presbyterian practice with the disputes of the Great Awakening and should serve to remind us of the differences between that later tumult and the more quiet ministerial cohesion of the 1710's.

VI. REFORM WITHOUT CHURCH: THE SHAPE OF ANGLICAN FAILURE

Historians always have believed that the Church of England failed in the colonies. It was legally established only in the south where its domination by laymen, or at least by vestries of rich laymen, significantly altered the Church's English constitution. In all the colonies Church activities never fell under the effective control of a bishop, even though a bishop was the principal figure of authority in the Anglican ecclesiastical scheme. Outside the south most Anglican congregations were supported by the Society for the Propagation of the Gospel in Foreign Parts, the Anglican reform society organized by Thomas Bray in 1701. But according to the traditional historical view, S.P.G. assistance brought as much trouble as help. The society was too far from America. Its clergymen drank too much and were too immoral. And the prominent laymen who supported it as well as nearly all the ministers who were financed by it spent too much time in a fruitless and politically dangerous quest to install a bishop in America. In this view then, colonial Anglicanism was characterized by immense ecclesiastical chaos among scattered, drunken, and immoral clerics whose pursuit of hierarchical authority sealed its fate in the increasingly democratic colonies. [1]

More recent work on the fate of colonial Anglicanism suggests that these stereotypes need to be dismantled, however. Bruce Steiner's work in Connecticut demonstrates that the Church successfully established solid congregations there throughout the eighteenth century and that its communicants increasingly held public offices previously held by Congregationalists. John Callam counts much of the S.P.G. program in colonial education a distinct success, although he also argues that the Society was institutionally overextended in the colonies. A recent article

---

[51] Quoted in M. W. Armstrong, *et al.*, eds., *The Presbyterian Enterprise: Sources of American Presbyterian History* (Philadelphia, 1956), pp. 27–29.

[52] *RPC*, p. 93.

[53] *Ibid.*, p. 94.

[1] For expressions of these views see William H. Seiler, "The Anglican Parish in Virginia," in: *Seventeenth-Century America: Essays in Colonial History*, James M. Smith, ed. (Chapel Hill, N.C., 1959), pp. 119–142; John Callam, *Parsons and Pedagogues: The S.P.G. Adventure in American Education* (New York, 1971), pp. 55–61; Richard Hofstadter, *America at 1750: A Social Portrait* (New York, 1971), pp. 204–208; Sydney E. Ahlstrom, *A Religious History of the American People* (New Haven and London, 1972), pp. 184–229.

by William Hogue turns the bishop question around too. Where in *Mitre and Sceptre* Carl Bridenbaugh suggested that in the 1760's Anglicans plotted to install a colonial bishop who might curtail some of the settlers' religious liberties, Hogue demonstrates that the Anglican search for a bishop involved no plot at all, and was consistent with Anglican ecclesiastical and theological principles that had been discussed in America since the 1690's. Finally, in the broadest vein, John Murrin has argued that in the eighteenth century the colonies were more often becoming "Anglicized" than "Americanized" as colonial middle classes and elites sought to duplicate the style and substance of British aristocratic and upper class culture. Murrin does not consider the role the Anglican church might have played in this process—indeed, similarities of spelling should warn us against confusing Anglicization with Anglicanism—but if his assessment proves accurate, Anglicization would only have aided the growth of Anglicanism; it certainly would not have hindered it.[2]

These revisionary studies do not suggest that Anglicans succeeded in America as Quakers, Presbyterians, or Baptists did. But they do suggest that we reconsider the nature of their defeat. Anglicanism did not fail because the S.P.G. was too far from America, because too many Anglican clergymen were immoral drunkards, or because the S.P.G. was an autocratic anachronism in an emergent democracy. London proved to be surprisingly close, Anglican clerics were no less dedicated, hardworking, and moral than other Protestant ministers, and, as we should realize already, Anglicans scarcely were the only colonial Protestants committed to upholding hierarchical schemes of church government.

In fact, other facts make the Anglican case even more puzzling. The number of Anglican ministers and congregations multiplied rapidly as the S.P.G. increased its activity in America by paying clerical salaries and distributing thousands of books and tracts throughout the colonies.[3] Yet on the eve of the Revolution the Church's stoutest defenders still counted the American colonial experience a failure. In fact, in America the Church grew but never matured. This happened because, unlike other English Protestants, Anglicans never established their own familiar ecclesiastical institutions in America, while the society they did establish, the S.P.G., which itself was founded on a Dissenting model of religious activity, proved to be a contradiction in terms.

From the very first years of settlement there, the Anglican presence in the Delaware valley was tied to the work of the S.P.G. Before 1701 only two Anglican congregations existed there and after 1701 virtually all the Anglican congregations established in the Delaware valley were organized by S.P.G. missionaries and sustained by S.P.G. aid. As was true elsewhere, however, the S.P.G. intended to do more than provide ministers and money for America. It was a reform organization designed to promote the kind of awakened Anglicanism in America that Thomas Bray and the English reformers were sponsoring at home. Bray insisted that the Society should select only "good, substantial, well studied Divines" for America. They should demonstrate "such nice Morals, as to abstain from all Appearance of Evil." They should be men of "exact conduct" in the management of parish affairs. If they were not, they would "unavoidably fall in Contempt, with a People so well versed in Business, as even the meanest Planter seems to be." And they should be thoughtful men, "well experienced in the Pastoral Care" but "not so grown into years, as to be uncapable of Labour and Fatigue."[4]

Yet certain darker elements vied with the S.P.G.'s reform ideals. They were rooted in the reformers' envy of Dissenting organizational techniques, especially of those developed by Quakers since the Restoration. Not only were the S.P.C.K. and S.P.G. modeled in a general way on the Quaker institutions, but considerable evidence exists to suggest that between 1701 and 1703 the colonial missionary tour of the ex-Quaker George Keith was part of a scheme developed by Keith and the S.P.G. founder, Thomas Bray, to

[2] Bruce Steiner, "Anglican Officeholding in Pre-Revolutionary Connecticut: The Parameters of New England Community," *William and Mary Quart.*, 3d ser., 31 (1974): pp. 369–406; John Callam, *Parsons and Pedagogues: The S.P.G. Adventure in American Education* (New York, 1971), pp. 189–192; William M. Hogue, "The Religious Conspiracy Theory of the American Revolution: Anglican Motive," *Church History* 45 (1976), pp. 279–292; John M. Murrin, "The Legal Transformation: The Bench and Bar of Eighteenth Century Massachusetts," in: *Colonial America: Essays in Politics and Social Development*, Stanley N. Katz, ed. (Boston, 1971), pp. 415–449; John M. Murrin and Rowland Berthoff, "Feudalism, Communalism, and the Yeoman Freeholder: the American Revolution Considered as a Social Accident," *Essays on the American Revolution*, Stephen G. Kurtz and James H. Hutson, eds. (Chapel Hill, N.C. and New York, 1973), pp. 256–288.

[3] The growth in the Anglican communion is described in the following sources: Edwin S. Gaustad, *Historical Atlas of*

Religion in America (New York, 1963), pp. 6–10; C. F. Pascoe, *Two Hundred Years of the S.P.G.* (2 v., London, 1901) 2: pp. 830–831; [Josiah Pratt,] *Propaganda, being an Abstract of the Designs and Proceedings of the Incorporated Society for the Propagation of the Gospel in Foreign Parts* (2d ed., London, 1820), pp. 52–61; and Frank J. Klingberg, "The Expansion of the Anglican Church in the Eighteenth Century," *Hist. Mag. Protestant Episcopal Church* 16 (1947): pp. 292–301. Anglican activity among ethnic groups in the Delaware valley, which added significantly to their congregational strength, is described by Nelson R. Burr, "The Welsh Episcopalians of Colonial Pennsylvania and Delaware," *Hist. Mag. Protestant Episcopal Church* 8 (1939): pp. 101–122.

[4] Thomas Bray, "A Memorial Representing the Present State of Religion in the Continent of North America," *Rev. Thomas Bray, His Life and Selected Works Relating to Maryland, Fund Publications of the Maryland Hist. Soc. 27* (1901): pp. 167–168.

demonstrate how well Anglicans might succeed in America if they managed their ministers in the way Quakers did. Of course, Bray and Keith were well acquainted by the later 1690's. Even before the founding of the S.P.C.K. Keith apparently had convinced Bray that the Quaker schism he had led in Pennsylvania prefigured a massive upheaval among Friends that the new Society could exploit, and at its first meeting in 1699 the S.P.C.K. underwrote a plan that sent Keith on a two-year tour of England designed to produce so much discord among Quakers that they would flee for safety to the Anglican Church.[5]

The English scheme failed, of course. But by 1701 Keith had turned his thoughts toward America again. In September he spoke at the first S.P.G. meeting devoted to an appraisal of Anglican conditions in the colonies. Like others who offered comments there, namely Lewis Morris, a prominent West Jersey landowner and politician, and Joseph Dudley, then governor of Massachusetts, Keith told a familiar story. In the Jerseys he reported that "except in Two or Three Towns there is no face of any public worship of any sort, but People live very mean like Indians." Morris seconded this view by saying that Jersey colonists knew "no such thing as church or religion . . . they are perhaps, the most ignorant and wicked people in the world." [6] But where Morris and Dudley complained, Keith proposed that the S.P.G. solve its American problems by utilizing Quaker techniques. Faced with colonies where few ministers were employed and where no usable ecclesiastical jurisdictions then existed, Keith suggested to the S.P.G. that "such ministers as go over should not constantly reside in one place at present, but preach at several places through the whole Province, which they may safely now travel through from one end to another, with little charge or difficulty." They could speak to many people in this fashion and distribute tracts "against Swearing, Drunkenness, and Sabbath breaking," as well as books for the already divided Quakers "to persuade [them] to the Communion of the Church of England." [7]

Here was the Quaker model again, less obscure this time. Now, however, Keith also proposed to go to America himself as an S.P.G. missionary. His intent apparently was twofold: to harangue the Quakers and test Quaker ministerial techniques. Keith and Bray apparently discussed both aspects of the journey. A Bray manuscript headed "the chief stations from whence Mr. Keith may make his excursions," lists

those cities that Keith would use as centers from which to venture into the colonial countryside—Boston, New York, Philadelphia, Annapolis, and Williamsburg— and refers to some of the journeys as Keiths's "excursions against the Quakers." [8] After arriving in Boston, Keith asked the S.P.G. to appoint John Talbot, an Anglican chaplain aboard Keith's ship, as his assistant, which the Society agreed to do. Having thus reconstructed the Quaker ministerial team, Keith and Talbot headed south for New York City, stopping in Rhode Island and Connecticut to debate Quakers and Baptists and everywhere urging their listeners to return to a Church of England now ready to serve its colonial populace.[9]

Keith's attempt to bring Quaker methods to the S.P.G.'s task became especially obvious in New York. He dominated a ministerial conference organized there by Francis Nicholson, governor of Virginia and sometime patron of the colonial Church.[10] As usual, the conference report suggested that Anglican congregations and ministers still were faring poorly in America. But it also contained a long and unusual section entitled "How Quakers and others support their Meetings and Schools." This obviously came from Keith. Never mentioning the "others," the section named twenty-four ways by which Friends prospered in America. They established meetings "in all places where they can find access." They kept ecclesiastical order "by their having George Fox's Orders and Canons duly and orderly read." They reinforced doctrinal orthodoxy by spreading thousands of Quaker books among their members, "dispersing them at cheap rates." They also kept trade "within themselves" and imposed a "strict correspondence and Intelligence over all parts where they are." The result was a complex but highly integrated model of spiritual and secular cohesiveness that Anglicans could well emulate.

The greatest envy of the Anglican clergymen was directed toward the Quaker handling of the Public Friends. English and American Quakers contributed liberally to a fund that financed visits from "great numbers of Missionaries yearly from England." These ministers, together with those in America, efficiently advanced Quaker interests and discipline. Quakers even managed the secular careers of the Public Friends. Ministers were advanced "into a way of Trade, especially Merchandizing," so that "many poor

---

[5] *A Chapter in English Church History: Being the Minutes of the Society for Promoting Christian Knowledge . . . 1698–1704,* Edmund McClure, ed. (London, 1888), pp. 18, 24, 27, 28, 30, 31, 53, 58, 72, 87, 92.

[6] Lewis Morris's comments are in SPG MSS., Journal, Appendix A, no. 2; the comments by Dudley and Keith are printed in *CPEHS,* pp. xi–xv.

[7] CPEHS, p. xii.

[8] SPG MSS., Journal, 21 February 1701/02; Bray Papers, Sion College MSS., p. 323, Library of Congress microfilm copy at University of California, Los Angeles; H. P. Thompson, *Thomas Bray* (London, 1954), pp. 72–74.

[9] Ethyn W. Kirby, *George Keith (1638–1716)* (New York, 1942), pp. 125–135.

[10] *Ibid.,* pp. 135–136; John Talbot called the gathering "a sort of Convocation." See his letter to Richard Gillingham, 24 November, 1702, in Edgar L. Pennington, *Apostle of New Jersey, John Talbot, 1645–1727* (Philadelphia, 1938), pp. 85–87.

Mechanics, Servants, and Women, that have no good way of living, pretending to the Ministry among them, [are placed] into such ways of trade and business whereby to live plentifully, by which means, many who had nothing are become rich." Could Anglicans compete with such a system? The New York ministers, or at least Keith, believed they could, "by using some of the like ways and means above mentioned, such as are lawful, proper and convenient." [11]

Whatever its exaggerations—the encouragement of the poor in the ministry being the most notable—the report demonstrated how the Quaker techniques still weighed in Keith's mind. Thus, whatever its fate in London, Keith and Talbot launched a two-year effort to demonstrate how some of them could work for Anglicans. Like the envied Public Friends, they traveled through the colonies in pursuit of converts and communicants. "G. Keith's home and mine is every where," Talbot wrote in 1703. "We have been now at our Journey's End in N. Carolina as far as we could goe, . . . Now we tak about, and start t'other way to Philadelphia again." [12] They ministered everywhere, "publickly and from house to house," and distributed countless tracts and pamphlets. Public response was overwhelmingly positive. "By these Means People are much awaken'd, and their Eyes open'd to see the good Old Way and they are very well pleased to find the Church att last take such Care of her Children." [13] Nowhere was their success more obvious than in the Jerseys. Where Lewis Morris had once described colonists there as worse than heathens, Talbot now reported that they were forming Anglican congregations.

> Mr. Keith and I have preached the Gospel to all Sorts and Conditions of Men, we have baptized Severall Scores of Men Women and Children, . . . we have gathered Several Hundreds together for the Church of England and what is more to build houses for her service. Here are 4 or 5 going forward now in this Province and the next . . . Churches are going up amain where there were never any before.[14]

The dramatic possibilities opened by Keith's proposals and his itinerant preaching with Talbot went unrealized, however. In part the failure stemmed from the ambivalent character of the Anglican admiration of Quakerism. Coupled with envy was the old strain of hate. This bitterness, together with Keith's hard battle for Quaker conversions in the colonies, increasingly obscured even his own achievement as an itinerant Anglican preacher. He had no success in converting orthodox Quakers and at best succeeded only among some of his old followers of 1691–1693.[15] Quaker leaders warned lesser Friends to stay away from him. When prestigous Friends did agree to debate him they cleverly engineered his embarrassment.[16] At a 1702 confrontation in Newport, Rhode Island, for example, they ridiculed his shifts from one church to another by showing the audience a new pamphlet printed by Quakers in London entitled *One Wonder More, Added to the Seven Wonders of the World. Verified in the Person of Mr. George Keith, once a Presbyterian, afterward about Thirty Years a Quaker, . . . and now an Itinerant Preacher (upon his Good Behaviour) in the Church of England: And all without Variation (as himself says) in Fundamentals.*[17] Then they departed, leaving Keith to ramble through his tiresome list of Quaker heresies and errors.

Reality slowly caught up with Keith. No massive exodus destroyed American Quakerism and Anglicans soon tired of his claims. As early as 1701 Elias Neau, later famous for his school for black slaves in New York City, told the S.P.C.K. that it had "been imposed on by the Accounts of the Conversion of Quakers." There were "but a few truly converted," Neau wrote, "and those which are live in great Remissness." [18] Keith's connections with the S.P.G. also faded after his return to England in 1704. Although the Society agreed to print a journal describing his American trip it insisted that he make deep cuts in the narrative. And in the version the S.P.G. printed, Keith treated his tour as one of epic confrontation in which he defeated Quakers from New England to the Carolinas. But it said little about the effort to demonstrate how well Quaker ministerial techniques might work for the S.P.G.[19]

---

[11] The document is printed in *CPEHS*, pp. xv–xxi. Kirby saw no special significance to the list of Quaker activities and treated it as a simple continuation of the usual Anglican complaints about Quakers. Ethyn W. Kirby, *George Keith (1638–1716)* (New York, 1942), p. 136. The document, together with Keith's journal of his American travels, also can be found in "The Journal of the Reverend George Keith 1702–1704," Edgar L. Pennington, ed., *Hist. Mag. Protestant Episcopal Church* 20 (1951): pp. 346–487.

[12] Talbot to Richard Gillingham, 8 June [1703], in: Edgar L. Pennington, *Apostle of New Jersey, John Talbot, 1645–1727* (Philadelphia, 1938), pp. 85–87.

[13] Talbot to S.P.G., 1 September, 1702, in *ibid.*, p. 95.

[14] *Ibid.*

[15] See Keith's letters printed in *CPEHS*, pp. xxi–xxxi; Ethyn W. Kirby, *George Keith (1638–1716)* (New York, 1942), pp. 138–139.

[16] *CPEHS*, pp. 18, 21. For a Quaker description of the Newport debate, see *An Account of the Life of John Richardson* (5th ed., London, 1843), pp. 104–127.

[17] (London, 1702).

[18] Quoted from the abstract of Neau's letter in: *A Chapter in English Church History: Being the Minutes of the Society for Promoting Christian Knowledge . . . 1698–1704*, Edmund McClure, ed. (London, 1888), p. 348.

[19] SPG MSS., Journal, 18 August, 1704; 15 September, 1704; 20 July, 1705; 17 August, 1705; 21 September, 1705; 17 January, 1705/06; 1 February, 1705/06; 28 February, 1705/06. Although at the end of the published journal Keith observed that "to many, our Ministry was as the sowing the Seed and Planting, who, probably, never so much as heard one orthodox Sermon Preached to them, before we came and preached among them," his comments appear as an afterthought. *CPEHS*, p. 48.

Even John Talbot, Keith's assistant, failed to advance the Quaker scheme for S.P.G. missionary labor. Although elated by his success, Talbot spent much time searching for a good town in which to settle permanently rather than developing new paths for itinerant ministers to follow.[20] As early as September, 1702, he told the S.P.G. secretary, "I have many places offer'd me but I know not where I shall settle," and when Keith left for England, Talbot moved quickly into the Anglican pulpit at Burlington in West Jersey, a congregation created in his itinerant work with Keith.[21] Thus by 1704 any possibility that the S.P.G. would utilize a Quaker model of ministerial endeavor in America had been overwhelmed by the drive to attack Quakers and by the inclination to follow traditional ministerial employment in a single congregation.

The demise of Keith's Quaker plan failed to end S.P.G. interest in spiritual reform, however. The Society's commitment to it was demonstrated again in 1706 when Bishop White Kennett collected and revised the Society's regulations for ministerial labor.[22] An elaborate selection process would catch only the most pious and learned clergymen for overseas service. It required guarantees of a formal education and numerous recommendations from bishops and ecclesiastical superiors.[23] Once chosen, clergymen were subject to rigid standards of personal behavior. Before leaving for America they were to "lodge not in any Publick House; but at some Bookseller's or in other private and Reputable Families." They should "constantly attend the standing Committee of this Society," and "employ their Time usefully; in reading Prayers, . . . in hearing others Read and Preach; or in such Studies as may tend to fit them for their Employment."[24] On route to America they were to be "remarkable Examples of Piety and Virtue to the Ships Company." The Sailors who were not known for their piety, might furnish a good introduction to colonial conditions, and the ministers could use the voyage to "Instruct, Exhort, Admonish, and Re-

prove, . . . with such Seriousness and Prudence as may gain them Reputation and Authority."

Then followed a set of thirty-one rules that became a code book for eighteenth-century S.P.G. missionaries. Describing the ministers as "good soldiers of Jesus Christ," the S.P.G. intended to prepare them for successful battle. They should become "masters in those controversies which are necessary to be understood." Their speech should be "grave and edifying; their apparel decent, and proper for a Clergyman." They should follow the liturgical calendar exactly and "excite a spirit of devotion" in their congregations. Sermons should deal with "great fundamental principles of Christianity." When instructing "Heathens and Infidels," a category that also included colonists, ministers should "begin with the principles of Natural Religion, appealing to their Reason and Conscience." Only when these principles were understood were clergymen to "show them the necessity of Revelation" and thus connect the settlers' natural religious instincts with scriptural Christianity. They should distribute tract literature and establish schools for children. These might even be operated "by the Widows of such Clergymen as shall die in those Countries," a useful but scarcely comforting thought. Finally, missionaries should write London regularly, reporting on the size of their congregations every six months and communicating "what shall be done at the Meetings of the Clergy, when settled, and whatsoever else may concern the Society."

The regulations reflected familiar concerns. But acting on them in America was difficult. The reason was simple. In England—but not in America—Anglican ministers could carry out reform programs inside legally established parishes. Although many parishes were impoverished and ecologically anachronistic (some had been created in the medieval period) they were established by law to do the business of the state's religion. In them a minister was maintained, church buildings kept clean and in good repair, and the poor and needy provided for, all through the work of a minister and lay vestry who together perceived the needs of the parish and, most important, laid the taxes to meet them.[25]

Few such parishes existed in the American colonies. Certainly none existed in the Delaware valley. In the southern colonies parishes parodied the English model, since colonists eschewed their responsibility for taxes but maximized the authority of the vestry.[26] Else-

---

[20] In 1703 Talbot told the S.P.G. secretary of one of the major benefits of traveling with Keith: "That by his free Conversation and Learn'd disputes both with his friends and enemies, I have learn't better in a year to deal with the Quakers, than I could by Several years study in the Schools." Talbot to S.P.G., 1 September, 1703, in: Edgar L. Pennington, *Apostle of New Jersey, John Talbot, 1645–1727* (Philadelphia, 1938), p. 95.

[21] Talbot to Richard Gillingham, 24 November, 1702, in *ibid.*, p. 86.

[22] These are conveniently printed in Nelson W. Rightmeyer, *The Anglican Church in Delaware* (Philadelphia, 1947), pp. 187–190.

[23] Alfred W. Newcombe, "The Appointment and Instruction of S.P.G. Missionaries," *Church History* 5 (1936): pp. 340–358, discusses this problem but fails to distinguish the early regulations from later ones.

[24] See note 22 above.

[25] Wallace Notestein, *The English People on the Eve of Colonization* (New York, 1954), pp. 240–249.

[26] H. P. Thompson, *Thomas Bray* (London, 1954), p. 15. This was especially true where the Church of England was supported by the colonial governments, a paradoxical development characteristic of Virginia, for example. See William H. Seiler, "The Anglican Parish in Virginia," *Seventeenth-Century America, Essays in Colonial History*, James M. Smith, ed. (Chapel Hill, N.C., 1959), pp. 119–142. Nelson

where they did not exist at all, at least not for Anglicans in any effective way. New York provided for tax-supported parishes in the four counties surrounding New York City, but not elsewhere, and the parishes that existed in New England were used by Congregationalists, not Anglicans.[27]

Yet Anglicans found it difficult even to write about Church affairs without referring to parishes. When describing colonial missionary work, Bishop Kennett's regulations and the S.P.G.'s early provisions for missionaries nearly always referred to parish settings for it. Only occasionally, and then often naively, did these Anglicans speak of the American peculiarities, as when Kennett acknowledged the problem of colonial ministers "whose Parishes shall be of large extent," this certainly an understatement, or when he wrote that because of the small number of ministers in the colonies missionaries might serve several contiguous parishes simultaneously and might "reside sometimes at one, sometimes at another . . . as the Necessities of the People shall require." [28]

To respond to American conditions the S.P.G. reshaped the English notion of the parish. In practice and apparently without any formal discussion, the Society discarded the English definition. Its members instead talked about the parish as a geographical area with changeable boundaries set by real and possible clerical labor. Thus the parish's most obvious sign of even simple existence became the presence of a gathered congregation, which the minister formed and struggled to maintain. In recognition of this reality the S.P.G. also expected missionaries to form additional congregations in other nearby places that the Society promised to supply with new ministers. In turn these men would repeat the process. Thus clerical vigor, which characterized Anglican reform activity in England, also became a crucial, even necessary, part of S.P.G. activity in America.[29]

Finally, the S.P.G. provided the one thing that the American parishes lacked—financing. The power to tax residents for maintaining church buildings and paying ministerial salaries—nonexistent in the Delaware valley—was supplanted by contributions from the "Noble Patrons of Religion" whose gifts to the

S.P.G. were distributed among its missionaries overseas. The support would not last forever. Bray proposed to guarantee ministerial salaries for three years. By that time the clergymen could organize their congregations and secure local support that would alleviate the Society of its responsibility, allowing it to use those funds in newer congregations the ministers had organized elsewhere.[30]

In the three decades after 1701 the number of congregations, ministers, and communicants increased dramatically in the Delaware valley. Where in 1701 only two Anglican congregations existed there, at least thirteen had been organized by 1727. New Jersey supported major congregations in Burlington, Hopewell, Salem, Elizabethtown, and Perth Amboy, and their ministers often preached in other places too, including Rahway, Newark, Piscataway, and Bristol in Pennsylvania. There were four principal congregations in Delaware, in New Castle and Appoquiminy and in Kent and Sussex counties, and small chapels in the countryside again were visited by the resident ministers. In Pennsylvania, well-established congregations existed in Philadelphia, Oxford, Radnor, Chester, and Concord, and requests for ministers were continually arriving from newly settled areas in the west.[31]

Paradoxically, this success exposed the limits of Anglican resources and increased the burdens carried by the very ministers who created it. One good example of the problem concerned travel. Where extensive journeying had long been a hallmark of the Quaker ministers, most S.P.G. clergymen viewed it as an undesirable part of the scheme for building the colonial Church. Although a few ministers believed in itinerant preaching, most thought that service in parishes other than their own was an unfortunate necessity designed to help congregations temporarily without a minister. Yet such travel often was necessary and profitable. Before 1730 two and sometimes three of the five major congregations in Pennsylvania often were without ministers and men like Evan Evans of Christ Church in Philadelphia either had to fill the empty places or see the hard-won communicants scatter. In 1707 Evans reported that in the absence of others he went "frequently to Chichester, which is 25 miles, Chester or Upland 20 miles, Maidenhead 40 . . . Concord 20, Evesham, in West Jersey, 15,

W. Rightmeyer, *Maryland's Established Church* (Baltimore, Md., 1956), pp. 14–36, 77–88.

[27] Carl Bridenbaugh, *Mitre and Sceptre: Transatlantic Faiths, Ideas, Personalities, and Politics, 1689–1775* (New York, 1962), pp. 116–121; Richard L. Bushman, *From Puritan to Yankee, Character and the Social Order in Connecticut, 1609–1765* (Cambridge, Mass., 1967), pp. 62–72.

[28] Quoted in Nelson W. Rightmeyer, *The Anglican Church in Delaware* (Philadelphia, 1947), pp. 188–189.

[29] These observations are drawn from the manner in which the S.P.G. assigned missionaries to the colonies and from Society regulations. See especially the assignment of John Brooke, which is described in SPG MSS., Journal, 2 March, 1704/5, and his letters of 20 August, 1705 and 11 October, 1706, SPG MSS., Letters, ser. A, v. 2.

[30] Thomas Bray, "A Memorial Representing the Present State of Religion in the Continent of North America," *Rev. Thomas Bray, His Life and Selected Works Relating to Maryland, Fund Publ. Maryland Hist. Soc.* 37 (Baltimore, Md., 1901): pp. 168–172.

[31] For Pennsylvania see the document printed in *Historical Collections Relating to the American Colonial Church*, William S. Perry, ed. (5 v., Hartford, Conn., 1871) 2: pp. 145–146. For New Jersey and Delaware see Nelson R. Burr, *The Anglican Church in New Jersey* (Philadelphia, 1954), pp. 46–61, and Nelson W. Rightmeyer, *The Anglican Church in Delaware* (Philadelphia, 1947), pp. 5–20, 32–36, 44–52, 68–73.

Montgomery 20, and Radnor 15 miles distant from Philadelphia." The journeys were tiring and expensive because the congregations made little contribution for his travel. But he preached anyway, "till the Society otherwise Provided for them." [32]

Unfortunately, the Society did not always provide. Between 1708 and 1709 John Talbot reported that congregations in East Jersey were "falling to the Ground for lack of looking after." "I am forced to turn itinerant agen," Talbot wrote. "The care of all the Churches from East to West Jersey is upon me." The burden was heavy and Talbot sometimes bore it cheerlessly. "I preach't the Gospel at Marble Head where the people offered to subscrib some hundreds of pounds to build a church but I have resolved to build no more Churches till there are more Ministers to serve the Churches that are buil[t]." [33] The situation was no better in 1716 when George Ross, Anglican missionary at New Castle, in Delaware, pleaded with the S.P.G. to send more missionaries. Only two were then in Pennsylvania and they could scarcely supply the congregations there. Certainly they could not proselytize among Quakers and other Dissenters. They tried their best to remedy the deficiency, but Ross told the Society that, if more ministers were not sent, "we who endure so long the heat of the day must needs give out." [34]

Even when the ministers did arrive they faced a bleak future. Although the S.P.G. received large donations and lent money out for interest, its ministerial salaries were meager. In 1720, for example, the Society expended a total of £1261 on the colonial missionaries. Even had this been divided equally among the twenty-seven men then receiving its support, each clergyman would have received less than £47 that year, not sufficient to sustain a colonial family. [35] But the salaries varied from £20 to £70 a year and even the highest figure often provided for an inadequate living. Ministers also received little additional help from their congregations. Since the congregations could not levy taxes and since the ministers presumably were being supported from London, colonists were reluctant to provide additional support of their own. The Society tried to help by intimating that no missionary would be sent without some guarantee of local support and by trying to force the congregations to build houses and furnish glebes or farmland for the ministers' use. [36] But performance on these contracts left much to be desired. At New Castle the glebe was managed by the vestry, not the minister. Elsewhere it often existed only as the title on a legal document, the land being so poor or filled with rubble and brush that it could not be farmed. [37]

Other local support was equally elusive. Promises made to London proved difficult to collect in America. The supplemental salary, usually stipulated at from £20 to £50, often never materialized or, when it did, was paid in inflated local currency or rotting produce. Thomas Jenkins wrote that while in New Castle he received "but four pieces of eight, and tho' they have promis'd to pay for my diet, yet to this day it remains unpaid." Some ministers refused even to solicit contributions from parishioners. They tired of the endless arguments over money especially because the latter so visibly reinforced the complaints of Delaware valley Quakers that the "hireling clergy" were more concerned for their own purses than for their parishioners' souls. [38] As a result, many ministers found themselves caught between the Society's instructions to be "frugal in Opposition to Luxury" and to "avoid all Appearance of Covetousness." Since they received so little by way of salary or contributions, they easily obeyed the S.P.G. injunction against extravagant living. But their requests for better salaries from London and pleas for supplemental contributions from listeners gave the appearance of greed even when many were simply trying to survive.

These problems were summarized in the experience of John Brooke. In 1705, at the age of fifty-two, Brooke secured the assistance of the Archbishop of York in arranging to serve in the colonies and the S.P.G. assigned him to preach in Shrewsbury, Amboy, Elizabeth, and Freehold in eastern New Jersey. [39] Arriving in July, 1705, he found his parish large. Most of his parishioners were of a "Presbyterian" persuasion. But he told the Society that, if it reduced the size of his parish and would "allow me enough to subsist upon without depending upon the People, . . . I shall gain a considerable Congregation in a very few

[32] [Evan Evans], "The State of the Church in Pennsylvania, most humbly offered to the Venerable Society for the Propagation of the Gospel in Foreign Parts," in: *Historical Collections Relating to the American Colonial Church,* William S. Perry, ed. (5 v., Hartford, Conn., 1871) 2: p. 33.

[33] Talbot to S.P.G., 24 August 1708, in: Edgar L. Pennington, *Apostle of New Jersey, John Talbot, 1645–1727* (Philadelphia, 1938), pp. 119–120. Talbot's struggle with ministerial problems finally drove him to accept ordination as a nonjuring bishop in 1722. *Ibid.,* pp. 66–79.

[34] George Ross to S.P.G., 28 August, 1716, in: *Historical Collections Relating to the American Colonial Church,* William S. Perry, ed. (5 v., Hartford, Conn., 1871) 2: p. 101.

[35] See the chart of financial expenditures and numbers of missionaries in the colonies in [Josiah Pratt], *Propaganda, Being an Abstract of the Designs and Proceedings of the Society for the Propagation of the Gospel in Foreign Parts* (2d ed., London, 1820), pp. 52–55.

[36] Nelson R. Burr, *The Anglican Church in New Jersey* (Philadelphia, 1954), pp. 128–136.

[37] *Ibid.* Nelson W. Rightmyer, *The Anglican Church in Delaware* (Philadelphia, 1947), pp. 122, 138.

[38] Nelson W. Rightmyer, *The Anglican Church in Delaware* (Philadelphia, 1947), p. 125; Edgar L. Pennington, *Apostle of New Jersey, John Talbot, 1645–1727* (Philadelphia, 1938), p. 89. When Christ Church had no minister in 1718 visiting clergymen refused to be paid for their preaching. Minutes, Christ Church Vestry, 3 April, 2 May, 1718, Christ Church Neighborhood House, Philadelphia.

[39] SPG MSS., Journal, 2 March, 1704/5.

years." [40] Within a year Brooke was doubtful about even this mission. He had just received Bishop Kennett's instructions for the missionaries and he told London that he would be hard pressed to fulfill even one of its simplest demands, "vizt. to give you an Account of the Number of my Parishioners and their Way of Worship." He preached in seven places, his parish was over fifty miles in length, "and the Number of People is so great and their ways of Worship so many that I cannot yet give you a particular Account of them." Although he had been told that his parishioners looked forward to his arrival and would contribute £50 a year to supplement his S.P.G. salary, these promises were never fulfilled. "Instead of a Body of Church People to maintain me, I only met with a small handfull the most of which cou'd hardly maintain themselves much less Build Churches or Maintain me." By 1706 he had overcome some of these difficulties. A few of the towns he served were willing to erect church buildings, and his following had increased. But now, almost destitute, he heard that the Society intended to cut his salary. He reminded the S.P.G. that he had supported himself with personal funds and used S.P.G. moneys to contribute toward the construction of the church buildings. But he could have done neither "had not I been very well Stocked with Cloaths I brought from England." Neither could he continue his work on the Society's meager salary.

I ride so much I'm obliged to keep two Horses which cost me £20 and one horse cannot be kept well under £10 or £11 per year. It will cost a Man near £30 [per year] to Board here and sure 'twill cost me much more, who Pilgrim like, can scarce ever be three days together at a place. All Cloathing here is twice as dear at least as 'tis in England; and riding so much makes me wear out many more than I ever did before.

If the Society did not supply him with adequate funding, Brooke wrote that "I shall be much more capable, I believe of promoting the Glory of God in England than here, with a narrow precarious allowance, where to ask [for] any thing yet wou'd be a means to deter people from joyning with me, and wou'd be looked upon as oppression." Receiving no further encouragement from the Society, in 1707 Brooke left New Jersey to return to England. But he never arrived there because his ship was lost in an Atlantic storm.[41]

It is true that the distance between America and London sometimes made the S.P.G. an inflexible instrument of clerical reform and authority. Letters often took two or three months to arrive—sometimes, as in John Brooke's case, six months—and ministers continually feared that the correspondence demanded of them as well as their pay vouchers would be lost, mislaid, or sunk in the Atlantic. But historians have overemphasized these difficulties. In fact, it was the Society's own demands that often created major problems in administration. The reformed glances cast overseas from London sometimes became stiffnecked and unbending when implemented in America. For example, the S.P.G. disapproved of the movement of missionaries from one parish to another without prior approval from London. But this policy did not always work well, especially when missionaries thought the move would benefit everyone, including the congregations they intended to serve as well as those they were leaving. As a result, the Society became privy to disputes over lost or misunderstood correspondence, missing payments, confusion over instructions, and arguments about the duties of both clergymen and congregations. As it tried to adjudicate these disputes the welter of accusations flowing toward London only increased.

That these conflicts undermined S.P.G. programs is well illustrated by a Pennsylvania affair that dragged on between 1708 and 1716. In 1708 the congregation at Chester just south of Philadelphia was left without a minister when its pastor, Henry Nichols, moved to Maryland. To restore services there the Chester vestry asked George Ross, then at New Castle, to fill the vacancy, an invitation Ross accepted after consulting with Anglican laymen in Philadelphia, all of whom approved the move. In turn, the New Castle vestry began to search for a minister. They asked Thomas Jenkins to leave Appoquiminy, a small country parish, for New Castle. When Jenkins moved, the Appoquiminy vestry complained to the S.P.G. in London that Jenkins had violated his S.P.G. instructions by leaving for New Castle.

Other complaints soon followed. Disaffected persons at Chester wrote that Ross had forced Nichols to leave for Maryland in order to obtain the Chester position himself. This charge was supported by John Talbot, Keith's old associate and the new minister at Burlington. Tired of ministerial conniving over positions and fearing that such behavior was destroying the work which had been accomplished in the middle colonies, Talbot told the S.P.G. that Ross was a "wandering star" who was best "confined to some place where there is need," but not at Chester. In response, the S.P.G. stopped payment on Ross's and Jenkins's salaries and ordered Ross to sail for London to explain his behavior. After many interviews in London, Ross was exonerated. But the Society nonetheless returned him to New Castle to demonstrate its authority over the American missionaries. Unfor-

[40] Brooke to S.P.G., 20 August, 1705, SPG MSS., Letters, ser. A, v. 2.

[41] Brooke to S.P.G., 11 October, 1706, SPG MSS., Letters, ser. A, v. 3. Brooke's bitterness was strengthened by letters he had received from the Archbishop of York detailing the Society's promises of support and which he quoted in his letter to London. A brief biography of Brooke is in Nelson R. Burr, *The Anglican Church in New Jersey* (Philadelphia, 1954), pp. 587–588.

tunately Ross's ship was captured by the French while heading for America and he did not arrive back in New Castle until 1712, meaning that he was absent from New Castle for over three years. Not even this delay marked the end of the affair. When Ross returned to Delaware his fellow ministers asked the S.P.G. to pay him a bounty for enduring the rigors of captivity. Although their request was approved, the monies were not paid until 1716, four years later. Yet no one protested. The clergymen had learned to wait.[42]

Delaware valley Anglicans also were penalized by the Church's success elsewhere. As the eighteenth century progressed, the established churches of Virginia and Maryland offered attractive clerical livings to ministers serving in Pennsylvania, New Jersey, and Delaware. The relatively secure and high salaries acted like a magnet to clergymen tired of competing with Quakers or fussing with the S.P.G. Thus John Talbot told the Society in 1718 that "all your Missioners here about are going to Maryland . . . for the sake of themselves[,] their wives and children." [43] This had happened before, but Talbot was especially worried now because the latest to depart was Philadelphia's Evan Evans, the most distinguished Anglican clergyman in the Delaware valley. To Talbot, Evans's move summarized the Anglican difficulties there. Evans was tired of worrying about money and discipline. "He says no body will serve the Church for Nought," and was heading for Maryland. This occurrence did little to promote public confidence in Anglican promises, and was made even more devastating by the fact that, as Talbot expressed it, the S.P.G. still was "not able for their parts to send Bishops, priests nor Deacon nor Techures [sic] nor Catechist" in sufficient numbers anywhere.[44]

It is not surprising then that the S.P.G. program for reformed clerical labor met with only variable success. For example, Bishop Kennett's 1706 regulations encouraged missionaries to establish religious societies in their congregations. But their existence usually depended on peculiarly fortunate circumstances. When Philadelphia's Christ Church unexpectedly found itself with two ministers in 1704, the young assistant clergyman, John Thomas, collected a group of laymen to form such a society to read Scripture and hear sermons every Sunday evening. "We

Discover'd a visible Benefitt from Our evening Lectures," his superior, Evan Evans, wrote. "For those Quakers, that Durst not appear in the day at the Publiq Service of the Church, for fear of disobligeing their Parents or Masters[,] would stand under the Church windows at night, till many of them pluck't up so much Courage, as to come to the Church it selfe." But the Society apparently disbanded when Thomas left Philadelphia.[45] Few other congregations were even this fortunate. A Society for the Reformation of Manners was formed in Kent County, Delaware, by Thomas Crawford in 1708, but apparently was abandoned after Crawford was himself accused of bigamy and had to defend himself before the S.P.G. in London in 1710; and while John Talbot acknowledged in 1704 that the religious societies and the S.P.G. had secured "more Reputation to the Church and Nation of England abroad" than many other forms of Anglican activity, he apparently never established the societies in his own congregation at Burlington.[46]

This did not mean that missionaries failed to instruct or catechize. They did. But most found their work frustrating. Their effort to instill even rudimentary Church doctrine in listeners proved difficult. Worse, wider objectives were lost in the narrow quest for conversion. Ministers commonly reported that their communicants, especially former Quakers, were so ignorant of fundamental Christian doctrine that little could be done to reform their personal lives until their intellects had been cleansed of heresy. The search for morality was dominated by a simple-minded catechizing in which ministers propounded narrow questions to their listeners, while these students, many of them adult communicants, responded by parroting short answers cribbed from a small lesson book.[47]

Worse than this, the missionaries' financial straits and insecurities encouraged some ministers simply to preach and pray and to slight their active involvement in the S.P.G. schedule of reform clerical activity. In

[42] The affair is described in Nelson W. Rightmeyer, The Anglican Church in Delaware (Philadelphia, 1947), pp. 9–12, and in the letters printed in Historical Collections Relating to the American Colonial Church, William S. Perry, ed. (5 v., Hartford, Conn., 1871) 5: pp. 7–16, 19–26.

[43] Talbot to S.P.G., 3 May, 1718, in: Edgar L. Pennington, Apostle of New Jersey, John Talbot, 1645–1727 (Philadelphia, 1938), p. 145.

[44] Ibid. Talbot told the S.P.G. that he never would have encouraged settlers to build churches—"Nay Now they Must be Stalls for Quakers Horses"—had he known the Society would be so lax in sending missionaries.

[45] [Evan Evans], "The State of the Church in Pennsylvania, most humbly offered to the Venerable Society for the Propagation of the Gospel in Foreign Parts," in: Historical Collections Relating to the American Colonial Church, William S. Perry, ed. (5 v., Hartford, Conn., 1871) 2: p. 34.

[46] Edgar L. Pennington, Apostle of New Jersey, John Talbot, 1645–1727 (Philadelphia, 1938), p. 97; Nelson W. Rightmeyer, The Anglican Church in Delaware (Philadelphia, 1947), pp. 46–49; Thomas Crawford to S.P.G., 31 August, 1708, in: Historical Collections Relating to the American Colonial Church, William S. Perry, ed. (5 v., Hartford, Conn., 1871) 5: p. 18.

[47] John Callam, Parsons and Pedagogues: The S.P.G. Adventure in American Education (New York, 1971), pp. 43, 95, 103–104; [George Ross to S.P.G.], 30 December, 1712, in: Historical Collections Relating to the American Colonial Church, William S. Perry, ed. (5 v., Hartford, Conn., 1871) 2: p. 70. Nelson W. Rightmeyer, The Anglican Church in Delaware (Philadelphia, 1947), pp. 158–160; Nelson R. Burr, The Anglican Church in New Jersey (Philadelphia, 1954), pp. 180–184.

1707 Thorogood Moore, a former Cambridge scholar sent first to minister among the Indians at Albany, then to Burlington while John Talbot made a trip to England, was thrown into prison by New York Governor Robert Cornbury after refusing to administer communion to Cornbury's lieutenant governor, Richard Ingoldsby. The refusal resulted from Moore's effort to censure Ingoldsby's lewd behavior and the entire episode apparently terrified Delaware valley ministers for a decade.[48] Later, in 1710, William Black, Anglican clergyman in Lewes, Delaware, tried to solicit contributions from his listeners while instructing them in the ideals of Christian behavior. But he found the effort impossible; "For while the Minister depends upon the Precarious Contribucion of a very poor People for the greatest part of his salary, he is forced either to Connive at many of their irregular actions or to lose the next Years Subscription of every one he displeaseth by reproving their Vices." [49]

Of course, many historians have believed that among Anglicans the failures of individual clergymen were especially important in determining the Church's fate in America. The stereotyped Anglican missionary— drunken, ill-educated, morally loose, and spiritually indifferent, but too insecure to feign the haughtiness of the Anglican clerics in Fielding's *Tom Jones*—simply has no parallel in the historical literature of other early American denominations. In fact, the description makes good reading but poor history. Among Anglicans, minister after minister preached, catechized, taught reading and writing (often because they needed the fees such work brought), and visited the sick with steady regularity. When neighboring parishes stood empty their duties only multiplied. Indeed, colonial clergymen may have served with greater distinction than did those who remained in England. Men like Evan Evans and John Talbot, for example, brought enormous reforming energy to their American work. Of course, this is not to deny that some clerics acted shamefully. The drunken John Urmstone, for example, blotched the reputation of Philadelphia's Christ Church in the 1720's. Worse, his behavior marked the second major scandal in a decade for that congregation, since in 1715 the Reverend Francis Phillips brought gleeful mobs into the city's streets after he told friends that he had "debauched three chief Gentlewomen" in the city.[50] Yet the Urmstones and Phillipses were rare. Certainly they were no more

scandalous than some Presbyterian and Baptist ministers. And if the remainder of the missionaries did not always meet the standards set by Evans and Talbot, they were nonethless loyal and industrious men living on small salaries and overburdened with work.

Why then did the Anglican mission fail? Were Anglicans too obsessed with Old World habits of government? Were they too needful of hierarchical institutions? Were they too undemocratic? If so, how can we then explain the success of the Quakers, Presbyterians, and even Baptists. Rather, in a comparative and eighteenth-century context, the cause related to the Anglican inability to establish the kind of non-democratic, hierarchical institutions that created order for them in England and were doing so in America for Quakers and Presbyterians.

Despite the presence of good ministers, a program of reformed clerical labor and the S.P.G., no Anglican institutions paralleled the meetings Quakers, Baptists, and Presbyterians established in America to handle problems of ministry, order, and even drunkenness. Anglican ministers sometimes held clerical conventions in the Delaware valley that superficially resembled the Quaker, Baptist, and Presbyterian denominational gatherings. Bishop Kennett's 1706 regulations had required the ministers to report on these meetings. In 1724 missionaries from Pennsylvania, New Jersey, and Delaware told London that they gathered "twice a year for Brotherly correspondence" and that these meetings included sermons delivered for the benefit of the gathered clergy and discussions of the ministers' parish problems.[51]

The Anglican meetings never emerged as continuing bodies, however. They possessed no authority, never assumed any, and never received any. Indeed, before 1730 they were held only fitfully, usually in response to some immediate crisis which the ministers could describe but were powerless to resolve. Thus Delaware valley Anglican ministers met in 1704 and 1705, apparently abandoned the meetings until 1711, met again in 1712 and 1713, met twice in 1714, then allowed the meetings to fall into neglect until 1721 or 1722 when they were revived in the fashion mentioned above in the report of 1724.[52]

---

[48] Nelson R. Burr, *The Anglican Church in New Jersey* (Philadelphia, 1954), pp. 625–627; Edgar L. Pennington, *Apostle of New Jersey, John Talbot, 1645–1727* (Philadelphia, 1938), pp. 45–48, 58.
[49] Quoted in Nelson W. Rightmyer, *The Anglican Church in Delaware* (Philadelphia, 1947), p. 125.
[50] Robert Jenney to S.P.G., 4 January, 1715, in: *Historical Collections Relating to the American Colonial Church*, William S. Perry, ed. (5 v., Hartford, Conn., 1871) 2: p. 81. The

Pennsylvania clergymen refused to present Phillips for prosecution by the Philadelphia magistrates "to prevent the disgrace that must needs fall upon their Sacred Order." John Talbot *et al.* to S.P.G., 17 March, 1714, in *ibid.* 2: p. 86; Minutes, Christ Church Vestry, 11 May, 1723; 6 August, 1723; 29 October, 1723, Christ Church Neighborhood House, Philadelphia.
[51] Robert Weyman *et al.*, to the Bishop of London, [1724], in: *Historical Collections Relating to the American Colonial Church*, William S. Perry, ed. (5 v., Hartford, Conn., 1871) 2: pp. 136–137; Nelson W. Rightmyer, *The Anglican Church in Delaware* (Philadelphia, 1947), pp. 187–190.
[52] Notices of the meetings are found in many sources. Among them are *Historical Collections Relating to the American Colonial Church*, William S. Perry, ed. (5 v., Hartford, Conn.,

Under the guidance of a reform-minded bishop the clerical meetings might have blossomed into dynamic gatherings that would have paralleled the Dissenting denominational meetings. But instead they only produced a monotonous series of reports complaining about conditions in America. In them the ministers fussed about the lack of missionaries, that they were forced into arduous journeys to vacant parishes which obliged them to neglect their responsibilities at home, that their salaries were low, that their congregations offered them little supplemental income, that they were plagued by Quakers and other well-organized Dissenters, that communications from England were irregular, and that the S.P.G. failed to comprehend conditions in America.[53]

Of course, the main complaint concerned the absence of a bishop in America. Nearly every missionary pointed to the correlation between the lack of a bishop and the chaos reigning among American Anglicans. If the S.P.G. wondered why American missionaries demanded "the Constant Residence of a Mitred head among them," Evan Evans offered a simple reason as early as 1707:

I take it for granted, that the Ends of the Mission can never be rightly answered without Establishing the Discipline, as well as the Doctrine of the Church of England in those parts; For the One is a Fortress and Bulwark of Defence to the other, and once the Outworks of Religion come to be slighted and dismantled it is easy to foresee without the spirit of Prophecy what the Consequence will be.[54]

And by "discipline" he meant institutions of ecclesiastical authority. The S.P.G. could furnish books and missionaries. But only a bishop could force missionaries to "doe their duty, and to live in Peace and Unity among themselves or with the populace." Only a bishop could force communicants to observe Christian behavior and to "pay a greater Regard to their Spirituall Guides." And only a bishop could make everyone "submit to Church Discipline, and Censures, without which, tho' a church may be planted, and gathered, yet it can never be of any long Growth or Continuance."

The desperate call for a bishop reflected the tragedy

of the S.P.G. endeavor in the Delaware valley. In significant ways, especially in the number of ministers and congregations, Anglican worship obviously prospered there. Ministers did not always stay in their proper "parishes," they were not always well supported by their congregations, and they sometimes lost listeners to Presbyterian or Baptist preachers. But certainly by 1730 the sight of enlarged numbers of parishioners in more and more congregations was as common for Anglicans as it was for Dissenters.

Yet no Anglican Church existed in the Delaware valley because for Anglicans, as for Dissenters, the Church was more than ministers and lay men and women gathered together for worship. As Evan Evans had put it in 1707, the Anglican Church was a true place of worship only when it also acted as an organ of spiritual and ecclesiastical discipline activated by a bishop. All these elements, not just a few of them, had to be present. As John Talbot put it, paraphrasing James I, the colonies needed a bishop so "that we allso may be a Church; for I count, No Bishop no Church, as true as No Bishop no King."[55]

In this context the S.P.G. proved unable to fulfill all the roles it eventually assumed. It had been organized by English reformers. These men worked within an ancient Church which they intended to change, not leave, and they enjoyed the Church's institutional security even as they reformed it. But in the Delaware valley no Church existed, not even a miserably imperfect one. Only congregations, ministers, communicants, and the S.P.G. were to be found there. Thus the S.P.G. could not function as an agent of church reform because the object to be reformed did not exist there. And it could not function as the Church itself because it was not. It was only a voluntary society managed by reforming bishops and ministers.

This impasse never was broken. Year after year, from 1700 to 1730, then on to 1776, missionaries thanked the Society for its aid, then asked for a bishop. Like Evan Evans and John Talbot, they argued that neither reform nor Anglicanism could prosper where no bishop, and hence no Church, existed. All these pleas failed. Sometimes success seemed imminent. In 1713 the Society purchased a home for a bishop in Burlington, New Jersey. But the death of Queen Anne in 1715 brought the scheme to an end.[56] By the time success again seemed possible in the 1770's, the effort to obtain a bishop would be viewed by many colonists as part of a sinister plot to impose British tyranny on the American settlements.

The result was ironic. In England, parishioners

1871) 2: pp. 62–63, 69–73, 122–125, 131–133, 155, 173–174, 508; 5: pp. 40, 49; "Journal of Rev. John Sharpe," *Penna. Mag. History and Biography* 40 (1916): pp. 261–266, 291, 421, 423, 425; Nelson R. Burr, *The Anglican Church in New Jersey* (Philadelphia, 1954), pp. 282–285; Nelson W. Rightmyer, *The Anglican Church in Delaware* (Phliadelphia, 1947), pp. 174–175; Edgar L. Pennington, *Apostle of New Jersey, John Talbot, 1645–1727* (Philadelphia, 1938), pp. 38–40, 101, 107, 126. See also the article by Pennington, "Colonial Clergy Conventions," *Hist. Mag. Protestant Episcopal Church* 8 (1939): pp. 179–189.

[53] These are frequently printed in all the volumes of *Historical Collections Relating to the American Colonial Church*, William S. Perry, ed. (5 v., Hartford, Conn., 1871).

[54] Evan Evans to S.P.G., 18 September, 1717, in *ibid.* 2: pp. 37–39.

[55] Talbot to S.P.G., 1 September, 1703, in Edgar L. Pennington, *Apostle of New Jersey, John Talbot, 1645–1727* (Philadelphia, 1938), p. 96.

[56] Nelson R. Burr, *The Anglican Church in New Jersey* (Philadelphia, 1954), pp. 340–344.

complained about a Church lax in worship and devoid of spiritual sensitivity. While bishops and ministers in rich parishes prospered, in other parishes faith waned and slid toward a humdrum calendar of services led by the competent and incompetent alike. Yet in the Delaware valley a decent Anglican worship and even some reforming activity existed despite the inherent weaknesses of the S.P.G., problems with individual ministers, or the absence of a bishop. Faith there was not always more vigorous than at home. Certainly it never reflected any universal success in applying the S.P.G.'s reform program. But the growing number of ministers, congregations, and communicants meant that larger numbers of settlers increasingly found satisfaction with Anglican worship and willingly became Anglican communicants and parishioners. This success, which was all the more spectacular because it accumulated steadily, then produced its own strange drama. Increasingly after 1701 colonists in the Delaware valley saw more and more Anglican ministers and congregations. Some of them worried about the work of the S.P.G. Others wondered what the Anglican ministers were doing in their occasional clerical meetings. But they never saw an Anglican Church established there. At best they only witnessed the labor of reforming ministers whose salaries were paid by a voluntary reforming society. Thus it was England's Anglicans rather than its Dissenters who were forced to colonize America without the aid of their Old World institutions, and who paid a heavy price for their bravery.

VII. CONCLUSION:

THE ORIGINS AND CHARACTER OF EARLY AMERICAN DENOMINATIONAL ORDER

We began this study with a simple observation. For a long time historians of American religion have emphasized the democratic roots of American religious life—democracy in the congregations, revivalism in the pulpit, and common-sense morality in theology. To test the accuracy of these views it seemed useful to look at the evolution of denominational order among the four English Protestant groups that settled in the Delaware valley before 1730. The plan offered two main benefits. First, it would allow for a real comparative examination of patterns in early American denominational authority. The Delaware valley was the institutional home of three of the five English Protestant groups active in the colonies—Quakers, Baptists, and Presbyterians—and the scene of intense proselytization by Anglicans. Only Congregationalists were absent there. Second, the Delaware valley offered fertile ground for the growth of democracy in church government. Its colonial governments supported Christianity in a general way by requiring public officials to proclaim their belief in Jesus in order

to hold public office.[1] But they also upheld voluntary principles in their dealings with Christian groups. None of them taxed colonists to support state churches and none of them imprisoned Christians for their religious beliefs. Finally, since the Delaware valley's religious history before the Great Awakening was less well known than that of other places, and since it never had been studied comparatively, it seemed that such a study might clarify some broad issues in American religious history while contributing to an understanding of the history of each group separately.

The results suggest that we turn away from the stress historians have traditionally placed on the rise of democracy and the consequent importance of laymen in colonial American religious affairs. In the Delaware valley English Protestants shaped a history before the Great Awakening in which only ministers, or ministers and but small numbers of laymen, consistently managed religious affairs. These colonists sustained rather than rejected the hierarchical patterns of church government they brought with them from home. In England, ministers had dominated religious reform and denominational organization from the rise of the early Puritan movement in the 1580's to the rebirth of Anglican reform a century later. They did so through ministerial meetings, like those of the First Publishers of Truth, the Scottish presbyteries, or the English Baptist assemblies. These meetings survived difficult times in the Old World and were successfully transplanted in the New.

Of course, not all English religious groups found success in the Delaware valley. The Church of England failed to prosper there despite the fact that it was England's state church and that these were England's colonies. Sometimes the failure is taken to support the theory that the state church tradition common to England was unsuited to American conditions.[2] This probably was not true, although the Delaware valley is a poor testing ground for this suggestion because no state-supported churches existed there. Nonetheless, in the northern and southern colonies the state-supported churches always had larger followings than did their competitors and their inability to prevent the growth of Dissenters was no more marked than that of the Anglican Church at home. Thus the state church tradition probably fared no worse in the colonies outside the Delaware valley than it did in eighteenth-century England itself.

More to the point is the fact that the Anglican failure also is wrongly taken to demonstrate that institutions built on non-democratic, hierarchical models were anachronistic in America and doomed to failure there.

---

[1] Anson P. Stokes, *Church and State in the United States* (2 v., New York, 1950) 1: p. 168.
[2] The general view is best expressed in Daniel J. Boorstin, *The Americans: The Colonial Experience* (New York, 1958), pp. 123–139.

Such a conclusion would have shocked American Quakers and Presbyterians. It was an English meeting system developed and sustained by a minority of Friends, not a more open "American" one, that sustained Quaker order in the Delaware valley. Similarly, Presbyterian denominational order emerged out of a clerical cohesion created in the early Presbytery of Philadelphia, not out of the activity or agitation of laymen. Even after 1730, when Presbyterian ministers divided bitterly over theology, they still defended their mastery of the Presbyterian order. In 1735 they condemned Philadelphia's Samuel Hemphill for cribbing his sermons from the published works of others. Many years later Benjamin Franklin flippantly observed in his *Autobiography* that he had "rather approved of [Hemphill's] giving us good Sermons composed by others, [rather] than bad ones of his own manufacture." But Hemphill's colleagues acted because they worried that "wolves in sheep's clothing are invading the flocks of Christ every where in the world"; their description of the shepherds who should stand guard not only expressed their own views but those of Quakers and even Baptists: "We who are pastors by office and station should exert ourselves in an active and vigilant manner for the safety and preservation of our flocks committed to our care, [to protect them] from the assaults of those devouring monsters that are numerous abroad in the world." [3]

Laymen seldom challenged this ministerial domination. The Keithian schism among Quakers failed despite significant signs of discontent with some Public Friends before 1692 and George Keith's trenchant criticism of them afterwards. The later rise of weighty Friends in Quaker church government did little to change the Quakers' oligarchic habits. Weighty Friends usually served long terms as overseers and elders and were appointed, not elected, so that Quaker leadership remained in the hands of only a few Friends. Elsewhere the story was much the same. Rather than seeking power themselves, Baptist and Presbyterian laymen sought leadership from their Association and Presbytery. And why not? True, the record of these gatherings never was perfect. The Philadelphia Baptist Association never secured enough pastors to serve all the congregations that wanted them, and the Philadelphia Synod sometimes censured erring ministers so lightly that its action seemed to sanction the drunkeness, womanizing, or indolence of which the ministers had been accused.

But what happened when laymen acted alone? Here the record was abysmal. When the disgruntled Presbyterian congregation at Cohansey hired a minister without consulting the Presbytery, it had to turn to the Presbytery for help after the man proved

incompetent. And when Piscataway Baptists ordained the bigamist Desolate Baker (or Henry Loveall, as he sometimes called himself) without waiting for advice from the Philadelphia Baptist Association, its foolish behavior only substantiated the Association's claim that it provided careful leadership for Baptists willing to listen. As a result, for both laymen and ministers denominational order in the Delaware valley meant following the judgments issued from regularized meetings of those involved in the ministry, whether Quaker, Baptist, or Presbyterian.

The ministerial cast of this early denominational order does make it more difficult to explain the later evolution of American denominationalism, however. Historians are almost unanimous in the judgment that nineteenth-century American religion eagerly matched the enthusiastic democracy of secular society. Yet our attention has been riveted upon these democratic features for so long that we have paid relatively little attention to other possibilities. For example, while we know a great deal about popular revivalism between the election of Jackson and the coming of the Civil War, we know very little about clerical professionalism, the actual exercise of power in the Protestant denominations, or any connection between these subjects. [4] It may be that the kind of examination made here of seventeenth- and eighteenth-century patterns might reveal new facets of American religious life if applied to the nineteenth century.

In the meantime, our work here should help us understand some problems in colonial American religion. One of them concerns the Great Awakening. In the last several decades the Awakening has come to be viewed as both a symptom and cause of enormous social and political upheaval in the colonies. [5] With colonists everywhere turning out to hear the Anglican itinerant George Whitefield and thousands more forming new congregations that upset the old religious order, the Awakening offers fertile ground for the joint study of religious and social history. Yet historians have written too broadly about the

---

[3] *RCP*, p. 118; *The Autobiography of Benjamin Franklin* Leonard W. Labaree *et al.*, eds. (New Haven, 1964), pp. 167–168.

[4] Timothy L. Smith, *Revivalism and Social Reform in Mid-Nineteenth Century America* (New York, 1957); Alice F. Tyler, *Freedom's Ferment: Phases of American Social History to 1860* (Minneapolis, Minn., 1944). Works that describe the changing concepts of the nineteenth-century ministerial profession include Daniel H. Calhoun, *Professional Lives in America: Structure and Aspiration, 1750–1850* (Cambridge, Mass., 1965), pp. 88–177, and Burton J. Bledstein, *The Culture of Professionalism: The Middle Class and the Development of Higher Education in America* (New York, 1976), pp. 171–178.

[5] Two interesting views on this subject are Richard Bushman, *From Puritan to Yankee: Character and the Social Order in Connecticut, 1690–1765* (Cambridge, Mass., 1967), pp. 164–290, and Rhys Isaac, "Evangelical Revolt: The Nature of the Baptists' Challenge to the Traditional Order in Virginia, 1765 to 1775," *William and Mary Quart.*, 3d ser., 31 (1974): pp. 134–368.

Great Awakening as an event with common characteristics in all the colonies.

Among the Delaware valley's English settlers the Awakening touched only the Presbyterians in a profound way and its social impact never equaled that of the New England Awakening. It is true, as Martin Lodge has recently argued, that part of its cause lay in a shortage of ministers that prompted some ministers to question the classical training demanded by the Philadelphia Synod.[6] But if an awakening came in response to a paucity of ministers, ministers created the awakening—laymen did not—and they never allowed it to undermine their place in the Presbyterian system. However much tinged with democratic rhetoric, the Presbyterian awakening in the Delaware valley distinguished itself by the way laymen listened while clergymen preached. It was no egalitarian dance of the Holy Spriit. Instead, it was a careful (and sometimes not so careful) performance orchestrated and conducted by ordained Presbyterian ministers. It was a logical extension of the long-brewing dispute over ministerial discipline and behavior that began in the Synod of Philadelphia in the 1720's and which finally centered two decades later on the demand that a ministerial candidate present evidence of grace before his ordination. This last demand did not attack the ministry. Nor did it come from laymen. Instead, the proposal was sponsored by clergymen who sought to enlarge the ministry by purifying it. It was Gilbert Tennent, himself an ordained minister and son of a minister, who in 1734 offered the resolution to the Synod that expressed concern "with respect to the trials of candidates, both for the ministry and the Lord's Supper, that there be due care taken in examining into the evidences of the grace of God in them, as well as of their other necessary qualifications." And it was Tennent's famous sermon on *The Danger of an Unconverted Ministry* that became and remained the central document of the Presbyterian awakening in the Delaware valley[7]

In this context those who made the Presbyterian awakening in the Delaware valley still were acting within the familiar boundaries of ministerial dominance in Dissenting religion. Their understanding of the origins of a religious renewal among laymen was remarkably similar to Richard Baxter's in the 1650's. Like Baxter, they believed that religious reform depended on clergymen. Without clergymen there would be no Word and without the Word laymen could not understand God. Supporters of the

Awakening thus strengthened the ministers' position in the congregation because they linked the broadening of Christian commitment firmly to ministerial leadership.

In addition, neither Presbyterian supporters nor opponents of the Awakening emphasized anti-institutional themes. When members of the Synod of Philadelphia divided in 1741, opponents of the Awakening remained in the old Synod while backers of the Awakening formed the new Synod of New York. Both synods continued to uphold clerical discipline and to sustain a denominational order for the laymen that followed them, so that while some ministers abandoned one synod for another they never abandoned institutions and institutional authority.[8]

In a different vein, the lack of an awakening elsewhere reflects consistent themes in the development of Baptist, Quaker, and Anglican history. The failure of Delaware valley Baptists to participate in it, which distinguished them from their New England counterparts, can be traced in good part to their caution in finding pastors for their congregations. In the late 1730's and 1740's the Philadelphia Baptist Association still centered much of its activity on the search for preaching ministers. However logical a lay awakening might have been, especially one that involved a return to the egalitarian ministry practiced in the Commonwealth period, it did not occur. Having warned congregations for three decades about the danger of allowing untested laymen to preach, it is not surprising to find the Association continuing to exercise this caution long after 1730.[9]

The Quaker reaction to an awakening also was reflective of the Friends' denominational development in the previous half-century. Some Quakers genuinely applauded the various awakenings stirring in the English-speaking world in the 1730's and 1740's. The Quaker minister, Thomas Story, reported that the spiritual renewal of John Wesley's Methodists was having a good effect among London Friends: "It looks like a fresh Spring a Coming on, by those budds, sprouts, and Blossoms in so many places and forms." [10] But as Frederick Tolles has observed, the general reaction in both England and in the Delaware valley was one of distance.[11] The Presbyterians and

---

[6] Martin E. Lodge, "The Crisis of the Churches in the Middle Colonies," *Penna. Mag. History and Biography* **95** (1971) : pp. 195–220.

[7] For general treatments of this subject see Charles H. Maxson, *The Great Awakening in the Middle Colonies* (Chicago, 1920), and Leonard J. Trinterud, *The Forming of an American Tradition: A Re-Examination of Colonial Presbyterianism* (Philadelphia, 1949), pp. 53–121.

[8] Charles H. Maxson, *The Great Awakening in the Middle Colonies* (Chicago, 1920), pp. 69–103.

[9] This point is best established by reading the Association minutes between 1730 and 1750 in *MPBA*, pp. 31–64. See also Norman H. Maring, *The Baptists in New Jersey, A Study in Transition* (Valley Forge, Pa., 1964), pp. 47–59, where much of the discussion centers on events of the 1750's and 1760's.

[10] Thomas Story to James Logan, 11 April, 1739, in: *The Correspondence of James Logan and Thomas Story, 1724–1741*, Norman Penney, ed. (Philadelphia, 1927), pp. 76–77.

[11] Frederick B. Tolles, "Quietism Versus Enthusiasm: The Philadelphia Quakers and the Great Awakening," in: Tolles, *Quakers and the Atlantic Culture* (New York, 1960), pp. 91–133.

George Whitefield wallowed in the doctrine of pre-destination and encouraged much unseemly behavior, which as Tolles points out, contradicted the Quaker understanding of the Light and their eighteenth-century quietism.

Another reason was important too. The dynamics of the Awakening violated the dynamics of Quaker history. Public Friends had scarcely disappeared. But they no longer sought converts and governed the movement jointly with weighty Friends outside the ministry. In a denomination where authority was now quietly shared, an awakening based solely on the preaching of the ministers and which also would have brought in many new members simply was out of phase with late seventeenth- and early eighteenth-century Quaker development.

Interestingly enough, part of the Anglican reaction to Whitefield paralleled the Quaker response, but stemmed from different causes. Resident Anglican ministers also opposed the Awakening because it was undecorous and spent much time gossiping about Whitefield. The Anglican minister at Lewes, Delaware, for example, eagerly told London authorities that the boy seen with Whitefield by day actually was a young woman whom the evangelist ravished by night.[12] This was more than vicious chatter. In a region where Church order of any sort was difficult to obtain, Whitfield threatened that which Anglicans had managed to build. He spoke from Dissenting pulpits and refused to encourage listeners to join the Church of England. Yet because the settled Anglican ministers lacked any institutional base from which they could oppose him they could do little more than attack him with crude rumors and slander.

If the English denominations in the Delaware valley leaned heavily on Old World institutions to sustain them in America, the experience was not deadening, however. For example, Dissenters understood that a European past renowned for its dynamism also was replete with difficulties and errors. However much Presbyterian ministers came to disagree about standards of ministerial behavior by 1730, they still felt free to chastise Irish colleagues for laxness in examining candidates for ordination. They ordered that for the future "no minister or probationer coming in among us from Europe, be allowed to preach in vacant congregations until first his credentials and recommendations be seen and approven by the Presbytery," despite pressing shortages of ministers in the Delaware valley.[13] Baptists separated the useful from the crippling past in similar ways. In 1726, when the

Philadelphia Baptist Association was asked what to do with settlers bringing letters of recommendation from congregations split by internal bickering in England, the Association suggested that Delaware valley congregations should ignore the disputes and accept the individual: "Churches here may take no further notice of the letters . . . than to satisfy themselves that such are baptized persons and of a regular conversation, and should take such into the church covenant as if they had not been members of any church before."[14] Obviously, there were some ways one could start fresh in America.

All of this points directly to the character of the colonial relationship and the ability of some religious groups to profit from it. Obviously, for many settlers the English colonial relationship was enlivening. The English institutions through which it thrived were creative and dynamic. For Dissenting denominations especially, those institutions proved to be remarkably malleable and allowed for a rich variety of forms within a coherent tradition. At the same time they were largely oligarchic and hierarchical rather than democratic. Yet each denomination survived many crises in the Delaware valley because these non-democratic Old World institutions continually responded with creativity to the New World problems they faced.

On the other hand, the very institution that epitomized non-democratic church government in England—the Church of England—failed to prosper in the Delaware valley. Judging by the history of Dissenting groups, this did not happen because a non-democratic church order was unsuited to America. Nor did it happen because Anglican ministers were inferior to others. It happened largely because Anglicans never succeeded in extending their own traditional non-democratic ecclesiastical institutions overseas.

But Quakers, Baptists, and Presbyterians did. Consequently, Dissenters all found in the colonial relationship itself a supple and efficient vehicle for transferring their English past overseas and for succeeding there after they had arrived. And because they developed in America in this way, rather than by overthrowing their European past, their experience in the Delaware valley again demonstrates the continuing centrality of Old World tradition to the shaping of New World society.

A NOTE ON PRIMARY SOURCES

Since much of the secondary literature used in this study will be familiar to many readers, the bibliographical note concerns itself with the more difficult problem of locating primary source material for the early religious history of the Delaware valley. Unlike

---

[12] The Reverend William Becket, who made the charge, wrote Whitefield that he tried to keep it quiet "out of Christian Charity, a Doctrine which I find you leave out of all your Sermons." Becket to George Whitfield, 9 June, 1740, in Reverend William Becket's Notices and Letters concerning Incidents at Lewes Town from the year 1727 to 1735, HSP.

[13] *RPC*, p. 118.

[14] *MPBA*, p. 28.

New England, whose antiquarians and historians have published large numbers of town and church records, few collections of documents from the Delaware valley ever have been printed. The number of local histories is small and the available manuscripts usually are known to only a few specialists. Yet these materials are more numerous than one first suspects.

Quaker records are available in almost unmanageable quantity. For many years the manuscript minutes of many Quaker meetings were housed in the Department of Records of the Philadelphia Yearly Meeting. However, in 1976 this office was closed and its massive collections were divided between the Friends Historical Library at Swarthmore College, Swarthmore, Pa., and the Quaker Collection at the Library of Haverford College, Haverford, Pa. Nearly all the surviving records of Pennsylvania meetings are adequately listed in *The Inventory of Church Archives, Society of Friends in Pennsylvania* (Philadelphia, 1941). Records from New Jersey and Delaware meetings can be located through the card catalogs at Haverford and Swarthmore. Most of the meeting records have been placed on microfilm. Unfortunately, the rules of the Philadelphia Yearly Meeting make it impossible to use them through interlibrary loan facilities. But a research trip to either Haverford or Swarthmore is made easier by the fact that both libraries have microfilm copies of all the minutes formerly kept at the Department of Records, as well as of other materials, so researchers seldom need to scurry back and forth to check individual holdings.

Of course, the minutes of the Philadelphia Yearly Meeting are indispensable in studying all facets of American Quaker history. An extraordinary amount of valuable information also is found in the minutes of the many monthly, quarterly, and ministerial meetings in Pennsylvania, New Jersey, and Delaware. For the years before 1730 the minutes of those in Philadelphia, Delaware County and Bucks County are especially useful. In addition, important collections of Quaker epistles and printed journals can be found at the Haverford and Swarthmore libraries. Together with documents from the Pemberton Papers in the Etting Collection, the Maria Dickinson Logan Papers, the Penn Papers, and occasional materials in the massive Simon Gratz Manuscript Collection, all at the Historical Society of Pennsylvania, these manuscript sources are crucial to a study of Friends' behavior in the Delaware valley.

Some Quaker records have been published. Minutes of the Philadelphia Monthly Meeting between 1683 and 1699 were printed in the *Publications of the Genealogical Society of Pennsylvania* 1–4 (1895–1911), but with some significant omissions. Ezra Michener's *Retrospect of Early Quakerism; Being Extracts from the Records of Philadelphia Yearly Meeting and the Meetings Composing It* (Phila-

delphia, 1860) contains valuable quotations from many different monthly and quarterly meetings arranged under topical headings, and James Bowden's *History of the Society of Friends in America* (2 v., London, 1850–1854), contains extracts from important manuscript materials that now are lost. Equally important letters and documents are found in Samuel Smith's "History of the Province of Pennsylvania," *Register of Pennsylvania,* 6–7 (1830–1831), which despite its title is a history of Quakers in the province.

Anglican congregational records are scarce. The vestry minutes of Christ Church in Philadelphia dating from 1717 are housed at the church library, and those of St. James's and St. David's parishes at Radnor, and St. John's in Concord are at the Historical Society of Pennsylvania in the form of nineteenth-century copies. Unfortunately, they provide only very limited information. The voluminous and more important records of the Society for the Propagation of the Gospel in Foreign Parts now are available in a microfilm edition from Micromethods, Ltd., Wakefield, England. This edition is owned by many American university libraries and includes the Series A, Series B, and Series C manuscripts (most of them letters from Anglican missionaries in the colonies), the Society's Journal (a record of its proceedings in London), and an Appendix that contains several long reports on religious conditions in the early eighteenth-century colonies. The early records of the S.P.G.'s predecessor are printed in *A Chapter in English Church History: Being the Minutes of the Society for Promoting Christian Knowledge . . . 1698–1704,* Edmund McClure, ed. (London, 1888).

Some S.P.G. letters relating to the Delaware valley have been published in *Historical Collections Relating to the American Colonial Church,* William S. Perry, ed. (5 v., Hartford, Conn., 1875); volumes two and five contain letters from ministers and congregations in Pennsylvania and Delaware. *The Collections of the Protestant Episcopal Historical Society for the Year 1851* (New York, 1851) contains important letters from George Keith and John Talbot written between 1702 and 1704 and reprints the journal of Keith's trip to America that he first published in England in 1706. Additional letters from Talbot together with a short biography are in Edgar L. Pennington, *Apostle of New Jersey, John Talbot, 1645–1727* (Philadelphia, 1938). *Rev. Thomas Bray, His Life and Selected Works Relating to Maryland,* Bernard C. Steiner, ed., *Fund Publications of the Maryland Historical Society* 37 (1901), reprints important documents describing Bray's understanding of the colonies, while David Humphreys, *An Historical Account of the Incorporated Society for the Propagation of the Gospel in Foreign Parts* (London, 1726) is an important contemporary account of the S.P.G.

The manuscript minutes of the Pennepek Baptist

Church, 1687–1894, are at the American Baptist Historical Society, Rochester, N.Y. They are crucial to the history of Particular Baptists in Pennsylvania and New Jersey. A smaller register of the congregation's births, deaths, and baptisms, originally bound with the minutes, now is at the Historical Society of Pennsylvania. The American Baptist Historical Society also holds the letter book of the Philadelphia Baptist Association, but its contents do not begin until the early 1730's. Records of the Brandywine Baptist Church in Chadds Ford, Pa., and of the Church in the Great Valley, Valley Forge, Pa., are conveniently available on microfilm from the Southern Baptist Historical Society, Nashville, Tenn. Two sets of Baptist minutes have been printed: *Records of the Welsh Tract Baptist Meeting, Pencader Hundred, New Castle County, Delaware, 1801 to 1828, Papers of the Historical Society of Delaware* 42 (Wilmington, Del., 1904), and "Record of the Baptist Church, Middletown, N.J.," in: John E. Stillwell, ed., *Historical and Genealogical Miscellany* (5 v., New York, 1903–1932) 2: pp. 256–275.

Minutes of the Philadelphia Baptist Association from A. D. 1707 to A. D. 1807, A. D. Gillette, ed. (Philadelphia, 1851) contains a reconstruction of the Association's proceedings made from congregational minutes and Association manuscripts by Morgan Edwards in the 1740's. Edwards's *Materials Towards a History of the American Baptists* (2 v., Philadelphia, 1770, 1792) originally was designed to cover all the colonies. Only the volumes on Pennsylvania and New Jersey were printed. A microfilm copy of the unpublished portions is available from the Southern Baptist Historical Society, Nashville, Tenn., and an additional section, "History of the Baptists in Delaware," has been printed in the *Pennsylvania Magazine of History and Biography* 9 (1885): pp. 45–61.

Despite the large numbers of Presbyterian congregations in the Delaware valley, only fragmentary portions of the minutes of two congregations before 1730 still exist. These are from the congregations at Abington, Pa., and Woodbridge, N.J., and now are at the Presbyterian Historical Society in Philadelphia. Thus the historian must depend on the records of the various presbyteries and synods published as *Records of the Presbyterian Church in the United States of America . . . 1706–1788* (Philadelphia, 1904), plus "The Records of the Presbytery of New Castle upon Delaware [1717–1729]," *Journal of the Department of History* 14–15 (1930–1933). A few manuscript letters from Jedidiah Andrews of Philadelphia and Joseph Morgan of Freehold, N.J., are scattered through the collections of the Historical Society of Pennsylvania, the American Antiquarian Society, and the Massachusetts Historical Society, but no other significant Presbyterian manuscript materials seem to be available until after 1730.

The explication of English ecclesiastical developments has necessarily depended on published sources. Fortunately, primary materials are available in surprising quantity. For Quaker leaders no biography ever has replaced *The Journal of George Fox,* John L. Nickalls, ed. (Cambridge, Engl., 1952). Many editions of Fox's journal exist, but Nickalls's is the most recent scholarly one and his introduction explains the confusing background of the several manuscript sources from which the published versions are drawn and points out the important earlier versions. Fox's shorter works were published after his death as *Gospel-Truth Demonstrated, in a Collection of Doctrinal Books, Given forth by that Faithful Minister of Jesus Christ, George Fox* (London, 1706), and many of his letters are found in *Selections from the Epistles of George Fox,* Samuel Tuke, comp. (Cambridge, Mass., 1879). Additional correspondence of the early Friends was printed in *Letters, &c., of Early Friends,* A. R. Barclay, ed. (London, 1841). This volume was in turn reprinted in *The Friends Library* (14 v., Philadelphia, 1847) 11. Unfortunately, Barclay's texts sometimes are garbled and need to be used carefully. Other materials can be found in *Early Quaker Writings, 1650–1700,* Hugh Barbour and Arthur O. Roberts, eds. (Grand Rapids, Mich., 1973) and the voluminous published writings of Friends are listed in Joseph Smith, *A Descriptive Catalogue of Friends' Books* (2 v., London, 1876).

Useful English Quaker meeting materials include *The First Minute Book of the Gainsborough Monthly Meeting of the Society of Friends, 1669–1719,* Harold W. Brace, ed., *Publications of the Lincoln Record Society* 38, 40, 44 (London, 1948, 1949, 1951); *Minute Book of the Men's Meeting of the Society of Friends in Bristol, 1667–1686,* Russell Mortimer, ed., *Publications of the Bristol Record Society* 26 (Bristol, Engl., 1971); and *A Collection of Epistles from the Yearly Meeting of Friends in London to the Quarterly and Monthly Meetings . . . 1675 to 1805* (Baltimore, Md., 1806).

Materials on English Baptists are relatively scarce, although some nineteenth- and even seventeenth-century histories contain many important documents. Three classic works are Thomas Crosby, *History of the English Baptists* (4 v., London, 1738–1741), Joseph Ivimey, *A History of the English Baptists . . .* (2 v., London, 1811), and Joshua Thomas, *A History of the Baptist Association in Wales* (London, 1795). All quote extensively from manuscript materials. In addition, important church records and letters are found in the *Publications of the Hanserd Knollys Society* (10 v., London, 1846–1854), in *Minutes of the General Assembly of the General Baptist Churches in England* [1654–1811], W. T. Whitley, ed. (2 v., London, 1908), and especially in *Association Records of the Particular Baptists of England, Wales and Ire-*

land to 1660, B. R. White, ed. (London, 1971–1973), and *The Records of a Church of Christ in Bristol, 1640–1687,* Roger Hayden, ed., *Publications of the Bristol Record Society* 27 (Bristol, Engl., 1974).

Records of Commonwealth classes and ministerial associations have been printed in several places, sometimes without appreciating the differences between them. These include *Minutes of the Bury Presbyterian Classis, 1647–1657,* William A. Shaw, ed., *Remains Literary and Historical of the Chetham Society,* n.s., **36**, **41** (Manchester, England, 1896, 1898), which also contains minutes from the Nottingham classis, 1656–1660, the Cornwall Association, 1655–1658, and the Cambridge Association, 1657–1658, and *The Register-Booke of the Fourth Classis in the Province of London, 1646–59,* Charles E. Surman, ed., *Publications of the Harleian Society,* **82–83** (London, 1952–1953). Published records of later associations include *The Exeter Assembly: The Minutes of the Assemblies of the United Brethren of Devon and Cornwall, 1691–1717, as Transcribed by the Reverend Isaac Gilling,* Allan Brockett, ed., *Publications of the Devon and Cornwall Record Society,* n.s., **6** (1963), and *Cheshire Classis Minutes,* Alexander Gordon, ed. (London, 1919). Among the more important ministerial materials are *The Note Book of the Rev. Thomas Jolly . . . ,* Henry Fishwick, ed., *Remains Historical and Literary of the Chetham Society,* n.s., **33** (Manchester, Engl., 1894), *The Life of Adam Martindale . . . ,* Richard Parkinson, ed., *Remains Historical and Literary of the Chetham Society,* 1st ser., **9** (Manchester, Engl., 1845), and, of course, *Reliquiae Baxterianae: or Mr. Richard Baxter's Narrative of the Most Memorable Passages of his Life and Times,* Matthew Sylvester, ed. (London, 1696), which covers both the Commonwealth and Restoration periods.

INDEX

125